Poverty and Democracy

Poverty and Democracy

Self-help and political participation
in Third World cities

edited by
Dirk Berg-Schlosser and Norbert Kersting

Zed Books
LONDON AND NEW YORK

Poverty and Democracy: Self-help and political participation in Third World Cities was first published by Zed Books Ltd, 7 Cynthia Street, London N1 9JF, UK and Room 400, 175 Fifth Avenue, New York, NY 10010, USA in 2003.

www.zedbooks.demon.co.uk

Cover designed by Andrew Corbett
Set in Monotype Dante by Ewan Smith, London
Printed and bound in the United Kingdom by Biddles Ltd,
www.biddles.co.uk

Distributed in the USA exclusively by Palgrave, a division of
St Martin's Press, LLC, 175 Fifth Avenue, New York, NY 10010.

A catalogue record for this book is available from the British Library

ISBN 1 84277 204 X cased
ISBN 1 84277 205 8 limp

Contents

Tables and Figures

Tables

Figures

Notes on Contributors

DIRK BERG-SCHLOSSER is at the Institute for Political Science, Philipps University, Marburg. His publications include *Tradition and Change in Kenya*, Paderborn, 1984; *Politische Stabilität und Entwicklung*, München, 1988 (with R. Siegler); *Vergleichende Politikwissenschaft*, Opladen, 1997 (with F. Müller-Rommel); *Einführung in die Politikwissenschaft*, München, 1995 (with Theo Stammen); *Perspektiven der Demokratie* (edited with H. J. Giegel), Frankfurt, 1999; *Empirische Demokratietheorie*, Frankfurt, 1999; *Conditions of Democracy in Europe 1919–39*, London, 2000 (edited with J. Mitchell)

BARBARA HAPPE is the author of *Armut und Politik – Politisches Denken und Handeln von städtischen Armen in Brasilien*, Mettingen, 2000

NORBERT KERSTING is Assistant Professor at the Institute for Political Science, Philipps University, Marburg. His publications include *Armut und Demokratie in Zimbabwe*, *Urbaner Lebensstil und politische Partizipation*, Münster, 1994 and *Urbane Armut – Überlebensstrategien in der 'Dritten Welt'*, Saarbrücken, 1996

CLAUS-DIETER KÖNIG is the author of *Politisches Handeln der städtischen Armen in Kenya*, Münster, 1998

SYLVIA SCHMITT is the author of *Städter und Bürger? Lebenswelten städtischer Armer in Zeiten politischer Umbrüche in der Côte d'Ivoire*, Münster, 2001

JAIME SPERBERG F. is the author of *Urbane Landbesetzungen in Santiago de Chile und Buenos Aires. Soziale Bewegungen in Chile und Argentinien in den 80er Jahren*, Hamburg, 1997 and *Von Stadtteilbewegungen zur Zivilgesellschaft*, Münster, 2000

Preface

Research on problems of poverty and democratisation and their possible interactions remains one of the most pressing concerns of our times. Can the apparently ever-widening gap between the rich and the poor both within countries and on a world-wide scale be reduced? How can those who are most seriously affected become active in such a process? Has the recent wave of democratisation improved their chances in this respect? What can be done by multilateral and bilateral 'donor' institutions and non-governmental organisations of the 'North' and the 'South' to provide meaningful assistance in these processes?

These and similar questions are addressed in this study. Its focus lies on those parts of the population in 'Third World' countries where these problems have become most crystallised in a spatial sense, i. e. the inhabitants of 'marginalised' settlements in large cities, the ever-sprawling favelas, poblaciones, bidonvilles, quartiers précaires, slum and squatter areas or whatever the local terms may be. It is based on a larger comparative research project which has been generously funded by the German National Science Foundation (Deutsche Forschungs-gemeinschaft, DFG) and a predecessor supported by the Ministry of Science of the State of Hessen, Germany.

Such research by necessity must be inter-disciplinary and cross-cultural. Therefore, in the preceding project colleagues of the departments or institutes of economics, geography, medical informatics and political science of Philipps University Marburg and the Institute of Planning and Construction in Developing Countries at the Technical University Darmstadt cooperated closely (see HABITAT 1991). This time, the emphasis was put more strongly on comparative and cross-cultural aspects with regard to possibilities and problems of self-help, interest organisation and political participation. As leaders of this project we were also able to benefit from other previous experiences in this area including extensive fieldwork in Kenya and Zimbabwe (see, for example, Berg-Schlosser 1979, Kersting 1994).

The actual fieldwork this time was mostly carried out by four doctoral students, Barbara Happe (Brazil), Claus-Dieter König (Kenya), Sylvia Schmitt (Ivory Coast) and Jaime Sperberg (Chile) who in addition to their doctoral theses on these cases, which have been published separately (see König 1998, Happe 2000, Schmitt 2001, Sperberg 2000), also have contributed to the cross-cutting chapters of this volume. Barbara Happe has also been very active in the overall organisation of the project and this final report. Without a spirit of close cooperation, openness, personal sympathy and intensive mutually stimulating discussions a project of this scope and length (almost six years altogether) would not have been possible.

This also applies to our colleagues and friends in the four countries concerned who have been extremely cooperative and active in various stages of this project. This includes the two-way translations of the questionnaires into English, French, Portuguese, Spanish and Swahili, the selection of particular settlements, the establishment of manifold local contacts, selection and training of interviewers, discussion of relevant city- or country-specific aspects, etc. It all culuminated in a joint symposium at Philipps University in July 2000, again financed by the Ministry of Science of the State of Hessen, where the comparative research findings could be not only intensively discussed among many of those who had been previously involved and presented to other interested researchers and representatives of aid institutions and NGOs who are active in this field.

Among the many collaborators and helpers, we would like to most gratefully acknowledge the support by Doctors Michael Nzunga and Winnie Mitullah (Nairobi), Professors Alphonse Yapi-Diahou and Ousmane Dembélé (Abidjan), Professors Marcelo José Lopes de Souza and Maria Elisa da Cruz (Rio de Janeiro and Aracaju) and Doctors Vicente Espinoza and Jeanette Silva (Santiago de Chile). Their written contributions to the symposium containing extremely valuable suggestions and criticisms concerning a preliminary version of this book are also listed in the bibliography. We also want to thank our research assistants at various stages, Steffen Gross, Guido Tiemann and Tjark Albers, who contributed to the comparative data analyses and technical preparation of this book, and Johannes Lauber, who was in charge of the organisation of the symposium.

Inter-disciplinary and inter-cultural projects of this kind in some way are a never-ending story. They present and highlight some of the common concerns, but also reveal the different emphases and perspectives in an ever-changing subject area. We have become sensitised to important disciplinary and cultural differences in this regard, but we are convinced that a meaningful inter-disciplinary and inter-cultural discussion on a frank and equal basis such as we had the pleasure to experience in this project is the only way to overcome such problems and to further our common concerns. This study thus, at best, can only be a building block for similar research in these countries and further comparative work concerning other parts of the world. Any oversights are ours alone.

Dirk Berg-Schlosser and
Norbert Kersting, Marburg

CHAPTER I

. . . .

Poverty and Democracy. A Contradiction?

Dirk Berg-Schlosser and
Norbert Kersting

§ THE relationship between poverty and democracy has been a subject
of controversy for many years. Modernisation theory viewed economic
prosperity as a 'pre-requisite' for democracy (Lipset 1959, reprinted as
Chapter 2 in Lipset 1963). Although the methodological and statistical
basis for this theory was relatively weak and the existence of a number
of 'poor democracies', such as India, Botswana, Costa Rica, Mauritius
etc., stands in contradiction to it (for a detailed critical analysis, see
Berg-Schlosser 1985), to this day it attracts numerous supporters (see
Merkel 1999, p. 83 ff.). However, Lipset himself has modified the original
position somewhat and no longer speaks of economic prosperity as a
precondition, but rather as an 'encouraging factor' for democracy (Lipset
1994).

The reverse conclusion which was often extracted from this theory
and played a considerable role in US politics in the 1960s and 1970s,
namely that dictatorial regimes offer more favourable conditions for
economic development and that democracy is feasible only at a later
stage (see for example Löwenthal 1963), is even more dubious. This is
confirmed by the latest and empirically and methodically most extensive
studies by Barro (1996) and Przeworski et al. (2000). Dictatorships do
not produce development and then democracy, rather democracies in
poor countries often exhibit better conditions both for fighting hunger
and poverty, and for longer-term economic development (see also Sen
1984 and Sen 1999). The individual (and complex) mechanisms that
work at the 'macro' level of political regimes and the various historical-
regional 'paths of development' which become apparent require a more
differentiated analysis (see, e.g., Berg-Schlosser/Kersting 1996).

However, this debate will not be continued here. In contrast to other
analyses, which are based on 'macro' observations of the relationship

between economic development and democracy, this book examines this relationship at the 'micro' level of people and groups who are concretely affected. To what extent do those sections of the population who have so far mostly been excluded from the political decision making process view the latest attempts at democratisation as significant to them? Has democratisation offered, in the eyes of those affected, better, more promising and effective possibilities of improving living conditions in the longer term? And, can this contribute to long-term stabilisation and consolidation of the new democracies?

According to some observers, the latest 'wave' of democratisation (see Huntington 1996) has brought few real political changes. Some speak of 'low intensity democracies', which mostly serve the interests of the ruling classes and international capital, and have only limited meaning for the man (and woman!) in the street (see Gills/Rocamora 1992 and some contributions in Hippler 1995). In a somewhat different context, Guillermo O'Donnell (1994) speaks of a 'delegated democracy', which fulfils Dahl's criteria of a polyarchy (see Dahl 1971 and 1989), but which is mostly an elite affair and, in a 'republican' sense, is less anchored in the conscience and activity of wider sections of the population. Thus, it remains more susceptible to populist currents and authoritarian leaders. This concept is based on the current situation in many Latin American states, but is also potentially relevant for some of the 'new democracies' in Africa, Eastern Europe and elsewhere (see Merkel 1999).

This book aims to test these, and other propositions on the basis of the concrete living conditions and perceptions of poor and 'marginalised' groups in four countries affected by the 'third wave'. This 'view from below' should help clarify the relation between poverty and democracy at the 'micro' level, while at the same time taking into account the respective historical, institutional, political-cultural, etc., contexts. In this way, firmer conclusions concerning indications for realistic chances of development and further democratisation for those involved may be reached.

For a long period of time, the poor sections of the population in the 'Third World' (for the controversy concerning the further usefulness of this term, see e.g. Brock 1991, Menzel 1992) were subjected to two types of 'exclusion' (for a systems theoretical use of this term see Luhmann 1997). First of all, these countries were (and remain) at the 'periphery' of the world economy and mainly produce agrarian and mineral raw materials for industrialised states under mostly negative terms of trade (Hopkins/Wallerstein 1980, Nohlen/Nuscheler 1992). Furthermore, as a result of high population growth and rural–urban migration, many of these countries have increasing numbers of 'marginalised' sections of the population, which have specific settlement patterns and living conditions (see also Sassen 1996).

The populations of such shanty towns in the cities of the Third World are characterised by specific social and economic attitudes and behavioural patterns, which result from their special environment. Thus, individuals often seek various sources of income, while at the same time all members of a family capable of work are integrated into the reproduction process and make use of employment and income opportunities in both the formal and informal sectors. The lack of security in this economy of survival leads to a variety of patterns of social interaction in the 'marginal milieu' (Berg-Schlosser/Kersting 1988, Kersting 1996). The analysis of political attitudes and individual and collective patterns of behaviour in such 'marginal milieus' (for the term 'political-cultural milieu' see Lepsius 1966, for different definitions of marginality see Sotelo 1973, and Tironi 1990) is the main goal of this study.

For this field of study, the concept of politics in Third World countries requires a different emphasis than in industrialised countries, which usually possess historically developed, strongly institutionalised patterns of participation. Here, the definition is based on a more 'social' understanding, and the terms 'participation' and 'democracy' are also understood in an encompassing social sense (see Nohlen 1988). The subjective concept of politics amongst marginalised individuals is to a large extent dependent on the evaluation of their influence on the political process. For example, social activity in shanty towns often has a political component due to the fact that requests often meet with opposition from state authorities (Evers et al. 1979). Conversely, as a result of its inability to act, the state is often forced to leave wide fields of policy to individual initiatives of the marginalised population (Berg-Schlosser/Siegler 1988; Berg-Schlosser 1990). Thus, political participation in this wider sense also includes activities aimed at ensuring the fulfilment of basic needs, the reaction against social discrimination and the development of an organisational structure to proclaim these aims (see Schuurman/Naerssen 1989).

The living conditions in a total of 16 'marginal settlements' are at the forefront of this study. In recent decades, such settlements have increasingly shaped the appearance of many cities in the Third World. For example, according to local authorities, in Rio de Janeiro alone there are a total of approximately 600 such settlements with a population of about one million, that is 20% of the total population. A common superficial characteristic of such settlements is their precarious geographical position, e.g. on steep slopes, on the banks of rivers and the seashore which are often flooded, in swampy and other peripheral areas, which as yet have not been considered suitable for normal construction or commercial use. For this reason, in many cases their legal status remains controversial. In so far as public land (municipal or national, etc.) is concerned, legal recognition and political acceptance of the established settlements is often lacking. Private (large) property owners normally let such areas lie fallow and only demand their rights for clearance or suitable compensation after spontaneous colonisation.

Not even the basic elements of infrastructure are present in such areas. Because such settlements often proliferate wildly, they do not have paths or roads that can be used in bad weather. Provision of other elementary public amenities, such as clean drinking water, electricity, sewerage, and also social services, schools, health centres etc., is usually lacking. In many cases, 'improvised' structures, such as tracks, water supplies, illegally drawn electricity, but also self-help organisations for social centres and kindergartens, amongst others, have developed. The living quarters themselves are made of the most simple materials, such as waste wood, clay, plastic sheeting. In more 'established' settlements, there are sometimes also more lasting self-made structures of tiles and concrete. However, the structural engineering of these buildings leaves much to be desired, often causes accidents, and sometimes leads to catastrophes in cases of flooding or landslides.

Such living conditions, which will be examined in more detail in the chapters below, have been the focus of increased interest from social scientists over the last decades. The forerunners in this field were qualitative social anthropological studies, amongst others by Oscar Lewis (1961; 1966) in Mexico and Central America, which discovered unusual patterns of behaviour caused by unemployment or underemployment, lack of personal property, education etc. This deviant behaviour, which Lewis termed the 'culture of poverty', expresses itself, amongst other things, in high levels of criminality, especially amongst youth, alcoholism and drug addiction, and violence towards women and children. Furthermore, he observed a lack of social contacts and interaction amongst the residents. Social relations were mainly concentrated on the core family, often single mothers, while there was hardly any organisation within the settlement or social contacts with other families and groups in the settlement. Contacts with external persons or institutions were also rare. Settlement residents did not engage themselves in political parties, unions or private associations out of fear or lack of knowledge. Lewis registered a strong orientation of the 'marginalised personality' towards the immediate living environment and the present, and therefore a lack of long-term perspectives.

According to him, this experience of helplessness calls forth strong introversion and characteristic features of fatalism and resignation. Such value structures are passed on to children so that, in his analysis, a positive development, e.g. by vertical social mobility, cannot be expected.

However, other studies that deal with the phenomenon of social and economic marginality demonstrate that the concept of the 'culture of poverty' cannot be generalised in this way (see, e.g. Rabanal 1990). For example, studies on criminality in shanty towns demonstrate no above-average incidence of crime, although such settlements do not normally enjoy local police protection (Butterworth/Chance 1981; Linn 1984). Other authors have shown that a lack of social interaction and contacts does not exist (see Perlman 1976; Drakakis-Smith 1981). Thus, like other areas, shanty towns have social organisations, leisure clubs and cultural associations. In some settlements, the majority of residents come from a certain rural region or belong to a specific ethnic group and they organise themselves according to these criteria. Furthermore, many residents are active in church groups. Child care arrangements, information networks, credit systems, informal types of medical aid etc. can exist within shanty towns. Such social networks compensate for the lack of contact with people and institutions outside the settlement (Wülker 1991). Solutions to social, economic and medical problems are sought, and often found, primarily in the neighbourhood. The high level of solidarity and mutual help means that the enlistment of expensive external aid is often unnecessary (Semsek/Stauth 1987). An analysis of illegal occupations of unused municipal land for colonisation revealed that they often are planned, well-organised actions by large groups of settlers (Bennholdt-Thomsom 1979; El Kadi 1987).

As far as the economic situation is concerned, there is also a much wider spectrum of activities and sources of income than earlier studies supposed. The heterogeneous characteristics of the structure of employment have only been clearly perceived since the middle of the 1970s (see Leeds 1972; Quijano 1974; Lucchini 1977). In addition to informal activities, there is an area of subsistence production which can represent an important contribution to the provision of essential goods (H.-D. Evers et al. 1981). Some sections of the population in shanty towns are also active in the formal sector. Most research concerning the informal sector and subsistence production concentrates on a clear definition and demarcation of these areas, and on the analysis of the functionality of these sectors in the macro-economic context. Such informal and formal employment within shanty town populations is characterised by high work and time intensity, as well as uncertain income and employment relations (see DESAL 1967; Glembotski 1985; de Soto 1986, Portes et al. 1989).

Research into political-cultural aspects (attitudes and values, e.g. in relation to interest in political participation, understanding of democracy etc.) of marginalised sections of the population only began very recently. It has often placed special emphasis on the protest potential of these groups. The interest organisation, choice of strategy, political alignment and various forms of political participation have been dealt with less comprehensively. The evaluation of the protest potential of these population groups and the specific relations between neighbourhood organisations and the state is controversial. For example, O. Lewis (1966) described the population in shanty towns as politically apathetic, un-organised and apolitical. Elsewhere, in contrast, squatters are characterised as a frustrated, angry mass, with the potential to be a revolutionary force. Thus, Drakakis-Smith (1981) recorded increased popularity of radical left-wing parties in the poverty-stricken areas (Castells 1983). These two contradictory positions seem, however, to describe a peripheral phenomenon. Varying intensities and divergent forms of political participation exist not only in different cultures and political systems, but also in different settlements and within marginal groups themselves. This is the result of varying interests and levels of consciousness, which can be partly traced to divergent forms of political socialisation. Thus, a settlement's history and the reaction of a municipality to illegal occupation by squatters are important factors which influence the development of consciousness (see Adel Taher 1986).

The history of different neighbourhood organisations in squatter settlements shows that they are most often formed because of an acute worsening of a problem, the solution of which is viewed as existentially urgent, independent of employment and income structure. It has been shown that participation within an organisation is especially high when the basic needs of the whole group are involved (see Meinardus 1982; Kreft 1987). Organisation occurs where emergency situations lead to collective action. If sections of the marginal population feel individual solutions have a better chance of success, groups often split. Detailed studies concerning the structure of spontaneous neighbourhood movements are still lacking. Experience from planned self-help groups in urban marginal settlements points to a hierarchical structure. In the cases studied, women were mostly excluded from the planning process. General social structures, which are often exemplified by a high level of clientelism and a local leader (caziquismo), are reproduced within the organisational structure of such groups (Cornelius 1973; Eisenstadt/ Lemarchand 1981; Berg-Schlosser 1987; Weber Pazmino 1990).

The orientation of many neighbourhood movements towards representatives of the state channels conflict into regulated, institutional forms of political interest representation (Spessart 1980; Hanisch 1983; Müller-Plantenberg 1983). In a process similar to that during illegal occupation of settlement areas, organisations try to establish contacts with influential individuals in public life. In this way, possibilities arise of building clientelistic systems and integrating neighbourhood organisations vertically into party or organisational structures. In polyarchic systems in Latin America, a trend towards the institutionalisation of such neighbourhood organisations has been observed where the chosen strategies of the movements with regard to participation in the political system were conflictual, but not disruptive. Although the character of neighbourhood movements is overwhelmingly defensive and orientated towards basic needs and therefore limited (Sotelo 1973; T. Evers 1980; Augel 1985), there are different types of movements with an offensive orientation. Collective assertion of interests by neighbourhood organisations using a non-disruptive strategy is hindered by their relative lack of resources (material and political-institutional). Furthermore, neighbourhood movements must be prepared for negative consequences if, in addition to an offensive strategy, they employ violence, because this deters potential institutional coalition partners. In such a situation, no external increase in legitimisation can be expected and the movement is forced into isolation (Bader 1991). Thus, the 'choice' of an individual solution is most often a consequence of the frustrated search for possible collective solutions for specific problems within a respective neighbourhood movement.

If state institutions do not satisfy demands, political activities often take on extra-institutional, non-conventional forms of political participation. Demonstrations, opposition to settlement destruction and occupation of public offices are chosen as means of political activity. Institutional, legal, conventional forms of political participation and extra-institutional political opposition are therefore changing elements in patterns of participation. The marginal population orientates itself according to a strategy's potential for success. This results in dynamic change within organisations, which are characterised by weak, output-orientated party bonds and oscillation between conventional and unconventional forms of political participation (see Nie/Verba 1975; Barnes/Kaase et al. 1979).

In the discussions concerning forms of 'civil society' (see Hall 1995), the term 'social movement' is usually employed to place collective activities in a wider social context. Organised engagement of social movements is viewed as conflict-orientated action that aims to change social power relations in important areas of life (see Touraine 1988). However, continuing social disintegration and the accompanying splintering of social movements (and also neighbourhood movements), in addition to the often defensive character of the movements in the Third World, demand a new type of analysis which allows an organisational-theoretical and political-cultural 'view from within' these movements (Slater 1985; Friedmann 1989; Bader 1991). Indeed, neglect of this 'micro level' has often led to unacceptable generalisations (see Castells 1989, Touraine 1988, Camacho 1989, Eckstein 1989).

Apart from previous single case studies and the, sometimes, far-reaching hypotheses or political expectations of the respective authors, which, as demonstrated by the cited literature, were mainly carried out in the Latin American context, there have been no overall systematic comparative studies. This is true internally even in the otherwise relatively well researched societies of Brazil and Chile, and especially so for country and inter-continental comparisons. Of course, our study cannot deal with every aspect, but a systematic, comparative method does facilitate a better historic and regional classification and, where necessary, can qualify, and in certain circumstances modify, previous findings.

Focus and Methods

Thus, to locate our enterprise more precisely, it focuses on the intersection of both 'democratization' and 'poverty' research in recent decades. These are, of course, vast areas of investigation each in their own rights and traditions which, however, have not often been connected explicitly. Apart from the (selected) literature already mentioned, this research has been summarised in a number of overviews and handbooks (see, e.g., Sørensen 1993, Diamond 1999, Øyen et al. 1996). In spite of inevitably continuing controversies about appropriate definitions, approaches and theories we proceeded from the following concepts and emphases:

'Democratization' was understood to refer to a process of opening up avenues of broader political participation to large parts of the population in a political climate of greater freedom of expression and information and open political contestation with certain legally guaranteed procedural forms. This roughly corresponds to Dahl's (1971, 1989) well-known criteria of 'polyarchy', but here seen as the beginning of a process and not yet as any stable or 'consolidated' state of affairs (for a discussion of such criteria see also, e.g., Sørensen 1993, Diamond 1999). So, the protracted and still somewhat incomplete processes of democratic transition in Brazil and Chile which have led to a significant regime change were considered to satisfy these criteria and even though the introduction of multi-party systems, relatively free elections and greater freedom of information and expression have not led to a change of regime and dominant party in the Ivory Coast and Kenya in the period considered, it at least marked a significant beginning in this direction. If this will lead to fully 'consolidated' democracies in a more ambitious sense, relatively stable but deficient sub-types such as O'Donnell's (1996) 'delegative democracy', or still authoritarian forms in the African cases remains to be seen.

With regard to the broad field of poverty research, we explicitly focus on urban poverty which has mostly relatively recent social causes and not on rural forms where longer-established land-holding patterns, but also climatic conditions etc. play an important role. This we look at in a specific spatial dimension as it is manifested in the many sprawling 'marginal' settlements in Third World cities and includes cases of both 'absolute' and 'relative' poverty as well as particularly affected individuals and households, such as socially weak or handicapped persons, single-parent families etc. (for such distintions see, e. g., Samad 1996). In the 'great chain of poverty explanations' (Miller 1996) we do not take any explicit a priori position and there certainly are 'structural' (both in each society and on a global scale), 'cultural', and also some individual conditions and causes of the predicaments in which the majority of those living in such settlements find themselves. But what we are specifically interested in is how the recent political changes have affected the living conditions, perceptions and expectations of people in such circumstances and what this may mean for a possible improvement of their situation and, eventually a fuller integration in the overall social and political life. A detailed comparative investigation of this kind may then also lead to a more differentiated assessment of the causes and processes at work and certain possibilities and perspectives of ameliorating the overall situation.

Our study is based on a survey in four countries, Brazil, Chile, the Ivory Coast and Kenya. It was carried out between 1995 and 1998, by Barbara Happe, Claus-Dieter König, Sylvia Schmitt and Jaime Sperberg, who also assisted with this book, and led to detailed dissertations (see König 1998; Happe 2000, Schmitt 2001, Sperberg 2000). While these case studies are much more broadly based in nature and include important 'qualitative' elements related to the phenomena examined in intensive fieldwork, this book concentrates on the respective systematic-comparative aspects. The choice of cases was based on a 'most different systems design' (see Przeworski/Teune 1970 and Ragin/Berg-Schlosser/ De Meur 1996). This entails studying a group which, according to certain characteristics, is similar and comparable: namely residents of marginal settlements in certain 're-democratised' states in the Third World, but which exists under most different conditions; such as historical-regional factors, colonial system, political-cultural peculiarities, institutional-administrative structures, etc. This method aims to find out whether, despite such differences, certain over-arching similarities, in the sense of 'universal' theoretical conclusions, are apparent, or whether the specifics of each case dominate and facilitate, at best, theoretical statements of 'medium range' in the historical-sociological sense (for such concepts, see Merton 1957; Stinchcombe 1978, Flora 1999).

Two important 'development regions' of the Third World, or if one prefers, 'civilizations' in Huntington's sense (see Huntington 1996), are contrasted, namely Latin America and Africa south of the Sahara, with their very different historical-regional developments. In each continent, two states with different colonial, but also geo-political, political-cultural, etc. characteristics were contrasted. These were Brazil and Chile in Latin America, and the Ivory Coast and Kenya in Africa. In each country, two towns, which reflect different internal regional conditions, but also, for example, different possibilities of access to the central political decision making processes, were chosen. These were the metropolises of Rio de Janeiro, Santiago de Chile, Abidjan and Nairobi on the one hand, and medium-sized towns further away from the centre, such as Temuco in southern Chile, Aracaju in northeastern Brazil, Man in the north west of the Ivory Coast and Kisumu in western Kenya. Finally, in each town, two shanty areas were chosen: an older 'established' settlement, the existence of which had been, at least in practice, accepted by political decision-makers; and a younger settlement in existence for less than five years as the result, in some cases, of spontaneous land occupation the political and long-term legal status of which remaining uncertain. In one case in the Ivory Coast, this has since led to forced clearance. This multi-layered research design aims to increase the range of the results and conclusions which can be drawn. Thus, certain aspects, specified in the individual chapters, can only be applied to the town or country in question, while others apply to the general situation in the continent, or to far-reaching perspectives of democratisation and the 'urban poor' in general in the Third World. Despite this, we do not claim to be able to paint a representative picture of all aspects in these countries and continents. For this there are simply not enough similar studies for the entire populations of these countries or corresponding research in other states in these continents. Our concrete conclusions are, therefore, limited to the groups of the population and the settlements studied. However, this contrasting design can more clearly define their possible range.

In addition to these systematic-comparative and methodological considerations, as in all comparative studies, concrete pragmatic aspects played a role in the choice of country, town, and settlement. These related to the language capabilities and country knowledge of the person dealing with each case, their institutional connections and personal contacts, the geographical position of the towns and settlements etc. In certain cases, compromises had to be made between methodological postulates and actual realisation in the respective countries. Thus, our survey in a favela in Rio de Janeiro had to be suspended for a while due to violence from a local drug gang, and could only be completed under extremely difficult circumstances. However, we believe that our results explore important developmental, political and theoretical terrain, that until now has not experienced systematic comparison with a detailed empirical base.

Quantitative and qualitative methods were combined to develop and refine research instruments and to achieve the collection of more complete and detailed data. The survey was developed and organised with the help of local universities. Together with researchers from the respective country, the research instruments were discussed and refined in an intensive process, and it was here that one of the main problems of comparative research became apparent. Many of the aspects questioned were less relevant in some countries and were viewed, with hindsight incorrectly, as irrelevant and unimportant for their country by respective country experts. However, to remain comparative, intercultural comparative research must deal with such aspects or establish functional equivalents. In the final analysis, the quantitative research element of systematic comparison became the focus of attention, while the qualitative results examined specific cultural 'uniqueness'.

The qualitative instruments mainly served to formulate the hypotheses and the questionnaires, but also to further the interpretation of the quantitative results. Thus, the local elites, local leaders, organisation chairmen etc. in the marginal settlements were questioned in half-structured interviews. Helpers also questioned individual settlement residents in intensive qualitative interviews to supplement the quantitative results. Expert interviews were conducted with representatives from social organisations and groups, the town administration, social workers and teachers from the schools in the neighbourhood, nongovernmental organisations, Churches and clubs. Furthermore, important 'opinion leaders', who were identified via the questionnaires, were also interviewed. In the case of representatives of neighbourhood organisations, their personal function and level of information about other important people in the neighbourhood, as well as information concerning the organisation, its aims, history, size, membership structure, organisational structure and forms of participation were investigated. In this context, our main interests were horizontal and vertical forms of cooperation, as well as possible conflicts and dependencies within the framework of clientelistic systems. Another important area dealt with possibilities for improving living conditions, interest articulation and new forms of participation in the neighbourhood. The various expert interviews were compared according to different standpoints, taking into account respective interests. The interviews related thematically in part to the questionnaire and examined its results in more detail with relation to aspects of daily life. In these mostly narrative interviews, sensitive topics, such as alcoholism, drug dealing, prostitution etc., were addressed. Participant observation in marginal settlements and within neighbourhood organisations as well as an evaluation of related documents and publications rounded off the picture of the marginal settlements and neighbourhood organisations.

The core of the research project was the standardised questioning of more than 1,600 residents, that is approximately 100 people per settlement. This mainly dealt with the subjective perceptions of marginality. In this context, political knowledge and value structure, attitude towards the state and to forms of political participation, as well as towards political organisations and neighbourhood movements were also studied.

Helpers were chosen to carry out the interviews in each country, and were specially trained for the task. They were mostly students from the local university. The intention of the research and the questionnaire itself were explained, and instructions were given for carrying out the interviews. Even during the phase of data collection, the interviewer had the opportunity to clear up any uncertainties during the regular 'briefing' by the project coordinator. A pre-test of the questionnaire was also carried out. This served to improve intelligibility in the respective socio-cultural context and facilitate adaptation to local conditions.

For the random sample, a settlement or a certain part of a settlement was chosen. This involved finding out the total, that is the number of residents, and the concrete structure by studying the topography of the settlement using town maps etc. When choosing those to be questioned, it was important that each resident had statistically the same chance of being included. This was achieved by random choice of households and random choice within the household. The choice of household was organised using a Random-Route-Method. Households were chosen at regular distances on both sides of a randomly chosen street or footpath in the neighbourhood. In this context, the lack of clearly defined residential units was often problematic. If, as is common amongst the *allegados* in Chile, a number of households occupied the same plot, the owner's, or the tenant's, household was questioned in turn. Within the household, the 'last birthday' method was used to question those entitled to vote. If this method could not be used, women and men of varying age groups were chosen in turn. If there was no one at home, the process was repeated the next day. Approximately three quarters of the way through the survey, the samples were compared with existing social structural data. If there was an obvious discrepancy with the social statistical data, people from the missing social structural groups were added (according to age, sex, status in household). During this stage, various problems, partly country-specific, became apparent. Thus, in the Ivory Coast there was a strong tendency to refuse to answer amongst women and foreign immigrant workers. In both groups, refusal was based on fear of reprisals within the family, or from other social groups or the authorities. Especially in the case of the Ivory Coast, these deficits, which are noted, must be taken into account. In addition to this specific distortion, refusals were also linked to certain questions in the survey. For example, part of the population of a settlement in the Ivory Coast earned their living from smuggling. Thus, answering questions concerning income and employment structures became difficult. However, using this research method, we tried to obtain the most representative results possible. For the most part, our results can be viewed within normal statistical limits as representative for the chosen settlements.

During the creation of the survey, questions from other research projects were taken into account to facilitate a comparative analysis. These were mostly questions from the west European and north American context (e.g. Almond/Verba 1963, Barnes/Kaase et al. 1979) which had already been tested in the Third World. Thus, the questionnaire is based in part on surveys carried out in Kenya in the 1970s (see Berg-Schlosser 1979); other parts were tested in marginal settlements in Zimbabwe in 1992 and 1993 (see Kersting 1994). The focal points of interest are questions concerning political culture in marginal settlements. This means examining basic attitude patterns such as authoritarian orientations (Adorno 1950), conservatism (McClosky 1965), political cynicism and anonymity (McClosky 1964; McClosky/Schaar 1992), fatalism (Adorno 1950), or post-materialism (Inglehart 1992).

Further emphasis was given to the interest in politics and political knowledge of the population. The legitimacy of the political system, institutions and respective office holders, as well as satisfaction with 'political outcomes' were registered (see Barnes/Kaase et al. 1979; Berg-Schlosser 1979).

In a second area, the various forms of political participation and their affective, cognitive and evaluative dimensions were explored. In this case, partly modified questions from Anglo-American studies were used (Berelson et al. 1954; Campbell et al. 1960; Almond/Verba 1963; Dietz 1975). Questions concerning political contacts exposed existing clientele systems. Questions on collective forms of participation include attitudes towards political parties and social movements. In this case, the person in question was a member of a formal or informal neighbourhood organisation, detailed questioning about this organisation followed. For the most part, this section of the survey dealt with the organisation's founding history, goals, members, communication and power structures, as well as its external contacts (see Schenck 1982). The survey was rounded off by questions concerning life in general in marginal settlements. In addition to demographic aspects, habitation forms, complex income and employment structures, social contacts within settlements and with the rural population were also important (see Mitchell 1987).

Comparative research projects in Third World countries which must take account of different languages and cultures, and deal with marginalised groups, encounter a number of difficulties. First of all, there are problems of communication. The questions, in part, dealt with complicated situations. The double translation of the questionnaire by 'native speakers' had to be of high quality and comprehensibility, and willingness to respond was determined in pre-tests. Furthermore, country-specific, and sometimes town- and settlement-specific contexts had to be taken into account. The respective local colleagues were very helpful in this respect. The quantitative interviews sometimes lasted one and a half to two hours and demanded a high level of concentration and motivation from both interviewers and interviewees. Generally, the interviewees demonstrated a high level of acceptance of the research project and a strong interest in the results.

The comparative research process in four countries and across two continents also hindered the refinement of the individual surveys. Modern means of communication, e.g. the internet, were generally not available. Traditional means of communication, such as mail or telephone, were not suited for an ad hoc reaction to possible problems. As the four projects began a few months after one another, there were few possibilities for mutual coordination during the course of the research.

This is the cause of certain discrepancies in the respective questionnaires, but they are not related to any central points. The different emphasis and techniques are given more detailed consideration in the project collaborators' respective chapters. At the start of the project, the coordinators ensured a high level of homogeneity and comparability in the choice of settlement and adaptation of the questionnaire by their presence in the respective localities and basic knowledge of all five survey languages. The common set of data for all four projects, which was created according to uniform coding criteria, was able to take into account the original unevenness and compensate for it as far as possible.

Structure of the Book

This introduction is followed by a general background chapter, which gives a short overview of the most important national and local frameworks in the countries studied. This should give those who are not familiar with these countries a rough orientation and evaluation of the political situation, without claiming to be very original. More detailed analyses, which take more account of the historical dimension, are found in the respective country studies on which the qualitative interpretations in the following comparative chapters are based. The first of these deals with social structure, but also the subjectively perceived living conditions in the settlements. As far as possible, this is based on official statistics and on our own results. In this context, the respective objective living conditions, such as provision of local infrastructure etc., are clarified. The following chapter deals in more detail with the respective urban living conditions and state and non-state policies towards urban marginal settlements.

The subsequent emphasis is placed on possible self-help activities and the specifics of interest articulation and organisation in the respective settlements. This analysis is based on our survey, but also on the comprehensive additional qualitative interviews with members of and those responsible for the respective organisations, with municipal authorities, etc. This is followed by a broad stock-taking of the respective 'political cultures' in the cases studied, that is, the political attitudes and values expressed. These include, for example aspects of political interest, understanding of democracy, legitimacy of the respective regime and its office holders. This leads to concrete forms of political participation and types of behaviour, which are expressed in both 'conventional' (e.g. parties and elections) and 'unconventional' forms (e.g. demonstrations or land occupation). From this, various character-istic 'types' of political participation are developed which are used in the comparative analysis. This facilitates a more differentiated and realistic view than the still relatively common clichés of the 'apathetic mass' or 'revolutionary potential'. In this context, the concrete party political preferences of those questioned and their political perspectives for the future also play a role.

The concluding chapter of this section presents the respective cross-section analyses in a comprehensive multi-layered context. It points out the different layers within the systems studied (neighbourhood, munici-pality, country, continent), the different aspects of comparison, and also their respective range and limits. This provides points of comparison with similar studies which have already dealt with some of our cases, for example in Brazil and Chile, and also a fundamental basis for further complementary or continuing studies in other countries and regions. Finally, as some practical consequences should also be considered, the penultimate chapter explains some possible areas and means of applica-tion of our results for state and non-state development policies. The emphasis here lies on possible further self-help activities, but also on external points of contact and forms of 'advocatorial' interest representa-tion. The book is rounded off by some remarks and a short discussion of our results in the light of possible perspectives for both the urban poor in such countries, and the general chances of democratisation.

The named authors are responsible for their respective chapters. The project leaders and editors have tried to achieve a certain level of conformity. Where not otherwise stated, tables and results are based on our own data. As far as case numbers for individual questions do not deviate dramatically, the results of the whole survey (each settlement approximately 100 randomly elected persons) are used. For the respec-tive settlements, our data, which were validated as far as possible using other means, can be viewed within the normal framework of statistical limits as representative. The tables and values presented are all highly significant. There is, of course, a certain statistical margin of error, but basically, we are fairly sure, our results reflect the often neglected opinion of the urban poor in the marginal settlements studied.

National Contexts

Brazil: Barbara Happe

§ IN contrast to many of the neighbouring Latin American states, Brazil achieved independence without violence. In 1807, the Portuguese king and his court fled from Napoleon's troops to Brazil. 15 years later, Crown Prince Pedro I proclaimed Brazilian independence from the former motherland. After the – relatively late – abolition of slavery in 1888, the agrarian oligarchy lost confidence in King Pedro II; a year later the monarchy was toppled in a military putsch and the first Brazilian federal republic was formed (1889–1930). Until the 19th century, the focal point of the export economy and political power was based in the north east of the country. The increasing importance of coffee exports caused the centre of political and economic power to move to the south east. In 1930, precipitated by the world economic crisis and a drastic decline in export revenue for coffee and other raw materials, the political power of the 'coffee barons' was terminated by a 'revolution' led by the officer corps. The new man at the head of the Brazilian state, Getulio Vargas, tried to replace the export model, which had fallen into crisis, with import substitution and the development of national industry.

Even after the end of the Vargas era, the economic model of internally orientated industrialisation was continued, although this time with massive support from foreign capital. The attempts of presidents Quadros (1960–61) and Goulart (1961–64) to reduce external economic dependence and to introduce social reforms (agricultural reform, co-determination) led to deep political polarisation, which culminated in a renewed military putsch in 1964. This signalled the end of the 19-year democratic intermezzo (1945–1964). More than that in any other Latin American country, the military regime in Brazil strove to lend its rule a formal, democratic facade. To achieve this, it integrated democratic procedures into the authoritarian system of rule, for example a periodic change of the executive among members of the chiefs of staff, the creation of a representative body with an artificial two-party system (comprising ARENA (Alianca Renovadora Nacional) and MDB (Movimento Democratico Brasileiro)), and elections controlled by the executive (Moltmann 1989: 91). The regime gained its social and political support from a coalition made up of the military, technocrats and the bureaucratic elite. The Brazilian military regime has, therefore, been termed 'bureaucratic-authoritarianism' (O'Donnell 1979, Martins 1986: 76).

At first, the military regime continued the course orientated towards economic growth in the private economy that was begun in the 1950s. For a time this led to high levels of economic growth, although wages remained low. During this period, Brazil became a 'newly industrialising' country with a very uneven economic structure: highly dynamic industrial complexes and agro-enterprises, sometimes with foreign participation, on the one side and a 'survival' economy (high proportion of precarious employment such as 'small self-employed', seasonal workers, employment without work permits and/or social security) on the other. The main problem for the Brazilian model was the increasing inequality of income distribution and the high level of external economic dependence, which finally culminated in the debt crisis of 1982.

The military itself introduced political reforms of the regime in the middle of the 1970s. The maintenance of a democratic facade meant that, following liberalisation, the opposition movement was able to articulate its interests within existing institutional structures. The previously artificial two-party system created a real opposition in the form of the PMDB (Partido do Movimento Democratico Brasileiro).[1] It became a gathering point for social movements and the unions, which were once more increasing in strength. The eruption of the debt crisis and the free direct elections of the governors and representatives in congress in 1982, during which the regime suffered substantial losses, demonstrated that the regime was increasingly unable to control the transition process and that it was developing its own dynamic. In the final analysis, the regime change in Brazil represents a negotiated settlement ('transicao pela transacao')[2] (Mainwaring/Share 1986: 207) between reform-minded sectors of the military on the one hand and the increasingly strong actors of civil society on the other. The most important stages towards the renewed foundation of Brazilian democracy were:

- the free elections to congress in 1986, which the PMDB clearly won (PMDB: 54%, PDS: 7%), giving the congress constitutional powers;

- the new Constitution in autumn 1988; and
- the first free presidential elections in 1989, in which the liberal Fernando Collor de Mello (PRN, Partido da Reconstrucao Nacional) defeated his challenger Inacio Lula da Silva (PT, Partido dos Trabalhadores) in the second round.

The regime change, however, did not bring economic stabilisation. Brazilian democracy passed the first political test when it started the procedure to impeach President Fernando Collor de Mello for reasons of corruption. Collor's resignation pre-empted threatened removal from office by the congress. Until the next presidential elections in autumn 1994, the former Vice-President, Itamar Franco, took over presidential duties. The final period of Itamar Franco's rule saw the formulation of a new economic stabilisation plan, the Plano Real, which is still relevant today. Only a few months after the introduction of the new currency, the intellectual father of the Plano Real, the former Finance Minister, Fernando Henrique Cardoso (PSDB, Partido da Social Democracia Brasileira), became President. In October 1998, he was confirmed once more in office with 53% of the vote (FdSP 10.10.1998).

The most important goal for the Cardoso government was the stabilisation of the Real, the currency introduced in 1994. The currency reform of 1994 freed Brazil from high inflation for the first time in decades. The end of galloping inflation is advantageous for the poor population because after years of declining purchasing power, real wages have once more gained value. As yet, the problem of social inequality has not changed considerably during Henrique Cardoso's period in government. However, between 1994 and 1997, the national poverty quota sank continuously due to low inflation and low food prices. At the end of 1998, the Brazilian economy suffered its most serious economic crisis since the introduction of the Real. The dramatic worsening of state finances – the budget deficit was 8% of GDP at the end of 1998 – and continuous outflows of capital forced the Brazilian government to ask the IMF and the World Bank for a standby credit of US$41.5 (Frankfurter Rundschau 11.01.1999). In return, the government agreed to restructure state finances and reduce spending. However, neither the members of the congress, nor federal state governors made significant attempts to implement the required structural reforms and expenditure reductions. Between January and March 1999, currency speculators forced a 40% devaluation of the Brazilian currency. Since then, the Real has been stable and the feared recession has not set in. However, the lowest sections of the population are once more confronted with decreases in real wages and loss of purchasing power.

Social Structure and Social Inequality

The usual criteria, which differentiate societies into socio-economic categories of classes and strata, cannot be applied to Brazil. The key criteria of social structure in Brazil, such as aspects of regional differentiation and racial origin, are not taken into consideration in this form of analysis. Even today, Brazilian society is very hierarchical and unevenly structured. Until the start of industrialisation in the 1930s, there was hardly any middle or working class. As a result of rapid urbanisation and industrialisation, the agricultural sector, which had been dominant until then (both in relation to proportion of those employed and its contribution to GDP) continuously lost importance.

New classes formed in the large cities, especially in the industrial centres in the south and south east of the country. The industrial and public sectors employed more and more people and their importance for the economy increased. In 1980, almost half of the Brazilian working population was employed in the service sector, and 25% were employed in industry. The debt crisis in the 1980s caused a modification of the class and sectoral structure towards further tertiarisation, deregulation and increased flexibility of employment relations in the formal sector. As a result of the bad working conditions in the metropoles, more women joined the job market (proportion of women in working population 1996: 55%). The lowest urban classes are over-proportionally employed in the so-called 'informal sector', i. e., the 'area of the economy which is either not at all, or only under limited state control' (Elwert/Evers/Wilkens 1982: 283). Especially in the 1980s, this sector

Table 2.1 Brazil's economic structure 1970–97

Sector	1970	1980	1990	1996
Agriculture				
% of GDP	12	10	9	n.a.
% employed	45	29	23	25
Industry				
% of GDP	36	41	34	n.a.
% employed	18	25	23	20
Services				
% of GDP	53	49	57	n.a.
% employed	37	46	55	56

Source: Oliveira 1993: 9

often functioned as a reservoir for rural migrants and industrial workers not in employment.

The current tendencies in the so-called 'poor house' in the north east of the country stand in stark contrast to the developments in the industrialised south and south east in the cities of São Paulo and Rio de Janeiro. To this day, the industrial sector hardly plays any role in the north east. In 1996, 40% of the working population was employed in the service and agricultural sector. In contrast, in the south east, only 14% are employed in the primary sector. The agricultural sector is still unevenly structured. Enterprises with more than 1,000 hectares account for more than half of cultivated land. Farms which possess up to 100 hectares only account for 18% (Prange 1998: 7). Working conditions and earnings in the agricultural sector are very precarious, so the proportion of the poor population in the north east is 10% higher than in the south east. Thus, in 1997 approx. four times as many families in the north east (23%) as in the south (6.5%; Brazil 11%) had to survive on an income equal to the minimum wage (October 97: R$120 [=US$109]).[3] At the same time, only 3% of families in the north east have an income equal to at least 20 minimum wages per month. In the south east, this figure is 9.5% (Brazil: 7%). In addition to 'regional differentiation', 'racial origin' still determines chances of individual economic success and is a decisive factor for social stratification (Sangmeister 1990: 67). Forms of social and economic discrimination are part of the everyday experience of the Afro-Brazilian population, the majority of whom also live in the north east of the country and thus experience a double discrimination.

Political-Cultural Aspects

Brazilian society is characterised by a mixture of authoritarian, hierarchical and populist elements, which have hindered the development of independent structures of civil society. For a long time, clientelism and populism characterised the pattern of political relations between those in power and those governed. Such patron-client relationships involve an unequal exchange of e.g. political support for material benefits, administrative jobs etc. (see also Berg-Schlosser 1987: 208). By integrating the population into such a clientelistic pattern of relations, especially in the north east, the traditional elites (normally large estate owners) have been able to secure far-reaching possibilities of influence on the political process at the regional level to the present day.

Populism refers to political movements with an over-arching class base and a very personalised (sometimes) leadership. The goals of these movements, which are mostly found in an urban setting, are defined by the leaders. Personal contact between the leader and the masses is created using large rallies, and the fulfilment of social and political interests of the followers (social security provision, employment law, wage increases etc.) is usually promised. As the founder of populism in Brazil, Vargas secured himself such followers in the 1930s using authoritarian corporatist measures, in which he integrated workers into a state-controlled union system. To this day, populist voter mobilisation serves the directly elected Brazilian President, or the state governors, as a means of forcing the dominant conservative powers in parliament to make political compromises. Until shortly before the military putsch in 1964, those in power successfully employed a 'swing policy' for the lowest classes to prevent fuller democratisation of the pattern of relations between those in power and those governed. This policy was characterised by clientelism and populism, and oscillated between control on the one hand and attempts at integration into the hierarchically organised political structures on the other. In this way, until 1964 the state functioned not only as the motor driving economic development, but also as the organiser and controller of social development.

During the military dictatorship, the first large-scale forms of democratic self-help formed under the umbrella of the Catholic Church in the metropolises of the south. At the start of the 1980s, these culminated in the foundation of democratically organised unions, vocational associations, parties and the formation of social movements (amongst others neighbourhood organisations, also in the residential areas of the urban poor). Today, many of these social and political groups are silent. Some of them have dissolved themselves, or have been coopted by state authorities and integrated into clientelistic patterns of relations, while others have gone through a process of institutionalisation and replaced the visual expressions of their mobilisation strategy (e.g. demonstrations) by negotiations with the authorities. The latter have increased the scope of action in the political decision making process for those population groups who were previously totally excluded, or not independently active (Cardoso 1995; Doimo 1995),

Thus, following the transition process, some of the most important successes in the area of democratisation of interest mediation structures were achieved (e.g. basic human rights, enfranchisement of the illiterate, political competition). At the same time, there has still not been enough restructuring of the pattern of relations in the central political arena. Boschi et al. speak of a hybrid state (Boschi/Diniz/Lessa 1989: 60), in which the former pattern of corporatist integration of social and political actors into the political system and the clientelist structures of interest mediation exist in parallel to newly formed pluralistic structures. However, in the meantime, a far-reaching consolidation of democratic regulations in political practice can be observed in the urban and industrialised south and south east of Brazil, more so than in other parts of the country. In addition, the clientelistic structures of interest mediation, which remain important, are changing and becoming more short-lived and flexible. Thus, increasingly clients do not feel bound to adhere to their informally given (voting) promises.

System of Government

Brazil is a federal republic with a presidential system. Administratively, the country is divided into 26 federal states and the district of the capital Brazilia, as well as five large regions (north, north east, mid-west, south east, south). Directly below the federal states are the 5,500 local councils ('municipios'). The constitution of 1988 establishes the division of powers between the legislature, the executive and the judiciary. In accordance with the federal structure of the country, each federal state and the federal district have their own constitution, jurisdiction and state parliament.

The President, governors and local mayors form the executive at federal, state and local levels. They are elected directly by the population every four years according to the absolute majority system with two rounds of voting, if necessary (Art. 76). At the federal level, the legislative is comprised of a 513-strong chamber of representatives and a senate with 81 members. The representatives are elected by proportional representation for four years. The number of representatives is dependent on the population of the respective federal state. The senate is comprised of three directly elected members for each of the 23 federal states and the federal district. They are elected for eight years, although every four years one or two thirds of the senators are elected in rotation (Art. 46). At the state and local level, the legislative comprises a state or local parliament, whose number of representatives is dependent on the population of the federal state or local municipality. Those aged between 18 and 70 who are entitled to vote are subject to compulsory voting. Older citizens (above 70) and young people between 16 and 18 (exception: those doing national service) are relieved of this duty, but can vote *voluntarily* (Art. 14).

Traditionally, the executive has a relatively large area of competence, which was reduced for the first time in the constitution of 1988 and placed under stronger control of the congress. Thus, the President can still proclaim 'provisional laws' (Art. 62), but he must gain approval in retrospect from the congress. The lines of conflict in the congress do not run primarily according to party lines or political and socio-economically based camps, but rather follow state and regional loyalties.

The approx. 20 nationally active parties often only differ slightly from one another with regard to their programmatic statements. The PT is the only ideologically rooted party and is a product of the union and social movements formed during the transition process. The party of the current president, Fernando Henrique Cardoso, the PSDB, was only formed in 1988. It is a middle-left splinter group of the PMDB, which itself had functioned as a coalition of different opposition groups after the reform of the party law in 1979.

On the eve of the elections in 1994, the PSDB entered an electoral pact with the two conservative (offshoot) parties of the military regime, the PFL (Partido da Frente Liberal) and the PTB (Partido Trabalhista Brasileiro), which was continued in the following legislative period as a loose alliance. Since then, in addition to these two parties, the PMDB and the conservative-liberal PPB (Partido Progressista Brasileiro), as well as some other smaller parties also support Cardoso's government.

The numerous changes of party allegiance by representatives, the absence of an electoral threshold, and the numerous party foundations are witness to a lack of party discipline. Since 1985, they have caused substantial shifts in seat distributions in the House of Representatives and the Senate, which can also be observed at the state and local levels. This lack of party discipline makes it difficult for the current President to get the structural reforms he desires approved by Congress, since parliamentarians do not always feel bound to vote in accordance with the agreements between the leaders of the allied parties.

Table 2.2 Results of presidential elections in Brazil

Year	Winner	Alliance	Votes (%)
1990	Collor de Mello (PRN)	personalistic ad-hoc movement, no firmer party coalition	42.5 (first round) 61.8 (second round)
1994	Cardoso (PSDB)	loose alliance of PSDB, PFL and PTB	54.3
1998	Cardoso (PSDB)	alliance of PSDB, PFL, PTB, PMDB, PPB and PSD	53.1

Sources: Calcagnotto 1994: 189, Calcagnotto 1998: 11, FdSP 10.10.1998.

In this weak and highly fragmented party system, the parties have always been a vehicle for personal political entrepreneurs, whose aim is the fulfilment of their individual interests (see Mainwaring 1991: 54f.). The parliaments do not represent a corrective to a strong executive, but rather support traditional power relations, according to which the large estate owners at the state level, especially in the north east, to this day divide power, influence and control over finances amongst themselves (Brühl 1992: 45). Because candidates for public office must finance their campaigns themselves, they often turn to the dominant family clans for financial support (Mainwaring 1991: 43). This implies loyalty of politicians towards local and regional elites, rather than to a party or electoral basis. Politicians are therefore more the representatives of the ruling elites than the 'elected representatives of democratically defined parties' (Brühl 1992: 50). The reputation of the Brazilian parliament at the local, regional and national levels is quite negative. This is due to the fact that the independence of politicians from their parties expresses itself in corruption, nepotism or excessively high salaries.

Since the democratic transition, the military has increasingly withdrawn from politics. The military's lack of involvement in the conflict concerning the impeachment of President Fernando Collor de Mello in 1992 demonstrates the increasing de-militarisation of national politics.

Table 2.3 National election results in redemocratised Brazil (percentage of seats immediately after elections)

Parties[4]	House of Representatives				Senate			
	1986	1990	1994	1998	1986	1990	1994	1998
*PDS/PPB	7	8	10	12	7	4	—	6
PFL	24	17	17	21	21	19	22	25
PRN	–	8	–	–	–	4	–	–
PTB	4	8	6	6	1	10	6	–
PMDB	53	22	21	16	63	33	28	33
PSDB	–	7	12	19	–	12	14	20
PDT	5	9	7	5	3	6	7	3
PSB	0.2	2	3	4	1	1	–	4
PT	3	7	10	11	–	1	6	9
Others	4	12	14	6	4	10	16	1
Total no. of seats	487	503	513	513	72	81	81	81

* PPB in 1995 became the successor of PDS.
Sources: Calcagnotto 1991: 78; FdSP, 10.10.1998; Thibaut 1996: 259

The dissolution of the secret service in 1985 was crucial for reducing the military's power. The military has also increasingly lost importance in the political arena. In June 1999, the Army, Navy and Airforce Ministries and the Army General Staff were dissolved and replaced by a Defence Ministry. Since then, the Brazilian armed forces have been headed by a civilian for the first time (NZZ 05.06.1999). In comparison to many neighbouring countries, the finances which flow into the military budget are relatively low (below 2% of GDP). The rights of the military to function as guarantor of political order were pruned in the constitution of 1988. Today, the military can only become active in the area of 'internal security' at the initiative of the three state powers (Art. 142). Thus, it no longer acts to combat politically motivated violence; rather it is used by the government to defuse social conflicts, e.g. to put an end to collective plundering of supermarkets in the north east of the country (1997), or to fight organised crime in Rio de Janeiro (Operacao Rio 1995).

Urban Setting

The constitution of 1988 produced only few major changes in the institutional structure. In addition to the reduction of power of the executive, the second central point was the devolution of power to the federal states and local councils (Art. 18–31). Decentralisation was aimed to bring about an end to the uncontrolled and illegitimate use of power by local and regional elites, and to increase the transparency of the political decision making process. As a result of decentralisation, the local authorities were given the right to regulate 'affairs of local interest' (Art. 30). These are pre-schooling and primary education, public health, public transport and other services, and land zoning regulations. The constitution established the financing of these tasks by an increase in the local authorities' proportion of national tax income. It also gives them the right, in certain areas, to raise contributions and tariffs (Art. 29, 31). In political practice, decentralisation has been a means of shifting responsibilities without increasing the flow of finance from the federal level to the local authorities according to the increased burden of tasks (Schulz 1994: 222). In the face of empty coffers, the local authorities are sometimes forced to delegate the competencies given to them in the constitution back to the federal authorities.

Today, over 75% of the total population live in towns. In 1940, urbanisation was 31.2%; five decades later the relationships between the rural and urban populations have been completely reversed (Kaiser 1995: 69). The urban population is concentrated in a few centres. In 1991, approx. 30% of the total population lived in the country's new metropolises (Souza 1993: 86). Large currents of migration and a high natural population growth are the main determining factors for the quick growth of the Brazilian metropolises, especially in the south east of the country. In addition to the slowing down of the migration towards large centres, declining birth rates, resulting from different structural conditions (e.g. increasing employment of women) and modern values in the urban environment have, depending on region, led to a decrease in urban population growth over the last two decades. Migration has shifted towards the regional capitals and industrial centres. Between 1960 and 1990, the number of towns with a population of over 100,000 increased from 45 to 207 (Santos 1993: 87). However, the phenomenon of hyper-urbanisation, the (over-)concentration of economic activities and urban functions on a few cities, still remains. In the 1980s, the country's nine metropolitan regions registered a population increase of 22% the other nine cities in the country with a population of over 500,000 registered a growth rate that was twice as high, 44% (in absolute figures: 1980: 5.15 million, 1991: 7.42 million) (ibid.: 86f.).

The first favelas – illegal residential areas resulting from spontaneous or planned occupation of public or private land – formed in the two largest metropolises at the start of the 20th century. They often occupied difficult terrain (flood areas, steep slopes etc.). In contrast to other South American countries, the majority of the lowest social classes in Brazil were often unable to settle in run-down inner-city areas because this accommodation was used for other purposes (renovation and infrastructure). At first, former slaves and agricultural workers sought sanctuary in the favelas, but from the 1930s/1940s, they mostly accomodated migrants from the north east. The increasing importance of medium-sized towns (from 1960) led to an increase in inter-urban migration.

However, not all favelados are poor, and not all those who are poor live in favelas. Thus, at present in Rio de Janeiro, approximately 20% of the population lives in favelas, but 32% are considered 'poor' (Rocha 1996: 22). According to IPEA estimates, the poverty quota in the nine metropolises at the beginning of 1996 ranged from 22% in Sao Paulo, to just below 50% in Recife (Roche 1996: 22).[6]

Favelas differ widely from one another with regard to important criteria such as living conditions, infrastructure provision and socio-economic standards. In Rio de Janeiro alone, there are just over 600 such areas; 15 favelas have more than 10,000 residents (IPLAN-Rio 1995). Even though not all favelados live at the brink of existence, they can still be termed 'marginalised' because they do not have full access to developed urban infrastructure (water, sewerage, waste collection, access to transport, health centres, (pre-schools) and are often treated as 'second class citizens' by the state authorities (Bento Rubião 1993: 78). Only after redemocratisation did the state increase its attempts to improve the living conditions in the favelas.[7] Previous attempts to meet the demand for living accommodation in Brazil's cities with council housing construction programmes remained inadequate and did not concentrate primarily on the lowest social classes (see chap. 4).

In many places, a clear spatial segregation can be observed. Not everywhere have those in government been able to keep favelas out of city centres or away from 'better' residential areas, or to clear them. In such cases, modern security installations and walls ensure the isolation of the better-off social classes in homogenous enclaves. As a result of uneven social development over the past decades, the Brazilian cities and metropolises have become areas of strong social tensions. The extent to which such trends will seriously affect the ability to govern the cities in the near future depends on the political will of those in government to introduce social reform, and on the willingness of the population to accept the situation of social inequality.

Chile: Jaime Sperberg

§ CHILE gained independence in 1818 within the framework of the Latin American fight for independence against the Spanish colonial power. The 19th century was subsequently characterised by the conflict between supporters of a parliamentary model and advocates of a strong presidential regime. Until 1920, there were three phases. In the first phase, the parliament was dominant (1830–1860). In the second phase, both institutions were equal (1860–1890), and in the third phase (1890–1920) parliament once more gained the upper hand (Nohlen/Nolte 1992: 280f.). The land-holding oligarchy and the newly emerging urban classes increasingly carried out their conflicts in parliament, where, until 1920, they were represented by three parties. The Conservative Party's (Partido Conservador) social base was the large-estate-owning class, the banks and the Catholic clergy. Its most important goals were the centralisation of political power and prevention of secularisation. The social backbone of the Liberal Party (Partido Liberal) were mine owners, business people and a few members of the landowning class. Apart from the question of secularisation, they basically agreed with the conservatives on economic and political issues. The National Party (Partido Nacional), which formed an alliance with liberal and conservative forces at the end of the 19th century, represented the interests of the high-level bureaucracy, as well as those of banks, trade and industry (see Imbusch 1995: 72f.). Due to the high revenue the Chilean government obtained from taxing the export of raw materials, which was used to finance physical and social infrastructure, the state became autonomous relatively early on. Both relative independence from oligarchic interests and, in contrast to other Latin American countries, the limited importance of the military contributed to the enhancement of the political sphere and peaceful conflict resolution (see also Scully 1990).

This development was accompanied by important changes in social structure. Industrialisation and the mining industry in the north of the country led to the formation of an industrial proletariat, which organised itself in unions and political parties in the early years of the 20th century. In addition, the middle class began to grow in the larger cities in the 1920s. It was comprised of state employees, traders, intellectuals and small businessmen. These groups exerted pressure for political reforms and demanded their own economic and political integration.

The world economic crisis of 1929/1930 hit the export-orientated economy very badly. Mass unemployment and a decline in foreign capital were accompanied by political turbulence. 1938 was a turning point in Chilean politics (Imbusch 1995: 76f.). The new party of the middle class, the Radical Party (Partido Radical), played an important role in the integration of the two Marxist labour parties (PC and PS). From 1938 until 1952, the Partido Radical was a stabilising factor within the Chilean political system because it joined coalitions with both left- and sometimes right-wing groupings to gain a solid power base for its three consecutive presidencies (Collier/Sater 1996: 237ff.). The Chilean presidential system was dependent on compromise because there was parity within the left-right spectrum and no one political party alone could gain the presidency. In the period from 1930–1970, wider groups of the population were enfranchised. In addition, the electoral reform at the end of the 1950s and beginning of the 1960s cut back the control the large-estate-owning class exercised over the votes of agricultural workers and limited the possibilities of buying votes. The integration of more and more groups into political life enabled the parties of the middle class (the Radicals, and since the 1960s the Christian Democrats) to extend their political influence to industrial workers and the lower classes.

As a consequence of the world economic crisis, Chile had also changed its development model, which until then had been exclusively orientated towards the export of saltpetre and, later on, copper, to one that was more domestically orientated. Within this framework the state succeeded in becoming the most important economic and political actor. In 1939, the state development agency CORFO (Corporacion de Fomento de la Produccion) was founded. Its aim was to build up domestic industry in order to attain independence from foreign imports and create new job opportunities. Until 1973, state interventionism remained a central element of Chilean politics. The state sector was increasingly expanded, culminating in the nationalisation of the copper mining industry, which was carried out under the People's Front government of Allende's Unidad Popular (UP, 1969–1973), but which was supported by all parties in the congress.

The military putsch under the leadership of General Augusto Pinochet, which followed, ended this chapter of Chilean history. After the putsch, a neo-liberal programme was introduced which reduced the state's share in all areas, liberalised the markets, deregulated working relationships and transferred market principles to the social sphere. The military regime used violence for this restructuring. The improvement of the economic situation from 1985 onwards stabilised the authoritarian regime and caused the middle class to turn its back on the marches which had been held regularly since 1983 to protest against deteriorating social conditions. A large proportion of the urban poor took part in the protests and were therefore often victims of violent attacks by the representative forces.

However, the military regime could not prevent its defeat in the plebiscite of 1988 on the continuation of the dictatorship. This represents the beginning of the Chilean transition to democracy, with the result that in 1990 the freely elected Christian Democrat Patricio Aylwin took office. An agreement between the new democratic rulers and the old authoritarian powers ensured that high military officers remained free from prosecution for violations of human rights and also were able to preserve certain 'authoritarian enclaves'. This explains the continuing position of Pinochet as supreme commander of the military, a certain number of senators who are appointed by him and some other prerogatives (see Garreton 1995a).

This late democratisation in Chile contrasts with its very positive macro-economic data. Since the middle of the 1980s, GDP has increased by approx. 6%, and in 1997 per-capita income was US$9,520, the highest in Latin America (Imbusch 1999: 32). The most dynamic sector of the Chilean economy, the export sector, increased its share of GNP from 10% in 1970 to more than 35% in the 1990s. The demand for non-traditional exports resulted in the decrease in the share of copper in total exports to 40–50% in the 1990s. The new democratic government was also confronted with numerous well-organised business associations, which prevented any reform of the neo-liberal model (see Imbusch 1995: 202ff.). According to the plans of the new democratic rulers, Chile's export model, which was based mostly on primary goods with a very low level of processing, is to be integrated into the world economy in a second phase. In this way it is hoped to replace the previous basis of success – low employment costs, flexible working relationships, exploitation of natural resources – with technological innovations and better integration of the economic sectors (see Garcia et al. 1994: 172). Certain branches, however, which are especially involved in plundering nature such as the wood and fishing industries, still account for a substantial proportion of exports.

Social Structure

An important reason for the electoral success of the democratic forces ('Concertacion') in the presidential and parliamentary elections in December 1989 was the expectation that the new government would reduce social debts (deuda social) with a new social policy. A major characteristic of an extremely market orientated model such as that in Chile is social inequality, which can be measured using two indicators: the level of poverty and the distribution of income. In comparison to the period before 1973, not only did absolute poverty increase during the Pinochet regime, but also income distribution worsened. The poorest 20% of the population in 1969 accounted for 7.7% of private consumption; their share of consumption had decreased in 1988 to 4.4%. At the same time, the richest 20% raised their share of consumption from 43.2% in 1969 to 54.9% in 1988. Social expenditure as a percentage of GDP also decreased during this period, and minimum wages decreased markedly in the 1970s and 1980s (Nohlen/Nolte 1992: 323f.).

Table 2.4 demonstrates that the high level of poverty of the late 1980s has been drastically reduced by now. The proportion of poor people amongst the whole population was halved by 1998. The proportion of the extremely poor, the group of people whose available income does not suffice to fulfil the most important basic needs, was reduced by one third from 16.8% in 1987 to 5.6%. Thus, Chile once more belongs to the group of countries in Latin America which demonstrate 'low' levels of poverty (CEPAL 1999: 39). However, these figures disguise some discrepancies between the towns and countryside, as well as between regions. While in urban zones poverty ran at 20.7% in 1998, in rural areas it reached 27.6% (MIDEPLAN 1999a). There are also substantial differences between regions. Thus, in 1998, the proportion of poor in region IX, the historical settlement area of the Mapuche native inhabitants, was 34.3%, the highest in regional comparison. The Region Metropolitana, to which Santiago belongs, has only 15.4% poor. Regions IX and VIII, which both demonstrate the highest rates of poverty, in the past also exhibited the highest rates of growth in the export industry (wood) (see Aquevedo Soto 1998). This demonstrates that growth alone cannot overcome poverty.

Although the democratic governments since 1990 have successfully reduced absolute and relative poverty, contradictory tendencies can be observed with regard to income distribution. Since 1987, the share of income of the 20% of the most poor has slightly declined. The government's measures aimed at reducing unequal income distribution have so far had no redistributive effects. However, with regard to combating extreme poverty, there has been more success. This is related to the increased redistributive measures and the increase of minimum wages as well as minimum pensions (Minkner-Bünjer 1993: 78). Overall income distribution in Chile is still one of the worst in Latin America. In the period 1990–1996, the Gini-coefficient was 0.47%, a figure which is only topped in Brazil (CEPAL 1999: 63). The drifting apart between successes in reducing poverty on the one side and stagnation in the improvement of income distribution on the other are related to the specifics of the Chilean labour market. Wage increases have been enjoyed by the better-trained and people who were older than 35, that is, those groups who were already in a better position. Women also profited to a large extent from this increase in income (MIDEPLAN 1998). The lower wage groups profited from the increase in minimum wages to stay above the poverty line, but the income gap between them and the higher wage

Table 2.4 Development of poverty in Chile 1987–98

Year	Extreme poor (thousands)	Share of total population (%)	Poor* (thousands)	Share of total population (%)
1987	2,073.5	16.8	5,497.9	44.6
1990	1,659.3	12.9	4,965.6	38.6
1992	1,169.3	8.8	4,331.7	32.6
1994	1,036.2	7.6	3,780.0	27.5
1996	813.8	5.8	3,288.3	23.2
1998	820.0	5.6	3,160.1	21.7

Source: MIDEPLAN 1994b; 1999. * includes the extremely poor

groups did not narrow. An important reason for the reduction of poverty was therefore the increase in employment and the decline in the unemployment rate from 8.3% in 1990 to 5.7% in 1996. One can expect that in recession, unemployment and poverty will increase once more.

A further serious problem, which affects the urban poor in particular, is the increase in 'precarious' working relationships in the 1990s as well as very low incomes in the informal sector. In these cases, poverty is no longer a result of unemployment and marginality, but is also present amongst those employed in precarious working conditions (Díaz 1993: 25). In times of crisis, a further increase in poorly paid jobs in the informal sector and in unemployment can be expected. The government programme of the Frei presidency (1994–2000), which aimed to abolish extreme poverty and ensure a more just income distribution by the year 2000 must, at the end of his period in office, largely be viewed as a failure. The new president of the Concertacion, the socialist Ricardo Lagos, thus has a difficult inheritance in this sphere.

Aspects of Chile's Political Culture

Chile's political culture experienced a caesura as a consequence of the military seizing power. Until 1973, political parties were the deciding factor and society was divided into different political camps. After the neo-liberal restructuring of the economy and society, political moderation, pragmatism and in some cases an anti-party attitude dominated in the 1990s. The ideological polarisation between the parties, which still existed at the end of the 1980s, dissolved with the transition to democracy and made way for a basic consensus about the democratic rules governing the parties represented in parliament.

Chile's long previous democratic tradition as well as the negative experience of the military dictatorship enhanced acceptance of basic democratic values within society in general. The forms of political participation are more orientated towards west European examples than the clientelistic, populist practices in other Latin American countries. The introduction of a competitive market economy, which extends to almost all aspects of life and emphasises individual achievement, has served to increase individualisation. On the one hand, this is expressed in the limited rate of popular participation in political parties and unions, that is the political actors, who were important before the military putsch in 1973. On the other hand, since the start of the 1990s, the existing party system has been characterised by relative autonomy and isolation from influences from other areas of society. The parties have increasingly distanced themselves from the 'people' and have become more elite instruments to ensure efficient political decision making. Despite the three peaceful changes of government since 1990, a loss of political legitimacy can be observed amongst all sections of the population. Thus, trust in the political authorities has decreased and, to a lesser extent, in democracy itself (see Lagos 1995).

System of Government

The current government system is moulded by the constitution of 1980 and its partial reform in 1989. The members of the military still exert a disproportionate influence on the political process. They secure this influence through their dominant position in the national security council, via some appointed senators in the senate, and through the UDI (extreme right-wing) party, which remained loyal to Pinochet. The military uses its influence in its right of veto on questions concerning human rights and institutional reform. As a result, the scope of manoeuvre for the democratic governments since 1990 has been greatly limited.

In Chile, the president, who is elected directly by the population, exercises a considerable power. The president is at the same time head of state, head of government and head of administration. He has to ensure the country's internal order and external security (Nohlen/Nolte 1995: 327; Lauga 1996: 117). The congress is in a weaker position, but de facto the president needs majorities, which are difficult to reach, in order to implement his policies. This applies first and foremost to the governing coalition's efforts to change the constitution, to remove the enclaves of authoritarianism (Garreton 1995b). Thus, the Chilean presidential system presents a paradoxical constellation. On the one hand, the president has so much power that the description 'enlightened monarch' (Römpczyck 1994: 18) is justified, on the other his scope of activity, in relation to the necessary democratic reforms in the constitution of 1980, is limited due to the distorted majority in both chambers. Thus, he is dependent on the moderate right in parliament.

The Chilean party system which arose after 1990 is the result of the double experience of the collapse of democracy in 1973 and the military dictatorship from 1973–1989; and also the result of the regulations laid down in the constitution from 1980. Before 1973, there was no outright confrontation between the three major ideological camps. Thus, in the 1950's the centrist Radical Party entered into coalitions with both the right and left-wing groups (see Hunneus 1981; Scully 1990; Thibaut 1996). This served to moderate party politics because there was a willingness to rise above a specific camp and, in certain matters, agree on a compromise with the political enemy. The parties' ability to compromise declined rapidly in the 1960s and a 'transition from a moderate to polarised pluralism' (Thibaut 1996: 149) occurred in which the newly founded Christian Democratic Party (PDC) pushed the former centrist Radical Party (PR) aside. Before 1973, the Chilean party system was characterised by the strong influence of the parties on interest groups and social organisations. Vial (1986: 107) speaks of a 'colonisation' of social groups by the parties. The unions were completely infiltrated by the left-wing parties and, following the increasing polarisation in the second half of the 1960s, the neighbourhood committees (juntas de vecinos) also increasingly came under the influence of political parties. In addition, the formal recognition of the neighbourhood committees in 1968 made them directly dependent on the state and therefore on the then governing Christian Democrats.

The attempts of the military dictatorship to replace political parties with cooperative participation mechanisms failed. The parties did not always play the most important role in the organisation of protest against the authoritarian regime. However, during the transition to democracy (1988–1990) they took on a pivotal role in initiating constitutional reforms and ensuring that the military handed over power to civil authorities. The classical three-way division (right-middle-left) was maintained, but power has shifted to the advantage of the centre and right in comparison with the results of elections before 1973. In the right-wing camp, two new parties have been founded within the last ten years: the Independent Democratic Union (Union Democratica Independiente, UDI), which represents the interests of the former military dictatorship, and the Centre Progressive Union (Union de Centro-Centro Progresista, UCCP), which represents a new element in the Chilean party system. In addition, the Party of National Renewal (Renovacion Nacional, RN) is a conglomeration of various conservative tendencies, which expressed regime criticism in the run-up to the plebiscite in 1988, the first manifestation of its attempts to disentangle itself politically from former supporters of the authoritarian regime.

The current Chilean party system is determined to a large extent by the bi-nominal electoral system, which forces the parties to form alliances in order to increase their electoral chances. For small parties, joining an electoral alliance is the only way to ensure a minimal level of representation. The Socialist and Christian Democratic Parties are the most important pillars supporting the governing coalition, Concertacion de Partidos por la Democracia. The bi-nominal system distorts representation because it favours the second strongest political power in a constituency, which is usually the right-wing opposition. In this way minority party candidates in the two-member constituencies can still gain a seat in parliament, if they receive the second largest share. Two candidates of the same party must therefore gain at least two thirds of votes, to win the second seat in the constituency for that party. This system was aimed at creating a two-party system. It has failed to do so because, despite the necessity of forming alliances in parliament, there are nearly as many parties represented there as before 1973 (see Thibaut 1996: 267). The binominal system and the nine appointed senators are responsible for the distortion of representation in favour of the right-wing forces. To date, every attempt to change the electoral law has failed due to the veto of some of the appointed senators and the right-wing parties in parliament.

Responsibilities and Power Relations at the Local Level

The current organisation and administration of local councils can be traced to the authoritarian period. The democratically legitimated government, which has been in power since 1990, maintained the half-hearted decentralisation which was started at the beginning of the 1980's. Neither did it reverse the privatisation of public services. The internal administrative structure was also left basically intact, but the new democratic government was particularly concerned to reintroduce the democratic legitimisation of local political bodies. Since 1992, the mayor and the town councillors have been democratically elected.

The corporative organisation of the economic and social committee (CODECO) which existed under the military dictatorship was renamed CESCO (Municipal Economic and Social Committee, Consejo Economico Social Comunal). Its democratic legitimisation is based on the democratisation of the neighbourhood committees, which make up 40% of this institution. The creation of a town council, the members of which are freely elected, led to a reduction in the importance of CESCO, but it has retained its advisory function to the council and the mayor. The local authorities' areas of responsibility, which were given to them during the authoritarian regime, were further extended. However, no more financial means were allocated by the central government. Instead, various programmes and institutions should channel finances more efficiently amongst the poorer municipalities. But distribution is only in part related to the needs of the municipality. In order to gain access to the Social Fund FOSIS,[8] which has been in existence since 1990, established groups must formulate and send in applications. The local authorities carry out important aspects of social policy. Therefore, they have become the most important points of contact for the urban poor.

Under the new law of 1992, the local council is defined as an autonomous public territorial body which is recognised as a legal institution and has its own property (see Ministerio de Interior 1992). For administrative purposes, it is also part of a province. Functions which are the sole responsibility of the municipality include town planning and the formulation of building guidelines; support of socio-cultural development (desarrollo comunitario); and the formulation and implementation of a municipal urban development plan, which must conform to regional and national plans. Together with other state institutions, the municipalities must take on tasks in the areas of social security, public health, urbanisation and the construction, as well as allocation, of council housing. In addition to the town council and the mayor, the departments Desarrollo Comunitario (Department for Socio-Cultural Development) and the planning and advisory division (SECPLAC) also play an important role in the fulfilment of these tasks. The department Desarrollo Comunitario, with its numerous sub-divisions, is responsible for the formulation and implementation of measures and projects of social security (asistencia social) and for public health services. In the poorer towns, this department basically is concerned with implementing social policies at the local level and is therefore the institution with which the urban poor have most contact.

In contrast, SECPLAC advises the town council and mayor in the following areas: planning and coordination of policy, plans, programmes and development projects for the town. It advises the mayor on the implementation of town development and budgeting and has a controlling function in the formulation and implementation of the budget and development plans. Finally, this department is responsible for the collection and study of information for the evaluation and analysis of the current development of the municipality. Since the transition to democracy in 1990, SECPLAC has been no longer subject to directions from higher levels in the hierarchy. However this creates a problem, because the more influence SECPLAC has over policy formulation, the greater the danger of bureaucratisation of politics becomes. This hinders the participation of town residents in the formulation and implementation of policy in the municipality.

In 1968, for the first time formal legal recognition was given to the neighbourhood committees, junta de vecinos. These were recognised as territorially based, representative organisations which represent the interests of neighbours in a certain area of a town (unidad vecinal). Between 1974 and 1989, they were integrated into the hierarchical administrative structure of the military dictatorship and their chairmen were appointed by the mayor. After 1989, there was a rapid re-democratisation of the juntas, which were thereby able to regain their function as mediator between the neighbourhood residents and the town authorities and national government. Numerous other organisations, which are often territorially and thematically based, also exist at the local level. The numerous committees for the homeless (of the poblaciones comites de allegados) fall into this category. These have a direct relationship with SERVIU, the implementation organ of the Ministry for Housing Construction. However, the so-called *organizaciones de pasaje* or *comites de adelanto*, which, before 1973, were found within the junta organisation, tend to enter into direct negotiations with the state authorities which are responsible for their specific problems.

In comparison with other more spontaneous and less formally organised organisations from the 1980's, which were concerned with basic provisions and were often supported by NGOs, since 1990, the Juntas and other legally recognised organisations have gained more influence. The decline of the autonomous organisations is related to the demands from outside to channel participation into institutional forms (see Bultmann 1995: 220; Oxhorn 1995: 255ff). The increasing institutionalisation of participation within the new framework after 1990 has led to more autonomy from political parties for the representatives of the urban poor, but their dependence has been transferred to the state institutions. In this way, the specific and technical, bureaucratic manner in which the demands of the urban poor are dealt with impedes any unification of the inhabitants of the Poblaciones, as a social movement.

The Emergence of Poor Neighbourhoods (Poblaciones)

The increasing concentration of Chile's population in the towns began relatively early in the Latin American context. The proportion of those living in towns was already higher than that of those living in the countryside in 1940. In 1991, the level of urbanisation, that is the proportion of the population living in towns with more than 2,000 inhabitants, was approx. 86%. In the 1950s and 1960s, rural-urban migration reached its climax with approx. 4% annually in Santiago. The strong growth of the population of Santiago can be traced to the industrialisation strategy, which was orientated towards the domestic market. This attracted workers from rural areas and those from the saltpetre region in northern Chile, who had become unemployed. The migrants usually lived in so-called *Cites* and *Conventillos*. These two forms of accommodation were in the centre of town and comprised mass letting of very small 'flats'. Because landlords were not prepared to invest in the up keep of the flat, they became dilapidated. In this way, the first poverty belt arose around the colonial inner-city of Santiago.

Once the capacity of these flats had been reached, so-called Poblaciones appeared at the southern periphery of the town. These first 'marginal settlements' were given the name *'Poblaciones Callampas'* because they shot up from the ground like mushrooms (=callampas). The appearance of the Callampas had no particular political background, such as subsequent land occupations (*Tomas de Terrenos*), which in part came from these Callampas. In contrast to the Callampas, there was often a central, party-political orientated, organisation behind land occupation. In the 1960s and at the start of the 1970s, land occupation, mostly organised by political parties, was one of the most important forms of migration from the countryside and of accommodation for the urban lower classes. Other opportunities for migration were provided by the so-called *Operaciones Sitio* (Sites and Services) under the government of Frei Montalca (1964–1970) and by state housing construction projects under Frei and Allende (1970–1973).

During the military dictatorship, the Poblaciones experienced internal growth. This was due not least to the inadequate housing policy of the authoritarian government and the related lack of housing. This led to an increase in density of the plots and flats, which is described in Chile by the term 'Allegamiento' (see Gilbert 1992: 78f). The 'Allegados' engaged in extension or conversion of accommodation, either on the plot or in the house of the owner, to whom they were usually related.

Greater Santiago, with its population of 5 million, is the only Chilean city of such metropolitan extent. In 1986, almost 40% of the whole Chilean population were concentrated here. Current urban development in Chile is characterised by three trends. Firstly, the trend to further urbanisation has continued and in 1998 reached 86%. Secondly, Santiago has increasing importance in relation to the whole population. The third trend is a new phenomenon: the increase in importance of medium-sized towns of between 50,000 and 300,000 inhabitants (see Rosenfeld et al. 1994: 129). The growth of the medium-sized towns is greater than that of the centres Concepcion/Talacahuano and Vina de Mar/Valparaiso with approx. one million inhabitants, as well as that of small towns with under 50,000 inhabitants, which both demonstrate tendencies of stagnation.

There are only estimates as to the real extent of the Pobladores, and these often only deal with Greater Santiago. In 1993, Urmeneta et al. (1994: 13) calculated the proportion of pobladores in Greater Santiago at 41%. The same authors give a proportion of 33% for 1986. The poblaciones are also inhabited by groups who cannot be considered members of the poor population. There are not only great differences between the types of poblaciones, there are also heterogeneous social and economic structures within each poblacion. While economic hetero-geneity is mainly related to the employment and income situation, social heterogeneity is related to the relationship of groups or individuals to their human environment (organisation, contacts, religion etc.).

In the social sense, there is a clear desire for differentiation within the poblaciones. This can be explained by the pobladores' wish to defend themselves from their negative external image (criminality, alcoholism etc.) and therefore distance themselves from it and the 'other' pobladores (Campero 1987: 47). This phenomenon increases social differentiation and does not contribute to common action amongst the residents. This differentiation occurs in a way that allows both collective and solidarity relations to exist alongside individualistic orientations. However, the preference for collective social practices does not normally entail in-tegration into a larger movement aimed at overcoming the situation of poverty. Rather, collective action is limited to various smaller groups in a poblacion, which have only limited contact with one another, if any at all (see Espinoza 1994: 198f; 1993: 44ff; Guerra 1994: 206). The increased presence of numerous religious groups, or sects (Pentecostal Church, Mormons etc.) in the poblaciones has also encouraged the tendency towards social differentiation (Guerra 1994: 204ff).

Ivory Coast: Sylvia Schmitt

§ THE Ivory Coast was founded as a French colony in 1893 and re-mained subject to the general governor of French West Africa (AOF) until independence in 1960 (Ziemer 1978: 644). The Ivory Coast has been moulded in an economic, social, cultural and political sense by its first president, F. Houphouët-Boigny (Vogel 1991: 453). Since political independence the Ivory Coast was ruled by Houphouët-Boigny until his death in December 1993. Formal and informal power was concen-trated in the charismatic personality of the state founder. His leadership style has shaped the political culture of the country. In his role as 'père de la nation', he used his popularity and political legitimisation to achieve a level of political stability which is untypical of the region.

The traditional inner-African barter trade was largely substituted by the orientation towards western Europe during the colonial period (Wiese 1988: 34). Tropical hardwoods and agricultural products were exported from the Ivory Coast to France, and the wood industry became one of the pillars of the export economy. The predominant cash-crops were palm oil, coffee and cocoa (Wiese 1988: 34). Following the completion of the Vridi Canal in the 1950s, which provides an entrance to the port at Abidjan, the export of agricultural produce grew rapidly (Cohen 1984: 60). After independence, this orientation towards the needs of the world economy remained, and up to 90% of exports were from the primary sector (Jakobeit 1984: 14).

The economic system of the Ivory Coast can be classified as peripheral-capitalist (Ziemer 1978: 643). The coffee and cocoa boom of the 1960s and 1970s increased the need for workers on the plantations, which was satisfied by temporary workers and immigrants from the neighbouring states, especially Burkina Faso. The Ivory Coast is still one of the main exporters of coffee and cocoa in the world. At the end of the 1980s, these agricultural products accounted for nearly 50% of total export income (Jakobeit 1993: 199).

Nearly 25% of those who today live in the Ivory Coast were born outside the country. In the first two decades, 1.5 million of the total population of 8.3 million were foreign immigrants (Michael 1984: 78). Houphouët-Boigny integrated and assimilated the foreign workers from Burkina Faso, Mali, Senegal and other African countries. He gave them right of residence, the right to vote and propagated dual nationality (Vogel 1991: 452). It is important to note, that from 1904 until 1947 Burkina Faso was termed Haute Cote d'Ivoire and was administered as a single French colonial unit together with the Ivory Coast we know today. Many French citizens retained their leading positions even after independence (Ziemer 1978: 662).

In his role as a 'doyen' of politics in Francophone Africa (Jakobeit 1993: 209/210), Houphouët-Boigny played an important role within the region and maintained the orientation of the country's development towards the former mother country, France. The regime adhered to a centrally directed economic policy, which was orientated towards the world market. Society remained bound by traditional African structures, without negating the orientation towards the west. The political system was basically authoritarian-paternalistic (Medard 1982: 61/62). The economic crisis of the 1980s and the subsequent recession and austerity policies (Jakobeit 1993: 198) demonstrated the short life-span of the Ivorian 'economic miracle' of the 1970s. The prices of coffee and cocoa fell rapidly in the late 1970s and resulted in the Ivorian state taking large foreign loans to finance its investment programme (Michel 1984:

86). Under the effects of the economic crisis the 'welfare state' slowly crumbled. At the end of the 1980s, the prices of the two main export products once more dropped considerably. In 1989 and 1990, strict stabilisation and structural adjustment programmes (SAP) were agreed with the IMF to save the public sector and public finances from bankruptcy.

Until 1990, when the multi-party system was introduced, each Ivorian was a member of the state party, PDCI-RDA (Parti Democratique de la Cote d'Ivoire) by birth. The former single party still pervades important areas of society. The party organisation extends from village committees and neighbourhood committees, to Soussections in the administration and departments at the national level (Ziemer 1978: 652). Party organisation and the country's administrative apparatus are basically identical. Social protests and political unrest in 1990 led to some of the measures of the SAP being taken back. Political unrest and student strikes also characterised subsequent years. The decline in legitimacy of the regime was caused by the serious economic, social and political crises which had shaken the country since 1989/90. Houphouët-Boigny's long stay in a French hospital, the unanswered question of his successor and the effects of political events in the rest of the world after 1989/90 led to a climate of social and political tension. The introduction of the rigorous austerity programme finally led to open criticism of the political leadership and the president. The political conditionality of western development aid and the new realism of the French socialists ('La Baule') acted as a catalyst in the democratisation processes of Francophone Africa (Kanté 1994: 172ff). At the end of 1990, the first multi-party elections since the beginning of the 1960s were conducted.

However, in general, the rigid policy of structural adjustment succeeded in leading the economy out of crisis. In the long term, this consequent policy helped the new state president, Bédié (since the death of Houphouët-Boigny) gain legitimacy and he was able to present the fruits of this economic policy as his own success. Devaluation of the CFA-Franc, privatisation of state enterprises and the continuing debt problem marked the economic development of the 1990s. The devaluation of January 1994 once again demonstrated the dependence of the Ivorian state on external donor countries and organisations. The economic situation of the lower and lowest income classes continued to worsen, because these groups of the population were particularly hit by the increase in prices, e.g. for medicine and rice. Even though devaluation of the Franc led to an improvement of the situation in the countryside, and the urban elites had been the main group to profit from the over-valuation of the F-CFA, the generally poor economic situation and the price increases also hit the urban poor very hard. The level of debt of the Ivory Coast remains one of the highest amongst the developing countries.

Since the 1980s, increasing economic difficulties have forced the state to reduce the budget of the local authorities. Poverty has increased conspicuously in the towns and, since the devaluation in 1994, the financial situation of the local authorities has worsened. Necessary investment in physical and social infrastructure has not occurred. However, in comparison with other African states in the region, the Ivorian state still manages to provide relatively effective basic services. The elections of 1995/6 confirmed the existing majority, and the incumbent president was re-elected. The opposition increasingly lost profile and tempting offers of participation in government caused important opposition leaders to move into the government camp. The president, Bédié, campaigned both domestically and internationally for his policy of a form of democratic state which is adapted to African conditions. Without their leadership figures, the opposition parties can hardly make an impact on the Ivorian multi-party system, not to mention presenting effective opposition policies. The debt relief negotiations ended with generous conditions on the side of the donor countries and the Club of London. Domestic political scandals, as well as revelations concerning support of the electoral campaign from the old apartheid regime in South Africa, did not do much damage. Only the possible candidacy of the former prime minister and IMF Vice-President, Ouattara, presented a serious challenge. His candidacy, however, was finally prevented by a new electoral law.

The era of a stable and internally peaceful state came to an end with the death of Houphouët-Boigny. Anti-foreign and tribal tendencies are increasing in both Ivorian society and politics. Of ten major projects (such as bridge building and the extension of the international airport in Abidjan) aimed at demonstrating the dream of an African 'elephant' to the outside world, only a few have begun to date. Bédié's success in the region, and in foreign policy with France, has been far less than

Table 2.5 Level of debt

	1990	1991	1992	1993
External Debt (billion $)	16.62	17.56	17.99	19.15
Debt Service Rate (%)	34.2	37.1	32.3	30.0

Source: EIU 1995.

that of his predecessor. In addition, the external political setting has changed. France is reconsidering its relationship and with possibilities in Africa and the Francophone world. Ten years after the fall of the Berlin Wall, political relations have changed in a new world (economic) order. This is also true of the relations between France and the Ivory Coast and the former Ivorian state party. The December 1999 military coup and the (heavily rigged) presidential elections in the autumn of the year 2000, in which the opposition candidate, Gbagbo (FPI), was elected the winner, left the country in a state of limbo.

Social Structure and Social Inequality

The Ivory Coast is still an agrarian state, but its society can no longer be divided into a 'plantation bourgeoisie' and state class on the one hand, and an agrarian lower class on the other. Following Gibbal (1974: 27), one can discern three main groups: privileged classes (high-ranking officials and decision makers, rich plantation owners and traders), middle classes (teachers and other state employees, industrial workers), and the poor classes (lower employees, planters, workers and helpers). Since the 1970s, a 'state class' concentrated in the towns has evolved, whose economic base can be found in transport, the trade and service sector, and most of all in the administrative apparatus (Hille-brand/Mehler 1994).

Increasing urbanisation over the past decades has led, especially in the economic centres (Abidjan, Bouaké, San Pedro), to further social differentiation. The economic boom of the 1970s facilitated the evolu-tion of an educated elite in the towns, which today forms the middle class. Income distribution since the middle of the 1980s is as follows: the lowest 20% of households account for 5% of total income, while the highest 20% of households account for 52.7% (Jakobeit 1993: 206). The primary sector employs 64% of those actively employed (Hille-brand/Mehler 1994). The policies of privatisation and liberalisation at the end of the 1980s facilitated the formation of an economically defined middle class, but these policies also affected the extremely high number of those employed in state services (privatisation of previously state-owned enterprises). Impoverishment in this group has increased. Restructuring increasingly prevented the use of clientelistic practices, which until now had served integration into the socio-political as well as the economic system. The increasing impoverishment of the middle classes and the increase of absolute poverty as a result of the effects of the economic crisis and restructuring are causing social disintegration which goes beyond that of current social inequalities. In times of economic crisis, the high proportion of unskilled workers from the neighbouring African states provokes social tensions in the Ivorian population, which is hit by high unemployment. This enmity towards foreigners can express itself in open action against citizens of other African states. At the same time, the policy of liberalisation makes the economic situation of the Ivorian small farmers more difficult. This may also develop into a further powder keg for Ivorian society.

Political-cultural Aspects

Since independence, the political culture has been moulded by the personalistic and paternalistic leadership style of the founding president F. Houphouët-Boigny.This can be described as 'neo-patrimonial': 'Like a traditional monarch, the neopatrimonial leader often cultivated the image of the pater familias, who was directly responsible for the people's welfare' (Bratton/Walle 1997: 64). A further building block of this political leadership was, and is, a form of clientelism which maintains the political order by a patronage relationship between the state and society. Political contacts are still based on clientelistic relations based on ethnic-regional affiliations. At all levels of the state, the observation of ethnic proportionality in the policies of cooptation and patronage has had a great influence on the political stability of the country (Jakobeit 1993: 194). This form of political culture has outlived the death of F. Houphouët-Boigny. 'Patrimonial logic is internalized in the formal institutions of neopatrimonial regimes' (Bratton/Walle 1997: 62). But the legitimacy of the president can no longer base itself on these clientelistic relations alone. Bédié's policy of 'démocratie apaisée', which further split and weakened the opposition, did not change the basic political culture of the former one-party state. Membership in the former single party and the bureaucratic state class still decided control of political and economic power (Jakobeit 1993: 209). The demo-cratisation of society in an, at best, formally democratised state system is still in its infancy. Democratic rules governing daily political relations between the opposition and government remain dependent on the often arbitrary interpretations of the president. The introduction of the multi-party system and the changed geo-political situation have affected, nevertheless, not only the democratisation process, but also the everyday culture of Ivorian society. For the first time, the population, especially the lower and lowest income groups, have been given the opportunity to turn their back on the logic of clientelistic and neopatrimonial relationships and to make use of a pluralistic right to vote.

Characteristics of the Political System

The president is at the pinnacle of a state model which is based on that of the fifth French Republic.[9] Until 1990, the position of prime minister[10] did not exist. The president is both supreme commander of the armed forces and chairman of the governing party, and is elected for five years in direct general elections. He appoints and dismisses the ministers, who are responsible only to him. According to the French model, the national parliament advises and supports the president. It has 175 representatives, and the right to decide the budget and proclaim new laws are within its competencies (Ziemer 1978: 660). A further body is the economic and social council, which is also based on the French model. It has an advisory function in the formulation of economic and social policies. Its chairman is appointed by the president.

Sine 1980, decentralisation at the local level has created a semi-competitive system. Since then, numerous candidates within the single party have been able to stand for election for each seat. With the democratisation process, a multi-party system has evolved with a two-round first-past-the-post electoral law. In 1998, the parliament passed a law which extended the period of office of the president by two years to a total of seven. Every Ivorian citizen over the age of 21 has the right to vote. There are some exceptions to the rule, in particular for migrants from Burkina Faso. As a result of many years of residency, members of this immigrant group often have residential status and the right to vote. There are also cases where 'Ivorian passports', which carry with them the right to go to the polls on election day, are distributed.

Even though since 1990 the state party has no longer ruled alone, power remains almost totally in the hands of the president and a small leadership clique within the party. In the eyes of the population, the

Table 2.6 Results of the presidential elections 1990 and 1995

Year	Candidates	Winner	Votes (%)
1990	F. Houphouët-Boigny (PDCI) Laurent Gbabgo (FPI)	F. Houphouët-Boigny	18.3
1995	Henri Konan Bédié (PDCI) Laurent Gbabgo (FPI)*	Henri Konan Bédié	95.25

*The FPI, RDR and PIT alliance called for a boycott of the elections and Gbabgo withdrew his candidacy.

PDCI is still almost identical with the state, and its party colours are still those of the country; they are the same as those in the national flag. The representatives of the national parliament have so far not managed to gain much profile. However, the vast majority of representatives have neglected the regions they represent in favour of their own personal aims and function within the Abidjan circle of power (Medard 1982: 67; Ziemer 1978: 664). The limited number of representatives from the opposition party,the FPI, have not achieved any major political goals and do not enjoy much respect amongst the population.

Following 1990, many parties were founded.[11] Only the opposition social democratic party, FPI (Front Populaire Ivorien), the workers' party, PIT (Parti Ivorien de Travail), and the republican RDR (Rassemblement des Republicains), which was only founded in 1994 as a splinter group of the PDCI, have remained important. Even though the former have a longer tradition (the FPI was founded in the 1980s) and have a programmatic orientation, they are still concentrated around a single personality. Thus, the general secretary of the FPI, Gbagbo, who was exiled in the 1980s, still plays a very important role. Following the stabilisation of the power relations of the former state party after the second general elections since the return to party pluralism and as a result of President Bédié's successful policy of cooptation, only the FPI offered a personal alternative to the PDCI.

The results of the first democratic multi-party elections are said to have been manipulated. The role of traditional and cultural mechanisms in Ivorian society must be included in the analysis of the change. Such factors played an important role in the first pluralistic presidential elections because voters did not really look at the party abbreviation behind the name of the candidate, but merely at the candidate's name and their social and regional affiliations (Kanté 1994: 182/183).

The limited importance of the elections to the national parliament can be ascertained by the low turn-out. In 1980, turn-out was 43%, in

Table 2.7 Results of the elections to the national parliament

Year	Party	Seats
1990	PDCI	166
	FPI	9
1995	PDCI	148
	FPI	13
	RDR	13

1985 it was 46% and in 1990 it was 40% (Kanté 1994: 170). In comparison, the presidential elections enjoyed a turn-out of 98% (1980), 99.9% (1985) and 69% (1990) (Kanté 1994: 170). The electoral boycott in 1995 aimed to draw attention to discrimination during the drawing of constituency boundaries, and the fact that neither the opposition nor international observers were permitted access to the electoral committee. Unrest amongst the population and rumours of an imminent military putsch caused isolated incidences of violence. The tactics employed against critical reports by Ivorian journalists and also against politicians who supported the electoral boycott demonstrate the merely formal character of the democratic system to date.

The Urban Setting

The policy of decentralisation, which has been ongoing since 1980, demonstrates two clear trends: the first decade is characterised by the state's desire to retain control and make decisions at the local level; furthermore, state logic still views the delegation of competencies as weakening and contributing to the loss of respect for the role of the state. Attahi (1997: 162) describes the problem of an over-centralised, one-party state in the Ivory Coast, and also other countries in Francophone West Africa, as an inheritance from the colonial past which has been strengthened by more than three decades of continuous single-party rule. Since 1995, development programmes from donor countries, and in particular the World Bank, aim to support local authorities in the administration of their affairs.

Decentralisation created a formal platform for the participation of the local population. However, this is not adequately supported by the local authorities. A lack of seriousness on the part of the central government to create politically and financially autonomous political decision-making institutions in the municipalities can also be observed.

In 1965, three million inhabitants still lived in the countryside, and 25% of the population lived in towns. In 1972, nearly 13% of the population lived in the capital city, Abidjan (Borchert 1972: 25). It is estimated that in the period between 1965 and 1975, 715,000 migrants moved to the towns, which is equivalent to an annual average rate of migration of 5.6% (Becker/Homer 1994: 88). The birth rate in 1978 represented 38% of the increase in population in Abidjan, and 46% in other towns. In 1988, the natural rate of growth of the population of Abidjan was 3.5% (Antoine/Kouamé 1994: 145). This growth dynamic can be explained by the declining death rate and a high birth rate (INS 1994a: 5).[12]

Immigration from neighbouring countries was very important not only for urbanisation, but also for economic development. The policy of immigration began as forced labour during colonial rule. In the first decade after independence, the Ivorian state replaced this with an agreement with Upper Volta (since 1985 Burkina Faso) which deals with immigration (INS 1994a: 19). The vast majority of immigrants from neighbouring countries moved to the economic metropolis, Abidjan. The Burkinabes are also still vital as farm workers in the coffee and cocoa plantations. The proportion of foreigners has reached between 25 and 40%.[13] Between 1963 and 1995, 76% of the total population growth can be traced to rural–urban migration (Potter/Ademola 1990: 161), which is not limited to migration within the country. In 1990, the total population had officially grown to 11.4 million. The level of urbanisation in the Ivory Coast is 47%.

Marginalisation and Urban Poverty

The colonial period laid the foundations for the division between poor and rich areas within a town by segregation into white and African quarters. In total, there are 2.5 million people living in Abidjan, of whom approx. 400,000 inhabit so-called precarious settlements. These quarters are not a peripheral ring around the town; they are distributed throughout the city. The annual growth rate of the population in the precarious settlements has been 19%, while the city as a whole grows annually by 4% (Dembélé 1995: 21). In 1996, the poor neighbourhoods in the metropolis were home to between 20% and 30% of the population. For decades, town planners viewed the phenomenon of poor settlements in Abidjan as a temporary phenomenon - similar to the situation in other economic metropolises in the Third World. In the formative years, these quarters provided accommodation mainly to immigrant workers.

These 'quartiers populaires' (such as Yopougon, Treichville) remained very precarious and there was no other cheap accommodation available. Because the immigrants did not think they would stay for long, and because infrastructure in these poor areas was not provided by the state this precarious situation prevailed for a long time. The economic crisis in the middle of the 1980s caused the settlements to grow rapidly and the proportion of Ivorian citizens in them increased. Employment was largely transferred to the informal sector. From 1990, programmes aimed at renewal were implemented in more and more settlements. With the implementation of a housing programme, initiated by the World Bank in 1992, this situation begins to change. Legalisation and integration of certain settlements (from nearly 90 precarious settlements, 66 have been chosen) is also planned (Dembélé 1995: 22).

Kenya: Dirk Berg-Schlosser

§ WITHIN the territory of the Kenyan state there are, according to the official census, 42 clearly defined linguistically and culturally different ethnic groups. The five largest (Kikuyu, Luo, Abaluyia, Kamba and Kalenjin) combined make up nearly three quarters of the population. Their structures and composition are, however, very different. Some are clearly made up of different sub-groups (e.g. Kalenjin, Mijikenda and Abaluyia), which have only recently been given a common name. Others, such as the Kikuyu and Kamba, demonstrate a high degree of linguistic and cultural identity. In pre-colonial times, none of the groups had a common political structure. Apart from some minimal exceptions (on the coast and in the west), all the peoples were structured in an egalitarian and segmentary manner according to clans and age groups. Decisions were made consensually at the local level by councils of male elders.

Colonisation began towards the end of the 19th century and, with the construction of the railway line to Uganda, took the form of a European settlement colony. Large areas of fertile ('white') highlands were placed at the disposal of the not more than 3,000 families of colonisers. Some of the local African peasants were placeed into reservations, while others were made to work for the European estate owners via the hut and poll tax. Africans were not permitted to plant lucrative export products such as coffee and tea until the middle of the 1950s.

Economic Development and Social Structure

The rural population thus consisted of a landless rural proletariat (in the region of several hundreds of thousands of people) and a majority of small peasants who mostly engaged in subsistence production. There was also increasing social differentiation in the towns: workers (e.g. in factories which processed agricultural products, on the railways, or in the port of Mombasa) and mostly unqualified employees (in the households, offices etc.). In this period, the middle classes in trade, crafts and administration were mostly immigrants from the Indian sub-continent. Therefore, according to criteria of economic status and race, Kenya demonstrated a clearly sub-divided, almost caste-like, social structure with only limited mobility between the respective groups.

This only changed after the Second World War when increasing numbers of Africans, who had been educated at missionary schools, found their way into middle employment and administrative positions. In the meantime, population pressure in the countryside and the poverty and discontent of the rural farming population had drastically increased. This found expression in unrest from an independence movement (Mau Mau) in the 1950s, based mostly among the Kikuyu in Central Province, which no longer shied away from violent action. The unrest cost 95 European lives and more than 12,000 African victims. In order to deal with the social problems which had caused the unrest, a far-reaching land reform was introduced which concentrated fragmented African landholdings and gave title deeds to individual African families. At the same time, the ban on planting export products was lifted and increased production for the market was supported by loans. However, the White Highlands remained untouched. In this way, a class of relatively successful small and medium-sized farmers was created, although they faced an increasing number of landless people. Because the former group mainly consisted of people who had been more welcoming towards the colonisers (Loyalists), and the latter, as previously interned Mau-Mau supporters, were often not taken into account during land registration, the political lines between Africans were sharpened.

The internal pressure, and political independence, which was achieved in 1963, opened the way for members of the African population to take up top positions. The highest positions in the administration were quickly Africanised and taken over by members of the newly created educated citizenry (there has been a university in Nairobi since 1952). The White Highlands were divided: one third was divided into small plots and passed into African small-scale ownership; over time, another third also passed into African hands in the form of large estates, those benefiting coming mostly from the political elite of the country; and the final third remained as plantations owned by European-dominated companies. The elite members of the political administration also quickly gained access to well-paid supervisory positions in the private economy and in the 'para-statal' sector (e.g. in 'marketing boards' etc.).

In the meantime, the Asian population lost its dominance in trade and crafts. In so far as those who had not opted for Kenyan citizenship on independence had not been forced to emigrate, they turned their energies towards industrial production, the export economy and the academic 'liberal professions' (lawyers, doctors, engineers etc.). The

European dominance in the industrial and tourism sectors was left mostly untouched. On the contrary, the increasing presence of offices of multi-national corporations in the regional centre of Nairobi and the construction of foreign-owned hotels and lodges on the coast and in the nature reserves was met with political good will.

These upper and middle classes, although small and medium-sized farmers are also included in the latter, face a large number of dependent employees in private companies and lower level administration. In addition, the number of those involved in 'informal', but mostly poorly paid, occupations (e.g. transforming wrecked cars into cooking pans) under the hot sun ('jua kali') has increased dramatically. A clearly defined class society has arisen from the caste society, and its inherent conflicts are increasingly being expressed in the political arena.

The total population currently totals approx. 30 million. The vast majority (about 70%) is still employed in agriculture. These contribute approx. 30% to GDP. The manufacturing sector, services, tourism and the public sector each account for 15%. The non-monetary economy (excluding agriculture) accounts for approx. 8–10% of GDP (as of 1988). Approximately 30% of the population live in towns (with more than 2,000 inhabitants). The capital city, Nairobi, with more than 2 million inhabitants is by far the largest. Kisumu, the third largest town in the country, currently has 250,000 inhabitants (these are approximate figures because the results of the last population census in 1999 are not yet available).

After, in African terms, relatively successful economic development in the first three decades following independence in which GDP grew by an average of approx. 5%, mostly due to small farmers, certain sectors of industry, tourism and a very dynamic informal sector, the 1990s were rocked by crises. The prices for the main export products, coffee and tea, decreased; tourism declined, amongst other things as a result of political crises including some ethnic strife and increased criminality. Foreign debt increased dramatically. Per capita income which, with a rate of population growth of 3–4%, had increased considerably less than the National Product, also declined over the past years.

Political Development

To date, political development has clearly been dictated by the upper and middle classes who, despite some critical appearances, have been able to widen their material base considerably. The ethnic focus was first and foremost amongst the Kikuyu and Luo, who both dominated the governing party, KANU. The first president, Jomo Kenyatta, was a Kikuyu. However, the Luo became more and more isolated after the attempt to propagate a programmatic opposition to the governing party under the leadership of former vice-president Oginga Odinga and his Kenya Peoples' Union (KPU). At first this party had followers in the lower classes in other regions, including Central Province, but in the final analysis, it failed. After the murder of Tom Mboya in 1969, the last important Luo minister in Kenyatta's government, this isolation became more obvious. Other currents of opposition, such as that represented by the populist Kikuyu politician J. M. Karikuri, were suppressed. This occurred partly by way of laws inherited from the colonial period, such as 'preventive detention' (unlimited detention without a proper court hearing). In individual cases, naked violence was also employed (Kariuki was murdered in 1976).

After Kenyatta's death in 1978, a presidential transition was achieved using constitutional channels to the advantage of the former vice-president, Daniel Arap Moi, a member of a sub-group of the Kalenjin. However, the dominant class alliance remained, even though the ethnic weighting had changed to the advantage of some of the smaller ethnic groups, in addition to the Kalenjin, the Maasai (the present vice-president George Saitoti is of Maasai/Kikiyu descent), the Abaluyia and groups on the coast. This was especially true after 1982 when the 'grey eminence' of the regime, the justice minister Charles Njonjo, who had also been one of those responsible for the smooth transition from Kenyatta to Moi, was booted out because of a corruption scandal, and also for political reasons. An attempted putsch in the same year supported by members of the airforce, university students and other opposition forces failed.

As a result, the previously rather moderate policy of the regime became harsher (after gaining power, Moi had proclaimed an amnesty for all political prisoners, including the well-known writer Ngugi wa Thiong'o). Influential forces amongst the Kikuyu and Luo now increasingly tried to organise an effective opposition. In the last few years this has become easier as a result of international developments which, with the end of the east-west conflict, called forth a 'perestroika' for many of the authoritarian African potentates who until then had been supported by their respective international allies. In December 1991, strong pressure from international development agencies and creditor countries forced Moi to announce a return to a multi-party system. The opposition parties coalesced around FORD (Forum for the Restoration of Democracy), in which Oginga Odinga and prominent Kikuyu politicians, such as Kenneth Matiba, became active once more; and the

Democratic Party under the chairmanship of another former vice-president, Mwai Kibaki, a Kikuyu from the somewhat more northern Nyeri district in Central Province. Later, FORD split into 'FORD-Kenya' under the chairmanship of Odinga's son Raila, with an obvious ethnic regional focus amongst the Luo in Nyanza province; and 'FORD-Asili' under the chairmanship of Matiba. In addition, a large number of smaller, but basically meaningless parties were also founded. Before the elections in 1997, FORD-Kenya split once more and Raila Odinga founded the National Democratic Party (NDP). Because Matiba was no longer a candidate, FORD-Asili also broke up. The more strongly programmatic Social Democratic Party (SDP) was able to benefit from the two splits. In the elections, KANU profited from the first-past-the-post electoral law, based on the British system, and despite only a plurality of the total number of votes (less than 40%) was able to gain the majority of seats.

Despite the existence of various parties, which are reflected in the parliamentary and presidential elections (see Table 2.8), the basic pattern of Kenyan politics has remained the same. Influential personalities from various ethnic groups, who have also usually attained private wealth through political means, are surrounded by local and regional followers, who for their part expect material advantages in the form of jobs etc. in return for this support (e.g. by voting in elections). This sort of clientelism is independent of class, but remains strongly personalistic and therefore also regional and ethnically orientated. However, this does not mean that there is no competition within a constituency, even under the former one-party system, and a certain variation of emphasis and groupings within ethnic groups exist.

For a long time, at the national level this led to an ethnically overarching alliance between important people and groups because no one

Table 2.8 Parliamentary seats according to party

	1992	1997
KANU	95	113
FORD-KENYA	31	18
NDP	–	22
FORD-ASILI	31	–
SDP	–	16
DP	23	41
Others	10	10
Total	180	220

could totally dominate the others. Thus, a certain consociational pattern evolved, even though the ethnic accents were somewhat unevenly distributed. The most important patron of all, however, the president, remained protected from competition. The necessary political correction and feedback mechanisms failed at this level. One can thus speak of a 'semi-competitive' system, which increasingly fell into crisis the longer the highest patron remained in office. In the future, the now limited presidential period of office to two terms could help correct this situation. 'Competitive clientelism' in Kenya cannot therefore be equated with the European pattern of pluralistic and programmatically orientated party politics.

Administrative Structures, Urban Setting

Independent Kenya has retained the strongly centralist administrative structure and division into provinces and districts with their respective 'commissioners', who are appointed by the president, that it inherited from colonial rule. Local administration falls to the responsibility of the Ministry of Local Government. Larger towns have their own town or city council, with directly elected councillors. The mayor is also directly elected. However, local administration is headed, in line with the British system, by a civil servant, the town clerk. Due to recurring corruption scandals over the past decades, individual town councils, including that in Nairobi, have increasingly been placed under the direct control of the ministry.

The lowest level of the administrative structure is the 'Chief' (also directly appointed) 'Chief' of the respective 'location' (town neighbourhood, settlement). In contrast to the traditional, who hardly played a role amongst Kenyan ethnic groups in pre-colonial times, they are simply administrative officers, although with far-reaching competences, including control of the police in their area. In most cases, the Chief is also integrated into the structure of the dominant state party, KANU, and can therefore sometimes make use of the violent KANU Youth Wings for intimidation and also for his own personal goals. However, the Chief is, as shown in our study, the most important contact person and point of mediation, via whom clientelistic relations to higher levels in the administration and governing party are often formed. The elected town councillors and urban members of the national parliament, in contrast to their importance in the countryside, only play a limited role.

Notes

1. The Party Law of 1979 demanded the dissolution of the two existing parties ARENA and MDB. The PDS (Partido Democratico Social) was formed as the successor party of ARENA, and the MDB became the PMDB.

2. In the literature various forms of transition are documented. 1: transition via regime collapse (e.g. Argentina 1982/3), 2: transition via voluntary abstinence (e.g. Peru 1980, Bolivia 1979/80), 3: transition pacts (transition via negotiated settlements) (Mainwaring/Share 1986: 209).

3. At the time of the survey, in Autumn 1995, the minimum wage was R$100 (US$105).

4. PPB/PDS, PFL, PRN and PTB belong to the political right, PMDB and PSDB to the centre and PDT, PSB and PT to the political left.

5. Between 1986 and 1990, there were almost 200 changes of party allegiance within the congress (from a total of 570 seats before the 1990 elections). Between 1990 and 1995, more than 25% of parliamentarians changed party allegiance (Thibaut 1996: 257), and between 1994 and 1995 more than 100 parliamentarians changed once more.

6. Between 1980 and 1990, the population of Rio de Janeiro grew by 8%; during the same time the number of Favelados increased by 34% (IPLAN-Rio 1995).

7. In this connection, the urbanisation programme 'Favela-Barrio', which was started in 1996 is of great importance. The programme aims to convert 90 of the 600 favelas in Rio de Janeiro into normal parts of the city and represents an attempt to integrate the poor settlements.

8. FOSIS, Fondo de Solidaridad e Inversion Social, came into being as a result of pressure from the World Bank. It aims to fight absolute poverty, which increased as a result of the structural adjustment programme in the 1980s (see Stahl 1994).

9. Constitution of 31.10.1960 (see also Jakobeit 1984: 17).

10. In November 1990, with the introduction of a multi-party system, the national parliament agreed to the introduction of the position of prime minister (Munzinger Archiv 1994).

11. According to Hillebrand and Mehler (1994), by Spring 1994 as many as 42 parties were licensed, some of which can be considered 'administrative creations', whose aim was to weaken the opposition.

12. The extent to which AIDS is reflected in demographic developments remains unclear. For some years now the Ivory Coast has engaged in national awareness programmes and public health campaigns.

13. The proportion of foreigners is a political issue, and the vague figures result from this, see Le Republicain Ivorien. No. 262. 14.11.1996.

CHAPTER 3

Housing Conditions and Policies

Sylvia Schmitt

§ WITHIN each of the countries briefly presented so far there are specificities which affect settlement patterns and the respective state policies concerning the urban poor. In this chapter, first migration will be briefly examined as a cause of marginal settlements. Then, the concrete housing problems in the settlements studied will be analysed. Do these settlements in all four states show a similar lack of provision of water, sewerage, electricity or health centres and schools? Finally, the state housing policies and relationships to precarious settlements will be characterised. What framework does the state provide in each country? Do the four states behave in a similar manner towards the poverty-stricken population? Is it true that housing policy primarily serves clientelistic networks and the maintenance of existing power relations? In this sense, the degree of integration or marginalisation of poor neighbourhoods in both the respective towns and the democratic processes will be dealt with in regard to spatial, and socio-political aspects. This leads to the question of whether and how far specific social housing policies interact with or supplement individual initiatives by the poor population in such settlements.

Urbanisation and Precarious Living

Precarious settlements have a large influence on the spatial extent and demographic development of the towns in the countries studied. Migration into poor areas especially caused the towns to grow. At present, the settlements examined demonstrate the following situation:

In Brazil, only 6% of the favelados questioned still live in the neighbourhood where they were born. In Man (Ivory Coast) and Santiago de Chile, the proportion is 13%, and in Kenya, 19% for Kisumu, and 32% for Nairobi. Thus, change of place of residence is part of everyday life for the urban poor in all four countries. In Brazil, almost three quarters had left their town of birth (73%). Often, the urban poor move from rural areas or small towns to large cities. In Nairobi (52%) and Santiago (48%), however, about half of those questioned had only moved their place of residence within the boundaries of their city of birth. In total, almost two thirds were born outside the vicinity of their current place of residence. Our data also confirm the high proportion of foreign immigrant workers and their families in precarious settlements in Abidjan. The degree to which the current place of residence is the result of social advancement or decline can be determined by enquiring as to the previous place of residence. Approximately one third (31%) came from rural areas into the town, and half of those questioned (55%) had lived in a residential area with a similar level of infrastructure. The remaining about 15% had lived in a (somewhat) better area before and thus had experienced some social decline. Altogether a country-specific picture resulted as shown in Table 3.1.

The influx into marginal settlements in the metropoles of Brazil, Chile and the Ivory Coast directly from the countryside is thus, in contrast to that in medium-sized towns, limited. More often, those questioned had moved from another precarious neighbourhood into a similar settlement. In Kenya, direct migration from the countryside still dominates. Social decline is most apparent in Brazil, followed by the Ivory Coast and Kenya. In this respect, Chile is an exception.

The process of favelisation in Rio de Janeiro is closely related to the socio-economic changes which began in the 1930s. Improved transportation networks, new industries and the transformation of the city centre into a bank and trading centre in the 1940s and 1950s pushed the favelas to the periphery of the city. Migration from north eastern Brazil

Table 3.1 Place of birth (percentage of population)

	Brazil		Chile		Ivory Coast		Kenya	
	M	T	M	T	M	T	M	T
Same quarter	8	3	13	–	1	13	32	19
Same city	21	21	48	34	11	29	52	18
Other city/region	70	76	39	66	43	42	5	62
Foreign country	–	–	–	–	46	16	12	2

Note: M = Metropolis; T = Town
Source: Project Political Participation

doubled the poor population in Rio de Janeiro and Sao Paulo in the 1960s. In both cities, the debt crisis in the 1980s led to increasingly difficult living conditions in the favelas, which caused a general increase in migration to medium-sized towns. In Chile in 1940 the proportion of those living in towns was already higher than in the countryside. In 1990, the level of urbanisation reached 86%.[1] Between 1940 and 1952, the population of Santiago grew by 42%, which can be traced to increasing industrialisation. The poorer sections of the population from rural areas, small towns and the north of Chile moved to Santiago. This strong flow resulted in a lack of suitable accommodation. By the 1940s, the first poor settlements appeared on the southern periphery of Santiago.

After the colonial period, industrial development in the Ivory Coast remained largely limited to exports for the former 'motherland', France. Immigrants from neighbouring states were needed as plantation workers, as well as in the developing metropolis of Abidjan to fill employment requirements in the port and on large construction sites. Precarious settlements grew successively with the increasing need for workers in the industrial and nascent service sector. The increase of transport infrastructure and the high level of agricultural exports such as coffee, cocoa, wood or hevea (for rubber production), led to a high level of urbanisation in the 1960s and 1970s. Medium-sized towns became regional economic centres. With the decline of coffee prices in the middle of the 1980s and the economic crisis in the early 1990s, urbanisation became an expression of a rural-urban exodus, which hit Abidjan especially hard. The precarious settlements have grown rapidly since then and are increasingly home to Ivorian families.

In colonial Kenya, urbanisation, especially along trade routes, was forced by railway construction at the beginning of the twentieth

Table 3.2 Former residence (percentage of population)

	Brazil		Chile		Ivory Coast		Kenya	
	M	T	M	T	M	T	M	T
Rural	14	30	13	35	12	21	58	67
Similar quarter	69	50	86	60	53	68		
Better residential areas	18	20	1	5	36	11	15	9

Note: M = Metropolis; T = Town
Source: Project Political Participation

century. After the Second World War, the return of soldiers led to another rapid increase in the urban population. Land reform in the 1950s and 1960s caused further migration into the towns. Because restrictions on migration were lifted simultaneously with independence, the urban population grew by an annual 7.3% in the years between 1962 to 1969 (Aseka 1990: 62). In the 1970s and 1980s, this increased to over 8%. According to the latest census data, over 3.8 million Kenyans lived in towns in 1989. Precarious urban settlements in Kenya were at first the result of racist segregation. In the residential areas reserved for Africans, only 'semi-permanent' structures could be built. In addition, there were strict rules governing residential rights in urban areas, so that illegal settlements and dwellings formed at the fringes of towns. With independence and increased migration, the number of precarious settlements also grew.

The term precarious living conditions applies to the relative situation in the respective countries. This means that living conditions in Chile and Brazil differ from those in Kenya and the Ivory Coast. Today, almost one fifth of the population in these countries live in precarious residential areas. In Rio de Janeiro, almost 20% of residents, that means approx. 1 million people, live in the favelas. In Santiago de Chile, the proportion of urban poor is approx. 20–30% with a total of approx. 400,000 inhabitants. In Nairobi, more than one million people live in precarious settlements. In 1993, half the population of Nairobi and Kisumu lived in such areas (Karuga 1993: 24).

Problems related to lack of infrastructure such as sewerage, waste collection or electricity are compounded by high residential density. Where some kind of social infrastructure (schools, health centres) exists, in the African cases often Churches and other non-governmental organisations are in charge of them. In Brazil and Chile, many of these institutions owe their existence to collective social initiatives. In regional comparison, construction standards are clearly divergent and point to the differentiated economic development of the countries. In contrast to the African cases, most poor settlements in Chile and Brazil have adequate provision of electricity, water and schools. But the roads are often not paved, electricity is illegally drawn and primary schools are the result of private initiatives. In continental comparison, the existence of houses with several storeys, such as in the Favela Vidigal in Rio de Janeiro, or in the settlement Esperanza in Santiago, offer a disproportionately higher standard of living in comparison with African conditions.

In the medium-sized town of Kisumu in Kenya, the houses are in no better state than those in Nairobi. Basic infrastructure is completely

Table 3.3 Basic infrastructure

Quarter, city	Inhabitants	Water supplies	Electricity	Primary schools
Vidigal, Rio	8,500–15,000	Nearly all houses	Nearly all houses	3
Minha Deusa, Rio	500	Nearly all houses	Nearly all houses	2 in the proximity
São Conrado, Aracaju	ca. 2,000	100% in the old part, insufficient in the new area	Nearly all houses, some illegal	1; 4 in the proximity
Santa Maria, Aracaju	ca. 3,000	Insufficient, own water wells	ca. 100%, mostly illegal	1; 2 in the proximity
Galvarino, Santiago	2,400	100%	100%	In the proximity
Esperanza, Santiago	4,000	100% (in self help)	100% (in self help)	1
Lanin, Temuco	2,400	Nearly all houses	Nearly all houses	In the proximity
Los Boldos, Temuco	6,000	100%	100%	In the proximity
Washington, Abidjan	8,300	3–4, water sold	3–4, illegal	1
Vridi III, Abidjan	8,100	3–4, water sold	n.a.	1
Belle-Ville, Man	7,000	Water sold, water wells	Since 1997	None
Kennedy, Man	3,000	Water sold, water wells	1 or 2 houses	None
Majengo, Nairobi	13,200	Few, water sold in cans	Rare, too expensive	1
Mukuru Kayaba, Nairobi	30,000	Few, water sold in cans	Not available	1
Nyalenda, Kisumu	100,000	Few, water sold in cans	Rare, too expensive	3
Kaloleni, Kisumu	2,000	Few, water sold in cans	Rare, too expensive	1

lacking. In the Ivory Coast, the neighbourhoods in the medium-sized town have a more village-like character than in Abidjan. The houses are solidly constructed, the courtyard is often owned by a family and the grounds are often more extensive. However, provision of infrastructure is as much lacking as in the city. Unclean water in the courtyard wells is often used as drinking water. In Brazil, living and residential conditions in the metropolis Rio are different from those in the medium-sized town, Aracaju. Thus, provision of drinking water in the settlements in Aracaju is limited and the water quality dubious.

In Rio there is a qualitative distinction between older and newer settlements. In older settlements, provision of basic infrastructure has occurred because often residents received it as a present during pre-election campaigns. In the medium-sized Chilean town of Temuco, living conditions are much worse than those in respective settlements in the capital. The houses are mostly made of wood and the roofing material is little more than cardboard boxes dipped in tar, although there are some houses made of brick. In Brazil, favela houses are usually made of solid building material, although the construction often has an improvised character. In African precarious settlements, building materials are mostly recycled wooden planks, cardboard, corrugated iron or a mixture of clay and sand. In Kisumu, in Minha Deusa in Rio and Kennedy in Man the settlements are regularly flooded. The dwellings on the steep slopes of the settlement Washington in Abidjan were partly washed away during the long period of rains in 1966 and there were a number of casualties. The Favela Vidigal in Rio is threatened by erosion, and in Temuco the huts in Lanin often do not survive the winter.

These realities are not necessarily identical with the subjective perceptions of the basic infrastructure. Our survey shows that Brazilian residents are the most content with their living environment, which in this case can be traced to the relative improvement in living conditions over the past years. Only in Brazil do more than two thirds of those questioned describe the general condition of their housing as good or very good. In Chile, more than half of those questioned are discon-

Table 3.4 Evaluation of general state of housing (percentage)

	Brazil	Chile	Ivory Coast	Kenya
(Very) satisfied	8	4	6	61
(Very) dissatisfied	20	56	37	39

Source: Project Political Participation

tented or very discontented with their living environment. In both African cases, more than a third are clearly discontented.

With regard to sanitary installations, those questioned in Brazil and Chile give opposite answers. In Rio and Aracaju, the evaluation is the most positive, while in Santiago and Temuco, the responses are the most negative. In contrast to Latin America, sanitary installations do not exist for 60% of those questioned in Kenya and for 27% of those in the Ivory Coast, where existing toilets are mostly communal shacks.

Table 3.5 Evaluation of sanitary installations (percentage)

	Brazil	Chile	Ivory Coast	Kenya
Satisfied	71	31	43	17
Dissatisfied	23	67	30	23
Not available	6	2	27	61

Source: Project Political Participation

In Chile and Brazil, the evaluation of provision of drinking water presents a similar picture. One third are discontent and two thirds are content with the current infrastructure. In the Ivorian settlements, 72% are content or very content with water provision, and in Kenya, 75% are discontent or very discontent. However, neither in Abidjan nor in Man does individual water provision exist. It is usual to buy water in buckets from one of the few water taps. This also occurs in Kenyan settlements. In Brazil, the situation is very different from settlement to settlement and water provision is often only sometimes ensured. Although in Chile and Brazil almost every house has electricity, a total of 26% of those questioned are still discontented with the technical condition of the connection. These connections have often been laid

Table 3.6 Evaluation of water provision (percentage)

Brazil	Chile	Ivory Coast	Kenya
Satisfied	63	70	80	16
Dissatisfied	31	30	21	7
Not available	6	1	–	77

Source: Project Political Participation

illegally by the residents themselves. In the African cases, there are hardly any connections to the electricity grid.

Table 3.7 Evaluation of electricity supply (percentage)

Brazil	Chile	Ivory Coast	Kenya
satisfied	79	71	39	15
dissatisfied	17	26	17	5
not available	4	3	44	80

Source: Project Political Participation

An important factor for the integration of such settlements into the town and its social and economic spheres of activity is access to cheap public transport. Apart from Kenya, a majority of the residents in the chosen settlements are content with access to transport. The number of those in Kenya, 19%, and the Ivory Coast, 15%, who state public transport is deficient, is somewhat low, because in some settlements only collective taxis (matatus in Kenya) make transport possible. Access to transport is also differentiated amongst the Brazilian settlements. Transport problems often are a political issue in the conflict between governments and settlement representatives.

Table 3.8 Evaluation of public transport facilities (percentage)

	Brazil	Chile	Ivory Coast	Kenya
Satisfied	57	81	76	49
Dissatisfied	43	18	8	32
Not available	–	1	16	19

Source: Project Political Participation

Housing Policies

In this section, the responsible institutions, as well as the change in response and perception of public actors towards precarious or illegal settlements in the individual countries, will be described. Housing policy, depending on the regime, often forms part of a clientelistic system of patronage. Socio-political measures in the educational, health and social sphere, such as pensions and health insurance, or measures aimed at ensuring basic provisions have a longer tradition and greater importance in the two Latin American countries than in Africa. There, people are more dependent on support within the extended family, and only with the change from an agrarian to an urban society do these family ties begin to lose their importance. Thus, necessities of public welfare are moulded by the specific conditions in each state. The willingness of individual regimes to intervene varies greatly and the ability to intervene has reached its limit at various points in time. In all four countries, there was at least an attempt to facilitate basic provisions for the whole population, both in certain sectors (health and education) and in the creation of a public social security system. This, however, in all four cases requires a formal working relationship.

In *Brazil*, state authorities responsible for providing marginal settlements with basic infrastructure occupy different levels within the administration. In the north east (Aracaju) favela policy lies predominantly within the federal state's responsibility. The lack of municipal resources has led to the transfer of originally urban responsibilities, such as waste collection and provision of primary education, to the federal state. In Rio de Janeiro, the favelados turn to the municipal authorities, the so-called 'mayor's office for favelados'. Apart from the areas of health and pre-schooling, other local and regional authorities share responsibility for waste collection, security, property rights and sewerage. Since 1952, numerous institutions (often only for a limited time) have been created and given various tasks. Other federal and national authorities are also involved. At the national level only a few emergency housing programmes have been carried out so far.

In *Chile*, the central government has many years of experience (from the 1920s until 1973) in an outstanding social policy compared to most other Latin American states (Molina 1996: 154ff). The Ministry for Urban Housing (SERVIU) is responsible for the implementation of housing policy, e.g. distribution of subsidised accommodation. Since 1990, on the recommendation of the World Bank, Chile created a programme specifically aimed at combating poverty (FOSIS). In addition other successful housing programmes were inaugurated. Social policy is implemented by town authorities. They decide about the provision of health care, social security payments or food stamps. Since the decentralisation under the military regime, responsibilities for basic infrastructural provision and primary schooling have also been transferred to the local level.

Thus, in the Latin American countries, the development of policies and institutions specially designed to deal with problems of poverty and the favelas can be discerned. However, since the introduction of neo-liberal reforms in the 1980s and 1990s this has been largely limited to some social welfare measures.

In the *Ivory Coast*, housing and other areas of social policy are the responsibility of the respective central ministries. Following decentral-isation in the 1980s, local authorities received more decision making powers and technical and financial resources to deal with the tasks at hand. The mayor is both a representative of the state and responsible before the local council. At the same time, the mayor has an electoral political interest in ensuring residents of settlements which are due to be cleared remain within the constituency. For a long time, the lack of real decision making power in local councils was determined by state policy, which only reluctantly delegated control to lower levels. As a result of decentralisation, now local councils increasingly make use of their formal authority. This tendency is strengthened by cooperation with international development projects and the respective donors.

In *Kenya*, responsibility for housing and social policy for the urban poor is divided between the responsible central ministries, administration at the district level and town authorities. However, the districts have the most important coordinating functions, which were united in the person of the District Development Officer in the middle of the 1970s. This coordination function is formally strengthened by the so-called District Focus on Rural Development, which was introduced in 1983. Respon-sibility for squatter settlements lies in designing and implementing renovation measures or, as the case may be, demolition plans, or the support of self-help groups in precarious settlements. These represent the most important form of social policy for the urban poor.

In all countries, conflicts over the respective responsibilities, or lack of financial autonomy between the different levels, hinder an effective implementation of housing policies. And, one must not forget the factor of corruption. The point of contact for the urban poor is mostly the local council. But as a result of the desolate financial situation and lack of technical expertise, a higher level often decides about town planning and its implementation, for example in a medium-sized town such as Aracaju. The high degree of dependence of Brazilian towns on central state support limits their ability to react in an adequate and flexible manner to local tendencies of social fragmentation (Windhoff-Héritier 1993: 239ff). In Chile, decentralisation under Pinochet created local authorities, which are neither in a financial nor technical position to ensure provision of a suitable infrastructure (Molina 1996:157/158). Since 1980 in the Ivory Coast, the mayor is the major authority to whom the residents of precarious settlements turn, and is therefore viewed as representative of the state and the (unitary) party. In the case of conflicts, such as 'clearance' of an illegal settlement, these often occur not only between the residents of the settlement and the representatives of the state, but also between the local administration and the central government with its respective ministries.

In contrast to the African countries, in Brazil and Chile separate authorities, which were responsible for living conditions in urban areas and problems of poverty, were created at least for a while. Compared to the African countries, the stronger institutionalisation of housing and social policies in Latin America provides the population groups concerned with some explicit rights. Even though funds are still lost to corruption, the pressure for action and accountability on those politically responsible is much greater. In both Latin American countries, the creation of organisational structures in the settlements (neighbourhood organisations) as contacts for local and central political actors can be traced partly to state initiatives, and partly to the endeavours of the local population. In Kenya (local 'chiefs') and in the Ivory Coast ('chiefs' of the party committees), these institutional structures are elements of the former single-party states, and in both countries their main task is the administration and control of the population, as well as their electoral mobilisation (see chapter 7).

The four countries demonstrate a similar course of orientation in state housing policies. Different phases followed one another: conscious ignoring of precarious settlements in the towns, clearance policies, construction of public housing, legalisation and integration of settlements by specific measures. For a long time, violent clearance was the only answer to favelisation in town planning concepts. In the beginning, such actions occurred under the influence of 'modernisation' theory, which viewed such poverty-stricken settlements as temporary. The Kenyan development plan of 1966–1970, for example, explicitly envisaged the expulsion of the urban poor from illegal settlements. Until the start of the 1970s, such settlements were actually destroyed in Nairobi (Stren 1975: 271f.). In the 1970s in Abidjan, some precarious neighbourhoods were completely cleared in order to make space for the middle classes. From 1962 until 1974 in Rio de Janeiro, and especially under the military regime, the favelas were destroyed. In this period, a total of approx. 140,000 favelados were resettled (Valladares 1980: 23). Similarly, after 1973 in Chile the military regime met land occupation, which had increased rapidly between 1968 and 1973, with massive clearances and resettlements, which divided Santiago into rich and poor areas. The majority of precarious settlements in the Ivorian metropolis were to be cleared at the beginning of the 1990s.

Since redemocratisation in Brazil and Chile, such clearances have seldom occurred. However, large-scale illegal land occupation is still not tolerated. Some town planning concepts envisage clearance, without taking compensation or resettlement into consideration. In Aracaju, clearance of land, which estate agents are interested in, remains one of the goals of state policy. The poor settlements, 'invasoes',[2] the majority of which are not officially recognised, are cleared. In 1990, the Nairobi town administration destroyed the dwellings of approx. 40,000 residents. Today, the marginal settlements in the industrial area of Nairobi are especially threatened with destruction. In this area, the town authorities plan further industrial sites, as well as middle-class settlements.

Such clearances have different motivations. For example, they can be in the interests of certain groups due to land speculation (Gilbert 1992: 152). The massive favelas removal programme in Rio de Janeiro from 1962 until 1966 served to make space for a traffic concept (Gilbert 1992: 148), and in the years from 1967 until 1973 large-scale clearances were aimed at improving the city's image for tourists. In Abidjan, the clearance actions of 1996/7 should be viewed in the light of an economic policy which is based on privatisation and foreign investment. The settlements concerned lie exposed on main traffic routes to the upper- and middle-class areas and to the city centre, and do not fit the government's vision of an 'economic wonderland'. The official reasons for clearance are usually given as the welfare of those involved and poor living conditions. Clearances are not usually undertaken when the status quo and the social order seem safeguarded, or when the authorities are unable to provide alternative accommodation (see Stren 1975: 270; Gilbert 1992: 141ff.). Urban land occupation and existing marginal settlements have been, and are, tolerated when this can ensure the political support of the urban poor, or when the land is not private property. As a consequence, occupations increased massively in Santiago de Chile before the elections at the end of the 1960s (Cleaves 1974, quoted in Gilbert 1992: 149).

State social and council housing projects were copied from industrialised countries. In times of economic prosperity, the public authorities provided accommodation for the lowest income groups, although building projects were often over-expensive, the distribution of accommodation was determined by clientelistic practices and in the final analysis led to the creation of accommodation for the middle classes. Thus, in effect, official housing projects did not provide a solution for the urban poor in any of the four countries. The state construction companies failed and council housing projects for the lowest sections of society were increasingly abandoned. In the Brazilian town of Aracaju, for example, the need to act only became apparent in the middle of the 1960s. In an attempt to cope with the demand for accommodation, construction of council housing (mutirao) began here in the 1980s at the edge of the town. However, from 1986, the privatisation of state construction companies led to a reorientation towards accommodation for the middle and upper classes. In Rio de Janeiro, the foundation of the National Housing Construction Bank in the 1960s created a tool for council housing projects. Large low-cost housing settlements were built at the city periphery. Chile also met the increasing accommodation shortage in the 1960s and 1970s with such projects. Similar to Rio, low-cost apartment buildings were built on the fringes of Santiago. Following independence in Kenya, the para-statal National Housing Corporation attempted to meet the massive demand for accommodation with council house projects. However, due to the high cost of investment and rent, only those in the middle income bracket could afford this kind of accommodation, which still did not meet demand. In the Ivory Coast, public and private housing companies were founded in the 1960s. Between 1965 and 1975, state housing companies directly intervened in the construction and accommodation market (Antoine 1987; Paulais 1995: 42ff.). In its actual consequences, however, the great social project to create accommodation for all sections of the population excluded those who had the lowest income. Between 1968 and 1978, 76,000 housing units were created (Dembélé 1995: 15). After this period of economic prosperity and urban development, the economic crisis exposed the failure of this housing policy and only the construction of accommodation for the middle class was still subsidised.

Especially in the 1970s, 'site and service' programmes replaced clearance policies in Brazil, Chile and Kenya. The main forces behind this new policy were the World Bank and international development agencies (Brennan 1993: 86). This policy was also implemented two decades later in the Ivory Coast. Often, such programmes envisage clearance of precarious settlements and in return provide plots of land and basic infrastructure in other places. Actual construction of houses remains a task for the residents. Such areas are mostly at the periphery of towns and resettlement destroys existing economic, social and personal relationships (Gilbert: 1992: 143). These were followed by 'slum-upgrading' programmes (see Kersting 1996: 196ff.), which consisted of measures to improve living conditions in existing settlements. Such methods are only employed in Kenya, for example, to prevent the growth of squatter areas and cope with the increasing demand for low-cost housing. From 1964 until 1970, the Christian Democratic government in Chile used such projects to ensure electoral support (Kusnetzoff

1975: 292, quoted in Gilbert 1992: 143). Such programmes in all four countries are often initiated and financed by the World Bank and US-AID. Other development agencies are also beginning to take part and a greater number of NGOs and bilateral cooperation agreements support measures to improve infrastructure in such settlements.

Nevertheless, a certain tendency towards 'laissez-faire' can be discerned throughout all these phases of housing policy. This explains the toleration of settlements which were earmarked for demolition in the clearance phase. Legalisation of settlements stemming from illegal land occupation often concludes a phase of conscious ignoring of housing needs and problems. This behaviour is often characterised as tolerance towards the illegal practices of 'urban development from below', but is not rarely the result of the inability and the lack of political will on the part of the public authorities to combat housing problems by an adequate and financially viable concept of urban planning.

Since the 1980s, there has been a policy of state intervention in the favelas of Rio de Janeiro with the aim of improving living conditions. Thus, at the beginning of the 1980s, the national electricity company, LIGHT, connected the settlements to the electricity grid. With external support, upgrading was implemented in several favelas. These neighbourhoods were also integrated into the local garbage collection system and provided with some social infrastructure. Community (pre-) schools or health centres were the responsibility of town or federal state authorities. At the end of the 1970s, programmes were started with the help of the World Bank to improve the technical infrastructure (PDU, Programme de Dévelopement Urbain) of existing lower-middle-class neighbourhoods in Abidjan. Precarious settlements were only included in this programme after 1984. However, inclusion remained often arbitrary and not all those hit by clearance gained compensation or access to alternative accommodation. The World Bank's upgrading programme, which was envisaged to start in 1992 in all such areas in Abidjan, was only started in 1997 in the form of a pilot project. These upgrading and 'site and service' programmes are financed and organised by the World Bank, other multinational donors and the French. In the 1990s in Chile, 'help for self-help' programmes should increase private construction of housing by stimulating self-help initiatives in the area of infrastructure. This model can also be observed in Brazil. In addition, despite limited state involvement, the Brazilian population has meanwhile obtained improvements to infrastructure at the communal level in many settlements. In Kenya, 'site and service' as well as 'slum upgrading' projects often failed because, as a result of renovation, informal opportunities were destroyed by purchasers with more capital. Thus, the social solidarity of the previous neighbourhood often fell apart (McInnes 1995). The state now has withdrawn totally from such projects and NGOs, which invest in improvements to infrastructure in cooperation with local self-help groups and neighbourhood initiatives, have taken its place.

In the African cases, the provision of infrastructure in poor neighbourhoods often consists merely of the construction of central water taps, a road, or selective electricity connection. Only since the start of the 1990s has the World Bank carried out such projects in settlements in Abidjan. Thus, one settlement gained a coin-operated drinking water supply, another public conveniences. The devaluation of the CFA-Franc in 1994 facilitated further projects with French cooperation by increasing the value of external financial aid.

Developments in medium-sized towns have been different in each country. In Aracaju, with over 400,000 inhabitants in 1991 (IBGE 1995: 12), the process of 'favelisation' only began in the 1960s. From 1964 during the military dictatorship, settlements were established at the edges of the town. With the change of political regime, this was followed in the 1980s by a policy of public housing construction. However, after a short time, this policy, as elsewhere, was adapted to accommodate the demands of the middle classes (Karsch 1993: 27). Since the middle of the 1980s, a federal authority (FUNDESE) has taken over housing projects for the poorest income groups at the periphery of the town and conducts a programme of self-construction of accommodation (mutirao). In Temuco (240,000 inhabitants), developments were similar to those in Santiago. Land occupation in the 1960s and 1970s was followed by 'site and service' and public housing programmes in the 1980s and 1990s.

The African medium-sized towns became goals of migration only relatively late. However, demographic growth and pressure on the towns were varied. In the medium-sized town of Man (100,000 inhabitants) approx. one third of the population lives in precarious settlements. One settlement is inhabited by a large number of students of secondary schools whose families live elsewhere, while the inhabitants of another are mostly migrants from the north or immigrants from neighbouring Guinea. The other two precarious neighbourhoods resemble villages, around which the town has grown. Measures such as the extension of town garbage collection failed due to lack of equipment. The town budget often does not even cover the salaries of its employees. Large-scale French support began in February 1997 with the upgrading of these settlements. This included measures such as street lighting to protect the population and to fight criminality. In Kisumu (250,000 inhabitants), spatial segregation was regulated in colonial times. Thus, the poor settled at the periphery. Since independence, Kisumu has been neglected in the area of development aid compared to other regions and towns due to (party) political, which also means ethnic reasons. This led to a lack of industrialisation and housing projects.

The methods have, therefore, been similar in all four countries: first a policy of clearance, then some public housing projects, upon the failure of which followed in the 1970s and 1980s, with help from the World Bank among others, legalisation of precarious settlements, or at least their toleration, and measures to improve living conditions. The difference in the time period in Africa is explained by different political and economic developments. Only in the 1980s did the problems of the African countries become more pressing. The economic crises increased demographic pressures on the metropolis and precarious settlements grew dramatically. Until the 1960s and 1970s, housing policy in the four countries was not orientated towards the needs and living conditions of the urban poor. The intervention of external actors, such as the World Bank, was followed by a phase which aimed to orientate housing policy towards the poor via the provision of basic infrastructure. In certain cases this was successful, even though the total number of inhabitants thus provided for was, and remains, quite low. Since the 1990s, the now 'democratic' states have renewed attempts at housing and social policies orientated towards the needs of the poor. However, programmes such as 'site and service' spatially remove poor areas to the periphery of a town.

A look at state interventions in precarious settlements demonstrates the importance and role of external actors (e.g. the World Bank or US-AID) in relation to policies towards the urban poor. Over the years, the national authorities responsible for engagement in poor areas have changed. As a result of decentralisation and democratisation at the local level, more intensive negotiations with residents have become possible and greater insights into their problems can be gained. In the Ivory Coast, decentralisation has meant that in the respective town councils the mayor has gained more authority and settlement residents have in him (her) a direct contact person. In Latin America, the consolidation of the democratic systems improved the bargaining position of the urban poor and created corresponding demands and responsibilities. There, the political decision making process has shown more transparency over the last decade. In contrast, in the African cases, the relationship between the government and local residents is still often characterised by distrust, as in Kenya in the face of renewed clearances and experiences with only a formally democratic state. In the Ivory

Coast, the attitudes of settlement residents are characterised by lesser demands. Distrust is also present, but more decisive is the acceptance of their situation and living conditions. This may be based on the fact that, until the end of the 1980s, precarious settlements were mostly populated by immigrant workers, who placed great value on continued tolerance.

In addition to town planning policies, the various actors and aspects of technical implementation, clientelistic relationships play an important role in all the countries with the certain exception of Chile (see Kersting 1996: 111–18). In many Latin American towns, the provision of infrastructure is part of the barter relationship within the political system of patronage. In return for votes in elections, a precarious settlement can gain access to water, streets or telephone services (Gilbert 1992: 149).[4] Implementation of housing construction projects can, therefore, also be viewed as a safeguarding of clientelistic relationships, which, however, now due to increased party competition in South America may be reduced in the future. In the last elections for the office of mayor in Aracaju, for example, the candidate lost, after infrastructure measures promised for the favelas in his first term of office never came to fruition, and his voter base was precisely in these neighbourhoods (Cruz 1992: 111ff.). Strong ethnic clientelistic relations still dominate, however, the political systems in the African cases.

Summary

In Brazil, a development from paternalistic activities of a welfare character in the 1940s and 1950s towards a social policy more orientated to the needs of the poor, at least for Rio de Janeiro, can be observed. In this case, the political 'opening' resulted in an official urbanisation policy and recognition of the favelas. However, poverty was only later recognised as a structural rather than a temporary phenomenon. The democratisation process has now led to a substantial improvement in the standard of living for favela residents, although this is partly a result of their own potential to act ('pressure from below'). Redemocratisation in Brazil and Chile and the transition to a multi-party system in Kenya and the Ivory Coast have, therefore, provided opportunities, which the urban poor in Latin America have partly been able to take advantage of. But, there is still no more comprehensive urbanisation policy for any of the poor areas. Furthermore, the withdrawal of the state as the regulatory body to compensate for social disparities (because of neo-liberal economic concepts) had an adverse effect on the situation of the poorest sections of the population, as was the case in Chile for example, where a broader-based social security system had been in existence. In addition, the activities of NGOs have relieved the states of their social responsibilities. At the same time, the World Bank and the IMF have become important actors due to changes in their development policies (site and service, upgrading, decentralisation/participation).

The different decades of housing policies reflect these influences and changes. The 1960s and 1970s were characterised by programmes based on the considerations, initiatives and financing of the World Bank, the IMF and other large development organisations (amongst others US-AID). Concepts such as help for self-help and participation stand for a policy of cushioning poverty in the 1990s. In Chile, the state once more carries out housing construction programmes. In the Ivory Coast, democratisation has been combined with a strengthening of the local level. Economic development has also improved again. Housing construction, financed with help from the World Bank and other international donors, is once more explicitly orientated to the needs of the poor. In Abidjan, the government has been persuaded to start resettlement and legalisation programmes for precarious settlements. However, positive economic and political perspectives can be severely constrained by, amongst others, social developments. Thus, Abidjan has the highest number of AIDS cases of any city in west Africa, and the situation continuously worsens. Kenya also mainly reacted to aid programmes from multilateral donor organisations and NGOs. However, as external actors always carry out their projects in cooperation with the local political authorities, development activities often remain trapped in the net of clientelistic practices, and in the past years have increasingly contributed to a lopsided ethnic/regional distribution.

The processes of impoverishment and the concurrent demographic pressure have varying dimensions in the towns studied in Africa and Latin America. The high level of external debt is a factor in several countries, with the exception of Chile, which influences economic prosperity and the possibilities for improvement of living conditions (not only) of the urban poor. Only about half of those questioned in our surveys are in regular employment and, in the light of the lack of social security and the limited nature of social infrastructure in the respective countries, the chances for a 'better life' are relatively limited. Geographically, they find themselves pushed to the outskirts of the cities, especially after housing programmes such as 'site and service'. The living conditions of the urban poor, therefore, remain basically precarious and exposed to great economic and political risks.

Notes

1. Towns with more than 20,000 inhabitants.

2. The term refers to the illegal act of occupation of land and characterises the temporary nature of this form of living.

3. This is construction using forms of self-help.

4. In Rio de Janeiro (see Leeds 1969: 79, quoted in Gilbert 1992: 149) a large favela is in a better position to receive large favours (according to the principle of more votes for the politician), than a small favela, where nothing happens.

CHAPTER 4

Social Structures and Living Conditions

Barbara Happe and
Jaime Sperberg

§ A CURSORY glance at the realities of life of the urban poor is enough to show that their living conditions in the four countries we observed and sometimes even within the countries are very different. The following analysis of certain central indicators (employment and income situation, poverty rates, education chances etc.) should facilitate differentiated and comparative conclusions about living conditions and chances. This will not only provide an insight into the socio-economic similarities and differences between and within the countries, but also expose the influence these structures have on the thought and action patterns of the urban poor. Our observations, therefore, focus not only on the analysis of the socio-economic situation of those questioned, but also on their subjective perception of their living conditions. Study of the subjective judgement of the socio-economic situation is important because often the objective living conditions alone cannot explain social and political action. This is, for example, the case when individuals with similar objective living conditions show different political reactions (inactivity vs. political activity) (see chapter 7).

This chapter will first continue the discussion of 'marginality' because we are concerned with discovering the connection between material poverty and political action. The living conditions and poverty levels in the four countries will then be presented on the basis of comparative data from international organisations such as the World Bank and UNDP. In the next two sections, the objective living conditions and subjective evaluations of these by the urban poor will be examined. We close with a summary, in which the objective and subjective living conditions will be examined in relation to both consistencies and inconsistencies, as well as their relation to and relevance for political action.

Marginality and Extent of Poverty

The concepts of 'marginalisation' and 'marginality' were formed in the 1950s and 1960s and served to describe the peripheral economic, political and social position of the urban poor and peasants in the countries of the so-called Third World. In the course of modernisation, this peripheral position was interpreted partly as temporary and partly as a structurally conditioned phenomenon (for this debate, see Bennholdt-Thomsen 1979: 45ff.). The marginalised population was identified as a non-socially integrated group which demonstrated a lack of willingness to participate, (DESAL 1969) and cultural and social apathy (Lewis 1966). Marxist authors such as Nun (1969) or Quijano (1984) viewed marginality as an 'expression of global capitalism in its monopolistic capitalistic phase' (quoted in Bennholdt-Thomsen 1979: 48). Dependency theorists in the 1970s represented the position that marginality was the result of, from their point of view, false capitalist development (ibid.: 47). Marginality was viewed from this perspective as an economic, system-determined phenomenon, which could only be overcome in a socialist system. Marginalisation predominantly expressed itself in the poor employment situation of this group, members of which were seen either as an 'industrial reserve army' (Nun 1969), as 'informal workers' (Portes et al. 1989; Tokman 1990), or as 'subsistence workers' (Bennholdt-Thomsen 1979: 70). All these authors contributed to a certain 'myth of marginality'.

In contrast, on the basis of an empirical study in Brazil, the US-American anthropologist Janice Perlman (1976) succeeded in deflating this myth and showing that 'marginalisation', especially in the political and social arena, did not correspond to the picture of a politically apathetic or socially isolated group of people. In the case of Chile, Peru and Venezuela, Castells (1983: 179 ff.) also demonstrated empirically that even with regard to employment structure, marginality is not a phenomenon that lends itself to generalisation. At the end of the 1960s, he observed increased integration of members of this group into the formal employment market and thus contradicted the wide spread supposition that marginalised groups suffer from higher rates of unemployment and are predominately active in the informal or subsistence sectors (ibid.). In the 1980s and 1990s, partly as a result of debt crises and structural adjustment programmes, the employment situation in the countries we studied worsened (e.g. flexible labour markets, increase in informal employment, loss of jobs in the industrial and export sectors). This also affected the urban poor and contributed to the increasing heterogeneity of social structures within marginal settlements.

In the 1970s and 1980s, international organisations increasingly replaced 'marginalisation' with the neutral term 'poverty'. However, both terms are characterised by multi-dimensionality, which makes an empirical operationalisation difficult. The World Bank and the development programme of the United Nations (UNDP) deal with the problem in different ways. While the World Bank prefers to use income- and consumption-orientated measurements, the UNDP favours a definition of poverty on the basis of social indicators (material and non-material basic needs) (see Sangmeister 1993: 41). Accordingly, the definitions of poverty are different. While the World Bank interprets poverty as the failure to reach a certain level of income, which therefore prohibits the provision of basic consumer goods, the UNDP uses an extended definition. It views poverty as the lack of chances and possibilities of choice, which are crucial for human development: these prevent a long and healthy life, an acceptable standard of living, sufficient education, as well as access to private and public services. This method has been criticised because it mixes different dimensions, which would be better left separate (see Ravaillon 1997: 633). In 1997, the UNDP introduced the concept of the Human Poverty Index (HPI), a multi-dimensional instrument which measures deprivation using key indicators. In the following sections, the poverty and development level of each country will be described using both consumption-orientated measurements and social indicators.

Brazil: Poverty in terms of income of private households decreased in the period 1990 to 1996 from 41% to 29%. However, there was a striking urban-rural and north-south divide. While the total proportion of the urban poor in 1996 was 25%, 46% of rural inhabitants lived under the poverty line (CEPAL 1999: 38). Thus, in Latin American comparison, Brazil belongs to the group with a medium level of poverty (ibid.: 39). Despite the decline in poverty, low increases in real wages and the relatively low level of official unemployment benefit in the 1990s worsened the distribution of income considerably. In 1995, according to the World Bank, the Gini-coefficient reached the very high value of 0.60. In 1997 and 1999, Brazil was ranked 79th on the Human Development Index (HDI). The poverty index (HPI) was given at 15.8% for 1997 and is therefore considerably lower than income poverty. The low level of the HPI when compared to income poverty is typical for Latin America. In comparison with the rest of Latin America, Brazil has a very high level of illiteracy (16% in 1997) and a very low per capita income of the poorest 20%.

Chile: Income poverty of private households was reduced from 33.3% in 1990 to 17.8% in 1998 (MIDEPLAN 1999). Thus, Chile once more belongs to the group of countries in Latin America with a relatively low level of poverty (CEPAL 1999: 39). This strong decline is due to continuing economic growth of an average 6% since 1990, the increase in the minimum wage, and low levels of unemployment until 1997 (see CEPAL 1999). However, like Brazil, Chile has not improved the distribution of income, and the Gini-coefficient is 0.56 (1994). The rural–urban divide is not as serious as in Brazil, but regional differences are much greater. While in the city of Santiago a mere 12.4% of households are below the poverty line, in the IXth Region whose regional capital is Temuco, the figure is 27.6% (MIDEPLAN 1999). Chile occupies 34th place in the HDI and demonstrates the highest level of development of the four countries studied. The percentage of poverty lies at 4.8%, thus placing it with Cuba, Costa Rica and Uruguay amongst those developing countries with a higher level of development. With regard to life expectancy and literacy, Chile demonstrates values similar to industrialised countries. The per capita income of the poorest 20% of the population is three times higher than in Brazil, but is still very low. This explains the higher income poverty.

Ivory Coast: The proportion of the population below the income poverty line increased from 11% in 1985 to 36.8% in 1995 (World Bank 1997). This was the result of the economic crisis, which continued until 1993 and reduced living standards in the entire country. Between 1991 and 1993, real per capita income declined annually by 4%; the price of consumer goods rose by 35.4% in 1994 (IMF 1998: 7). Poverty in the Ivory Coast is regional and, with regard to certain groups within the population, very unevenly distributed. The highest level of poverty can be found amongst the rural population, which is partly active in the export economy (mainly cocoa), and in households participating in informal activities. Abidjan experienced a strong increase in poverty from 1985 (0.7%) to 1995 (20.2%), but this still lies below the national average (IMF 1998: 29). Distribution of income in the Ivory Coast is the most even amongst the countries studied. The Gini-coefficient was 0.36 in 1988 and the gulf between the poorest and the richest was 20% in 1994, only 6.5 times more.

Of the 174 countries which are covered by the HDI, the Ivory Coast ranks 154th. At 46.8% (1997), the poverty level is consequently very high. In contrast to the Latin American states, both income poverty and the HPI are very high. The high level of the latter index is explained by the high percentage (37.3%) of the population whose life expectancy is lower than 40 years, the high level of illiteracy (57.4%), and the high proportion of people who have no access to clean drinking water (58%).

Kenya: In 1992, 42% of the population lived below the income poverty line. By 1998, this percentage had increased to 47%. There are great differences between the town and countryside. In rural areas, 46.4% of the population belong to this category, in urban areas, this figure is 29.3%. Poverty is highest in the arid and semi-arid provinces of the country, as well as in households with female heads. At 44%, urban poverty is more often found in medium-sized towns (Kismum, Nakuru etc.) than in Nairobi (25%) and Mombasa (33%). The distribution of income in Kenya is similar to many Latin American states. The gulf between the 20% poorest and the 20% richest is 18 times. The Gini-coefficient of 0.57 is also a very high value in African comparison. The Human Development Index places Kenya in the lower midfield (place 136). The HPI is 28.2% and therefore considerably below the value for income poverty. The lower HPI, in comparison with the Ivory Coast, is related to the much higher level of literacy and higher life expectancy of the poorer sections of the population.

In the 1990s, therefore, Brazil and Chile greatly reduced income poverty, while in the same period in Kenya and the Ivory Coast more people fell below the poverty line. In both African countries, the proportion of poverty measured according to social indicators is also very high. In Brazil and Chile, on the other hand, these values could be reduced to below 20%. Even though income poverty in Latin America and the very uneven distribution of income remain central problems, the improvement of certain social indicators (life expectancy, better provision of infrastructure, higher level of education), demonstrates that the measures aimed at improving the living conditions of poorer sections of the population, which have been initiated by the governments and some international organisations, have had some positive effects.

In comparison to the national average, the indicators employed in the measurement of human poverty - low income and unfulfilled basic needs - are much worse in the marginal settlements of the four countries studied. The favelas in Brazil, the poblaciones in Chile, quartiers précaires in the Ivory Coast and the slums in Kenya combine the dimensions of income and poverty and low levels of social indicators and form a spatially defined area of poverty within the respective towns. In this way, social and spatial segregation is added to the previously described dimensions of poverty.

Objective Living Conditions

The study of objective living conditions is based on concepts of social classes and strata, which characterise social inequality and the related unjust distribution of chances with regard to income, employment, and education. This corresponds to a vertical differentiation which defines ´above and below´, that is those in a better or worse position, and therefore the rankings of the different groups (Hradil 1987: 14). In addition to the three vertical categories, ethnicity and religion will be treated as horizontal differentiations. They describe an allocation of opportunities in life, which is not directly related to a person's economic activity or level of education. A ranking, that is above or below, cannot be clearly defined in this case (see Hradil 1987: 40). These horizontal structures are relevant only in some of the countries studied.

The employment and income situations in market economies are the most meaningful indicators for material comfort or poverty. The urban poor's difficult access to the formal employment market as well as their low level of income are characteristic of this population group. On the other hand, social relations based on mutual help which try to compensate for lack of integration in the formal employment market do exist in slum and squatter settlements. With regard to employment and income, there are substantial differences not only between individual settlements, but also within them. This heterogeneous internal social structure also leads to different attitudes and political behaviour patterns.

Monetary income is only a partial indicator of the economic situation of the urban poor in the countries studied. This indicator is less relevant, the less opportunity the urban poor have to secure their livelihood by a monetarily rewarded main occupation (the more they rely on, e.g. neighbourhood help, subsistence production, state services). The income situation of the urban poor will be described and analysed according to the calculated poverty line for the respective countries. The official minimum wage is not used as a category of comparison because it is often not corrected for inflation (Brazil, Ivory Coast), and in Kenya does not even exist. Only for the Chilean case would it be a reliable indicator, because it is periodically brought up to date and lies somewhat above the poverty line.

In both the Ivory Coast and Brazil, members of the lower middle classes who have been hit by social decline often live in marginal settlements. Thus, the composition of the population according to income criteria is very heterogeneous in both these countries. This is especially true for Rio de Janeiro and Abidjan. The greater social homogeneity in the Kenyan and Chilean poor settlements has a historical explanation. The English colonial masters divided the population according to racist criteria, which meant Africans were allocated inferior settlement areas. After independence in 1964, racially motivated 'apartheid' was replaced by economic apartheid (see König 1998: 115). This is expressed to this day in the retention of a clearly defined social and spatial segregation in Kenya. In Chile, the military regime (1973–1989) followed a policy of social homogenisation. Thus, the poorer parts of the population were removed from the richer sector and re-settled in so-called receptor municipalities. This led to the southern periphery of greater Santiago being predominantly inhabited by low-income groups. This social and economic segregation increased dramatically in the 1980s (see Sperberg 2000; Rodríguez/Icaza 1993).

Lower income groups are more often found in medium-sized towns. It is conspicuous that the difference between the metropolis and the medium-sized town in Brazil and Chile is very great, while it is less marked in Kenya. In Chile, the extreme concentration of industrial production and the greater employment opportunities in the capital city, Santiago, mean that in the medium-sized town of Temuco, wage levels are much lower. In Brazil, the difference between the south east (Rio) and the north east (Aracaju) is characteristic. Examination of the settlements studied shows that, apart from Chile, the older and more consolidated settlements in the respective metropolises have the highest level of income. In Vidigal, Rio's older settlement, only 26.4% of its

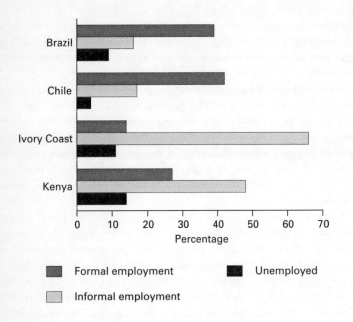

Figure 4.1 Economic situation of the urban poor (%), not employed (students, housewives etc.) excluded

inhabitants live under the poverty line. The poorest settlements are in the medium-sized towns. In Kenya's and Chile's medium-sized town, over 80% of the inhabitants can be classed in the low-income category. Income levels below the poverty line are most often experienced by women. In Kenya, the discrepancy between the sexes in this respect is especially strong. Here, 83.3% of women live below the poverty line, while only 53.1% of men fall into this category. Only in Brazil is the difference between the income levels of men and women not especially great.

Figure 4.1 shows the employment situation of the urban poor in the settlements studied. It is clear that the proportion of formal employment in both South American states is higher than in the African countries. In the Ivory Coast and Kenya, the unemployment rate is over 10% and informal activities reach a much higher level than in the two South American cases. In the Ivory Coast particularly, the proportion of those informally active, 66%, is very high, and 79% of those questioned also have a second job. In addition to the more widespread second job phenomenon in the Ivory Coast, it was also observed that in a number of the households questioned, more than one person was actively employed. This behaviour is partly a result of economic pressure and the very low income of the head of the household, but also due to the changing pattern of values, which clear the way for women to enter the labour market.

In Brazil and Kenya, in 70% of cases at least two people per household were in employment. In the Ivory Coast, this proportion is only 52% because here the breadwinner often had two jobs. In addition, female employment is at its lowest where the women's role is integrated into a traditional pattern (e.g. Islamic regions or settlements). Thus, in all four countries, there is a certain level of multi-occupationality. This expresses itself in the Ivory Coast in the breadwinner's acceptance of a second or third job, and in Brazil and Kenya in the form of numerous family members who earn additional income. After the height of the debt crisis in 1982, the numbers of those taking part in informal activities in Chile and Brazil clearly increased. However, in some cases, especially in Chile, the flight into informality represented only a temporary phenomenon of short-term adaptation to the crisis conditions (see Díaz 1993). Even though the urban poor's chances of returning to the formal sector have increased since the beginning of the 1990s, this cannot necessarily be evaluated as a positive change, because conditions of employment in the formal sector are worsening. In this sense, one can speak of increasingly 'precarious' and flexible formal employment (Sabóia 1994; Imbusch 1995). Precarious activities are characterised by irregular working hours, lack of social security protection, temporary working contracts and irregular income.

Kenya and the Ivory Coast are much more deeply affected by informal employment structures than the two South American countries. In these cases, informality does not represent a temporary phenomenon. More often, the inhabitants of marginal settlements have had to accommodate employment outside formally regulated activities from the beginning of the urbanisation process. Informal employment is mostly confined to trade and all kinds of odd jobs in the open air ('jua kali' in Swahili). Trade is often the domain of women, while production in the odd-job crafts is in the hands of men (König 1998; Schmitt 2001).

Comparison between the informal and formal sectors with regard to income showed a significant difference for Kenya. Here, the incomes drawn in the informal sector are much lower than those in the formal sector. In Brazil, the Ivory Coast and Chile, the differences between the two sectors are less marked. Thus, informality does not necessarily mean lower income because, especially in the Ivory Coast, incomes which are comparable to those in the formal sector can be achieved with the help of activities in small trade, which is mainly carried out by women. With regard to the precarious nature of employment, the formal sector, at least where employment relations have been subject to far-reaching deregulation and flexibility (most of all in Chile), has moved closer to the informal sector.

The possibilities of using subsistence production or other income resources to gain more independence from monetary income are limited. Only approximately one seventh of those questioned owned a garden suitable for self-provision and the same proportion own domestic animals. In the Ivory Coast and Kenya, the urban poor can rely much more on support from friends, neighbours or family members from the countryside (21% in Kenya, 38% in the Ivory Coast) than in the South American states. There, the proportion of those questioned who were supported by friends or relatives was only approximately 8%. This result demonstrates that feelings of solidarity and family ties are much more prevalent in the African countries than in Brazil or Chile. The African inhabitants of marginal settlements often maintain contact with their native region and support family members they left behind. Two thirds of all inhabitants of Kenyan marginal settlements and 58% of Ivorian squatters maintain such ties, in contrast to only 30% of those questioned in South America. The stronger social safeguarding in the African countries via family and other primordial networks can be traced not only to the higher level of 'suffering', but also to the lack of a system of public social security. Such a system was introduced in Chile in the

1920s, and in the case of pensions covers approx. one quarter to half of the urban poor (see Mesa-Lago 1994).

In addition to the income and employment situation, the resources of education and time are also important for the development of political activities.

Figure 4.2 shows a relatively low level of education for the Ivory Coast; 39% have not had any schooling and only 8% have been to school for more than eight years. In contrast, the level of education of the urban poor in Kenya and Chile is relatively high. In both these countries, the majority of the urban poor questioned (75–80%) went to school for more than five years. After the Ivory Coast, Brazil has the worst level of education of the countries in question. The proportion of those without any school education is approximately 14%, but a further 39% have only finished four years at school and as a result of the poor standards in Brazilian schools, only possess poor writing and reading skills.

In comparison with the other countries, the higher level of education in Kenya and Chile can be traced to the well-developed and easily accessible educational system. In Chile, universal access to a well-equipped school system was introduced in the 1920s, and eight-year compulsory schooling, which still exists today, was established shortly

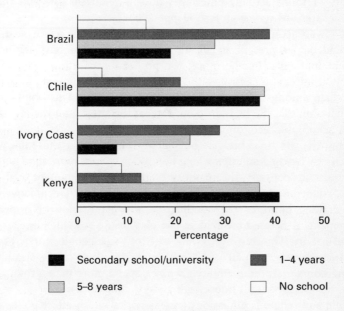

Figure 4.2 Education (%)

after. The national illiteracy rate in Chile is approx. 5%, and therefore one of the lowest in the whole of South America. Amongst those urban poor we questioned, illiteracy was hardly higher. In Kenya, the state spends approx. 20% of the budget on education. The state system is complemented by so-called Harambee schools, which are founded on private initiative. Thus, despite the lack of compulsory schooling, the country has a dense network of primary schools (Hofmeier 1993: 106). The literacy rate in Kenya is 77% (1996), and consequently high in African comparison. The education sector in Kenya is confronted with the problem of low school attendance of women and high costs for higher education. As a result of these high costs, access to higher education is barred for the poorest sections of the population. In Chile and Kenya, most population groups strive for formal education, which can facilitate social improvement.

In contrast, there is only limited state support of education in the Ivory Coast. Here, the national literacy rate is only 39.4% (1996). In Ivorian marginal settlements, as at the national level, women suffer greater discrimination. This is especially serious in the case of immigrants from neighbouring countries (see Schmitt 2001). Brazil's education policy concentrates to a large extent on supporting universal education facilities. Despite eight years of compulsory schooling, the numbers of those actually entering school is relatively low and the drop-out rates are very high (see Happe 2000).

The lower-income groups usually end schooling after eight years. This tendency is present in all the countries studied, but is most prevalent in Kenya. Furthermore, the proportion of those with no school education at all amongst the poorest (below the poverty line) is higher than amongst the more well-off slum-dwellers. This points to the conclusion that the high drop-out rate, at the latest after the eighth year of school, has economic reasons.

As regards the time budget, our survey showed that the Chilean poor have by far the longest working hours. They work more than nine hours a day. In contrast, the majority of those in employment in the African countries worked eight, or less, hours a day. The relatively short working hours of the Brazilian poor is a reflection of under-employment. A better time budget can also result in higher levels of political activity. This, however, is not true for those people working in the home (mostly women), who, although they have more flexible working hours than the main breadwinner, spend more than a total of nine hours engaged with housework and/or children.

Ethnic and religious affiliations are categories which affect political action in the Ivory Coast and Kenya. In the marginal settlements in the

Ivory Coast, 30% of those of non-Ivorian origin live alongside Ivorians. They are mainly immigrant workers from Burkina Faso, Mali, Ghana and Guinea. Immigrants from neighbouring countries were the original inhabitants of the quartiers précaires, especially in Abidjan. Only in the first half of the 1990s, as the country's economic situation worsened, did a large number of Ivorians also move into the slums (Schmitt 2001). Apart from a few exceptions (e.g. the Burkinabé), immigrant workers of various ethnicity have no political rights and are subject to the caprice of the political authorities. In the Ivory Coast, the Islamic faith is very wide-spread, especially amongst the urban poor in the medium-sized town of Man. By contrast, in Abidjan, Christian Churches have a relatively high number of followers, 60%. In the marginal settlements where the Islamic faith is dominant, social and political life is organised according to the rules of this religion.

In Kenya, only a few immigrant workers live in the marginal settlements. However, the distribution of ethnic groups in the four settlements studied is very heterogeneous. The newer slum in Kisumu is relatively homogeneous and has a majority of 81% Luo. In the other settlements, other ethnic groups - mostly the Kikuyu, Luhya and Kamba (only in Nairobi) - are more evenly represented. The Luos in the newer settlements in Kisumu and the inhabitants of the new settlement in Nairobi are predominantly Christian. In the older settlement in Nairobi and Kisumu, half of those questioned were Muslims. Ethnicity is also closely linked to political loyalty in Kenya (see chapter 7).

In the Latin American marginal settlements national and ethnic cleavages are rare. There are no immigrant workers or refugees from neighbouring countries. In Chile and in Temuco a small part of the inhabitants belongs to the indigenous group of the Mapuche. This indigenous population possesses stronger links to the rural region. It is often a victim of discrimination. Since the end of the nineties a strong politicalisation of the Mapuche has become apparent. Together with a strengthened self-confidence, demands on government policies like agrarian reform, compensation, etc. are raised. In Brazil the proportion of the black population is particularly high in the favelas. Even after the democratisation process in Brazil they are still frequently subject to open discrimination especially on the job market.

In Chile and Brazil, new fundamentalist Churches (e.g. Pentecostal groups) play a much more important role than in the African countries. 13–15% of all those questioned are members of these groups or sympathise with them. The Pentecostal Church is mostly present in the newer settlement in Rio and in Temuco (Chile), where it accounts for 30% of those questioned.

Perception of Personal Situation

The previous description of living conditions shows that the urban poor are affected in various ways and to varying degrees by poverty. While the majority of those questioned in the two African countries concentrate on daily survival, over the last few years at least some of the Brazilian favelados and the Chilean pobladores have succeeded in obtaining a level of financial security which enables them to live a life above the existential minimum. In Chile and Brazil, poverty expresses itself today more in the lack of provision of social and physical infrastructure in the marginal settlements, and in social exclusion of the pobladores and favelados in comparison with other population groups in the same town (e.g. in relation to possibilities of access to education and adequate health care provision). In comparison to the two African states, the living conditions in the favelas and poblaciones are better and state authorities today are more interested in integrating the poor into urban society. To be a favelado or a poblador still means to be a 'second-class citizen', but the extent of the lack of public provision is still less than in Kenya or the Ivory Coast.

The following section illustrates how the urban poor perceive and evaluate their objective living conditions. The type of problems the urban poor encounter varies only slightly in the settlements and countries we analysed. Thus, the major problems they confront in daily life are very similar, e.g. lack of physical and social infrastructure, high rates of criminal delinquency etc. (see chapter 9). But this tells us little of how they evaluate their own living conditions and how far they perceive them as discriminatory. The following depiction of life satisfaction provides some insight.

The judgement of quality of life in the countries studied was very different. Only the Brazilians give a unanimously positive evaluation. The percentage of those who are dissatisfied in each settlement is approx. 10%. The high level of satisfaction in spite of many serious deficits, such as poverty and unemployment, or the lack of provision of technical and social infrastructure, demonstrates that the favelados have accepted their life situation to a greater degree than the urban poor in the other countries. Although the uneven distribution of income is in none of the other countries studied so great as in Brazil, the favelados tend to judge their chances in life relative to their neighbours and other favelados, and therefore seldom compare themselves to members of higher social classes (see also Karsch 1993: 103ff., Perlman 1976: 182).

In the other countries, only just half (46%) of those questioned are content with their life. It is noticeable that in all three cases, satisfaction does not increase with higher income, and that in each country, it is one of the new settlements in which the inhabitants are most content. This indicates that the level of internal social cohesion and experience of mutual solidarity determine the subjective feeling of satisfaction. The remaining 54% of the urban poor in Chile, the Ivory Coast and Kenya express discontent with their limited chances in life – in both African countries approx. every fifth person describes herself as dissatisfied. This bears witness to the fact that they live under a great deal of pressure, be it because their living conditions are characterised by great objective deficits (Kenya, Ivory Coast), or because they had hoped for more concrete improvements to their situation as a result of the return of their country to democracy (Chile). Dissatisfaction with the present situation does not mean passive acceptance of the fate of poverty. The majority of those we questioned believe in or hope for 'better times'.

Particularly those questioned in the Ivory Coast (89%) and in Chile (64%) demonstrate much more optimism concerning economic expectations for their future than for their actual situation. Approx. 30% of the Kenyans and Brazilians questioned are pessimistic about the future. In these cases, it is mostly women who find it particularly difficult to look to the future with optimism. In Kenya and Chile, one can also observe that those with a higher level of education more often believe in a better future. This leads to the conclusion that the per-

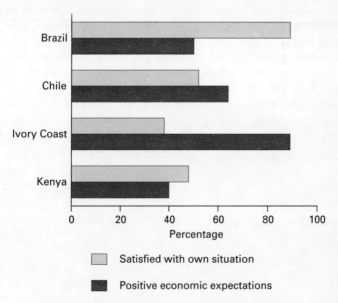

Figure 4.3 General satisfaction and economic expectations

ception of inequality and its interpretation within this group of people depends on how the individuals view their opportunities and chances of escaping poverty and improving their situation.

The processes of subjective perception and interpretation of one's personal situation in life are formed not only by common external environmental factors, but also by uniform interpretations of these and stable communication connections. The following section aims to examine how internal settlement relations and networks influence the life satisfaction of the urban poor, their evaluation of social inequality and finally their motivation to become active, in a political sense, to remove deficits.

The question concerning social unity in the settlements exposes clear differences between the countries. Unity is highest in the two African countries, in which two thirds of those questioned evaluated the internal social cohesion positively. In Brazil, a good half of those questioned, and in Chile in three of the four settlements only just 20%, evaluated the community spirit as high. If one compares the results for Chile and Brazil with survey data from marginal settlements taken at an earlier period in time (e.g. Perlman 1976), it is clear that the highly praised 'communal spirit' is no longer present to the extent it was during the transition phase to democracy and in the times of military dictatorship. In the meantime, individualistic tendencies have increased, a trend reflected in the increasing segmentation of accommodation according to income groups within the marginal settlements (Bento Rubião 1993). Good-neighbourly relations are still important, but community feeling born of common sufferings during 'emergency situations' (e.g. threats of evacuation) is (now) lacking. In Rio de Janeiro, the situation is complicated by the fact that the armed drug gangs present in the settlements foster a climate of intimidation and fear, and prevent feelings of unity and trust.

Table 4.4 Social distance (percentage)

	Brazil	Chile	Ivory Coast	Kenya
No unity in the neighbourhood	52	71	31	34
Trust in				
– nobody	32	29	17	25
– some	58	62	61	61
– all	10	9	22	14

Source: Project Political Participation

In the African settlements, those questioned viewed internal settlement solidarity much more positively. Because of the precarious economic situation of many of those questioned, and the insufficient social policies of the governments in Kenya and the Ivory Coast, good-neighbourly relations are much more important as a 'survival resource'. Neighbourhood groups in these cases are activated for small services, such as occasional donations of food, lending clothes or looking after small children during the mother's working hours. Small financial donations in emergency situations are rare, however, and when they do occur, it is mostly in the two older settlements where the standard of life is generally higher. This feeling of solidarity does not extend to a whole settlement, but is restricted to a certain selected group and neighbourhood. Thus, the urban poor experience help, support and solidarity in emergency situations within their ethnic-regional communities. However, that does not mean they also feel a duty to participate in more general communal activities, which aim at the improvement of the standard of living for the whole settlement.

The increasing tendencies towards individualisation also express themselves in answers to the question concerning trust in fellow human beings. The majority limited their circle of trusted people to family members and neighbours, or friends. The category 'residential area' or 'class' was hardly mentioned by the urban poor as a point of reference. In the two African cases, ethnically based loyalties are also prevalent.

Concluding Remarks

In all four countries, the individual socio-economic standard of living of those questioned is not the primary factor determining satisfaction with life in a larger sense. It is much more the learned values and internal interpretation patterns which decide individual priorities and personal goals. Whether the urban poor decide on passive or more active strategies to face their poverty situation, therefore, also depends on the social networks within which they operate (Putnam 1993; Espinoza 2000). For example, an unquestioned acceptance of inequality means that structurally determined discrimination is defined, according to the milieu, as normal and legitimate. In Brazil and Chile, however, one can observe that members of neighbourhood organisations are more inclined towards political actions, since they interpret experienced discriminations as illegitimate and amendable (see chapter 5). Thus, in addition to the individual factors (e.g. level of education, age, residential area, income, employment situation), the social networks within which the urban poor live are relevant for determining action.

Notes

1. The HDI combines in one index life expectancy, education and per capita income measured in purchasing power parities.

2. The following sources were used to define the poverty line in the respective countries: Brazil, Rocha 1996; Chile, MIDEPLAN 1999; Ivory Coast, IMF Staff Country Report 98/46; Kenya, Central Bureau of Statistics. The poverty lines, given in monetary terms (minimal basket of goods), are as far as possible those for the year of the survey, 1995.

3. Despite its theoretical lack of clarity, the term 'informal' will be used here. It is characterised by the following elements: low level of entrance barriers, because hardly any professional qualifications are required; a tendency towards low average wages with high work intensity (see Portes 1985; 1989); precarious working relations, that is, unstable and only sporadic employment which is not subject to national insurance; functional relationship to the formal employment market (see Sperberg 1997: 19f.).

CHAPTER 5

· · · · · · · · · · · · · · · · · · · ·

Collective Interest Groups

Barbara Happe and
Claus-Dieter König

§ WHEN dealing with transformation and democratisation processes in developing countries in political science, the focus is usually primarily directed to the institutional and procedural minima, which according to Dahl (1971, 1989) must be fulfilled in order to speak of democratic structures. Less often are intermediate spheres and the mediation structures between the state and its citizens (especially marginalised groups of the population) the focus of attention. However, precisely this area affects the long-term sustainability of transformation and democratisation. Only if governments can change potentially negative attitudes of citizens and groups towards the 'new' political system and establish its legitimacy, can democracies in the long run be consolidated. In this chapter we deal with the interest organisations formed by the urban poor and their integration into the political arena. In this context, the continuities and changes with regard to the urban poor's potential to influence political processes in the cause of democratisation will be examined.

The four countries, Brazil, Chile, the Ivory Coast and Kenya, have very different political and social traditions and differ considerably with regard to the extent of recent institutional and procedural restructuring. For this reason, our study of local organisational forms limits itself to the analysis of potential positive, as well as negative, influences on the organisation of political interest groups. In South America, the focal point of analysis are neighbourhood organisations, which are the most important local groups, and their aims, strategies and functions in the political process. In the case of Africa, we concentrate on the most numerous organisations: economic associations in Kenya and ethnic-cultural and social groups in the Ivory Coast. In these cases, the question is whether the potential for the expansion of group interests to include political demands exists and whether these groups have an opportunity of political participation in their own environment. Finally, the same question arises in all four countries: do the groups we examine act to express the interests of the 'discontented', who are distrustful of the dominant forms of interest mediation in their countries, or do they offer effective methods of participation and therefore act to further integration in and legitimisation of the political system? Our initial proposition is: the urban poor will only seek (Africa) or will strive once more (South America) for new forms of alternative organisation and action if state authorities can no longer maintain acceptance of the present system of interest mediation.

Characterisation of Shanty Town Organisations

In the literature concerned with South America, the urban poor of the 1970s and 1980s were sometimes depicted as the 'forces of basic social and political change' (e.g. Kowarick 1984, Moises/Martinez-Alier 1978, Evers et al. 1979). Such euphoric assessments stand in contrast to the opposite evaluations, which view these population groups as having limited organisational capability due to the fatalistic and passive attitudes moulded by their precarious existence (e.g. Rabanal 1990). In the South American cases examined, neither the theory of weak organisational ability,[1] nor that of above average (for each respective country) activity of the urban poor in social or political groups could be confirmed (see Table 5.1).

At almost 30%, the proportion of active Brazilians amongst those questioned by us lies within the national average (Ribeiro/Santos Jr. 1996: 16). At the same time, the Brazilian values are clearly below those

Table 5.1 Membership in voluntary organisations, Latin America (%)

Membership	Brazil	Chile
Religious groups	7	5
Economic groups	–	–
Local political groups	18	26
Local social and ethnic groups	1	20
Parties or trade unions	3	1
No membership	72	49
No answer	–	1

Source: Project Political Participation

in Chile (approx. 50%). This can be explained by Chile's longer tradition of a functioning system of interest mediation operating according to democratic principles, in which primarily the political parties (1920–1973) were the mediators between state and society. By contrast, in Brazil democratic mediation structures and interest organisations for certain population or vocational groups, which were not under state control, only began to form in greater numbers after the start of liberalisation at the end of the 1970s. Until this point, the political decision making process was dominated by a clientelistic relationship between the state and society (see chap. 6), and institutional possibilities for the participation of civil society were limited.

According to our survey, Brazilian favelados and Chilean pobladores most often join local political groups, so-called Residents' (Brazil) or Neighbourhood (Chile) Associations.[2] These organisations are voluntary, locally based groupings which are based on friendly, neighbourly relations, or political initiatives. The obligatory creation of the first neighbourhood organisations in Brazil in the 1960s by the state was aimed at improving the control and manipulation of the voting potential of the urban poor via the 'institutionalisation of the communications channel' (Diniz 1981: 1), and defending against communist infiltration. With its 'promocion popular', the Frei government in Chile (1968) aimed at a stronger integration of the poor in urban society. There, the government hoped that legal recognition of local urban organisations and the assurance of the right of articulation and representation of their interests in the political decision making process would stabilise the system. However, these measures could not prevent the subsequent politicisation and radicalisation of such organisations (Bultmann 1995).

Conceived as pragmatically orientated amalgamations, to this day these associations in Brazil and Chile have maintained their function of mediation between residents and state authorities. Their activities are mainly directed towards the correction of collectively perceived deficits in living conditions which can be solved quickly. In this context, the main priority is the demand for adequate provision of technical and social infrastructure in the shanty towns[3] (e.g. sewerage, water, electricity, garbage collection, health services and (pre-) schools) (Diniz 1981: 57f).

In addition to these neighbourhood associations, which have become weaker over recent years, other local social groups (e.g. Homeless Committees) are increasingly popular in Chile. After 1990, the Aylwin government encouraged their foundation using welfare measures, which gave the pobladores the chance of solving their concrete problems. According to a new law, informal contacts or party affiliation no longer decide the distribution of funds, but the level of need determined by the demands of the respective groups. As a result of this limited purpose, these groups no longer attempt to gain support for their interests in the political decision making process from parties and/or non-governmental organisations (NGOs). This bureaucratisation of the pobladores' demands also means that the potential for mass mobilisation of neighbouring areas is reduced since these are now viewed as potential competitors for state funds rather than partners in the fight for civic rights. Over the past few years, the Brazilian government has also furthered fragmentation and bureaucratisation of the favelados' 'lutas' (struggles) by constantly dividing the responsibilities of those sections of state administration concerned with favela matters. However, as yet there has been no reorientation of political activity in favour of social engagement in the local neighbourhood.

Declining membership of political groups in Brazil and Chile stands in contrast to increasing religious organisation, predominantly evangelical. Amongst our survey, in Brazil, the percentage of those active in a religious group, 7%, is clearly higher than the national average of approx. 3% (Ribeiro/Santos Jr. 1996: 29). Membership of such groups is divided between Pentecostal Churches and the Charismatic Renewal, a relatively new, conservative current within the Catholic Church. According to a recent study (Fernandes 1994), the various Pentecostal Churches in Brazil have mobilised approximately 15 million members, the same number that local Catholic parishes mobilised in the 1970s during the Theology of Liberation campaigns (Corten 1996: 68). In contrast to this movement, the vast majority of Pentecostal Church members are not interested in creating a link between religion and politics and devote themselves almost exclusively to pastoral duties and social activities. The Charismatic Renewal can be viewed as the Catholic Church's answer to its rapid decline of members in favour of Pentecostal Churches. This is also a purely religious movement with no desire to mix religious commitment and politics (Veja 20.09.1995: 74). In these groups, concrete socio-political measures are limited to sporadic welfare activities, e.g. food distribution.

Political parties and unions account for just 10% of all organisation members who were questioned in Brazil, and a mere 2% in Chile. The percentage of party activists in both countries, not only in the shanty towns but also nation-wide and irrelevant of class, is rather low (4% in Brazil (IBGE 1991: LIV) and 6% in Chile (Garreton et al. 1994: 67; Garreton et al. 1995)). Since 1992, Chile has suffered from political and party apathy because political parties are increasingly perceived as representatives of particular interests, rather than transmitters between the state and society (as was the case until 1973). Political parties have removed themselves almost completely from the shanty towns, where they were active as the organisers and mobilisers of the urban poor until the fall of Allende in 1973. The urban poor have, therefore, been unable to continue the tradition, which existed before 1973, of using local party political ties to further their own interests and have so far been unable to identify with the new means politicians employ in an attempt to represent social interests at the national level. In contrast to the Chilean party system, the Brazilian one has demonstrated a high level of instability and personalisation since its inception. With the exception of the Partido dos Trabalhadores (PT), none of the numerous and short-lived parties have been founded as a result of initiatives from below. To this day, parties function primarily as vehicle 'to fulfil the formal conditions for candidates and (...) to serve one's own interests and facilitate personal enrichment' (Cruz 1992: 134).

Although on a national basis, 18% of the Brazilian working popula-tion is organised in a union (IBGE 1991: KLV, LIV), the percentage of union members amongst the favelados we questioned and who are active in the formal sector is a mere 4%. This value is surprisingly low, especially as those with low incomes are proportionally overrepresented in the unions (1–3 minimum wages). The main incentive for joining a union is to obtain one of the free packages still offered by the 'pelego' unions[4] for their members. The package includes medical care and/or legal aid in an emergency. In the face of the limited efficiency of the social security system for low income groups, the unions have taken on the task of welfare provision for them. In Chile, the level of union organisation is approx. 12% (1995), which is ten times higher than that of the pobladores we questioned. From the perspective of a poblador, union membership does not promise any benefit because even in the democratically organised unions and vocational associations, the needs of the urban poor active in the formal sector only are selectively repres-ented in the organisation's activities. This is also true in the Brazilian case.

Furthermore, in both Chile and Brazil, frequent changes of employ-ment and/or activity and the increasingly precarious conditions of employment (e.g. seasonal work) hinder the development of solidarity and common interest patterns, which are the prerequisites for associ-ation organisation. The under-representation of pobladores in vocational associations is a consequence of the fact that, in contrast to those from other neighbourhoods, pobladores who are active in the formal sector are more often self-employed and are therefore not available for collec-tive organisation at the workplace. This is also true of shanty towns in

Brazil where people work more often as domestic employees or in very small enterprises and are, therefore, not available for organisation at a common place of work.

In contrast to the unions and parties, the central link and motive for membership in neighbourhood associations and social or religious groupings is the connection between the 'area of residence' and the interests formed by common experiences and living conditions. With regard to collective forms of interest organisation, the favelados and pobladores differ from other sections of the population not primarily in their level of organisation, but rather in the ways and means of their connection to organised civil society. The almost complete absence of political parties and unions is compensated for by above average activity in local residents' associations (e.g. Brazil: 17% of the urban poor, compared to 13.1% of all Brazilians (IBGE 1991: LIV)). This fact points to the segmentation of both South American societies in the area of association organisation (Ribeiro/Santos Jr. 1996: 109).

In both African countries examined, Kenya and the Ivory Coast, the comparison of forms and levels of organisation based on the data we collected was difficult due to differences in the concept and understanding of membership. Whereas economic associations in Kenya – material aspirations are usually most important for such associations – have a clearly defined and often formal membership, party membership is diffuse and is achieved by the single act of buying a membership card. Further payments are not required and regular local meetings or activities do not exist. The religious groups are Christian Churches or Islamic organisations. In Kenya two of the shanty settlements studied were strongly influenced by Islamic organisations, whose main interest was the observance of Islamic culture. Groups which are limited to the

Table 5.2 Membership in voluntary organisations, Africa (%)

Membership	Côte d'Ivoire	Kenya
Religious groups	2	6
Economic groups	–	25
Local political groups	6	–
Local social and ethnic groups	16	2
Parties or trade unions	3	3
No membership	1	55
No answer	72	9

Source: Project Political Participation

Islamic population and also fulfil a social, that is, an economic function are included in the category 'religious groups'.

In the Ivory Coast, 72% of those asked about membership in local groups did not respond. The social networks found here follow the pattern of traditional village communities and have, especially in the urban environment, also vertical links to different sections of the population. Thus, 'membership' of an organisation for those who migrated from a region in the north west of the Ivory Coast is often found in the shanty towns. Such associations often form as a result of particular circumstances, for example families from Burkino Faso in a certain neighbourhood may help each other in emergencies on the basis of their common nationality, and new arrivals join the 'family' solidarity. However, these social networks are selective and often only spring into action during an emergency, e.g. deaths, illness, births. Almost all associations and social relationships are based on ethnic-regional criteria and are not formalised. In the Ivory Coast, formal membership requires that an association is registered with the local authorities and its official statutes are deposited there. This is the case for local organisations such as youths' or women's associations and party organisations. This partly explains the low reported membership in the shanty towns. This observation is also true for the savings societies in Kenya as well as for the Luos' numerous 'funeral societies' in Kisumu, which contribute to the funeral costs and the transport of the deceased to their home town.

Even though our findings for the Ivory Coast are only of limited value, due to the reasons mentioned above, they do give an insight into local organisational structures. The respective leaders of ethnic-cultural groups function as mediators between their own group and the neighbourhood *chef*, who represents the residential area before the state authorities. The membership of various associations in the Ivory Coast is summarised within the category 'social organisations'. All these groups share one characteristic, they are socially active (e.g. night watches, hygiene associations), but are not explicitly ethnic-regional groupings. Formal self-help organisations are usually formed as a consequence of suitable directives from above. A mayor will often ask the *chef* of such a neighbourhood to get young people together to form a clean-up brigade, which manifests itself as a 'hygiene association', but is seldom long-lived. In reaction to the sudden increase in criminal activity in Abidjan in 1990–92, night watches were formed. These are seldom active today because the state police and private security services have taken over their function. In Man, one such organisation failed because of a disagreement between the younger members and the 'elders', the notables and members of the action committee. The younger members claimed that promised payment had not been forthcoming. There are also associations for neighbourhood hygiene in Kenya, but these are often groups of local health workers who work in conjunction with newly formed NGOs active in the medical sphere. Their activities considerably improve hygiene and basic medical provision in the shanty towns. To facilitate their continued survival, such groups have often combined these activities with wider functions of self-help groups, e.g. income-generating projects. The dividing line with economic associations then becomes blurred.

Membership of local political groups in the Ivory Coast is limited to youth and women's groups, which usually operate as subdivisions of the former state party, the Parti Démocratique de la Côte d'Ivoire (PDCI). While in some cases the youth groups have maintained a durable structure and represent their interests before the *chef*, women's groups are often only active during election campaigns. Official women's associations in Abidjan are ethnically dominated by the governing ethnic group and, in the medium-sized town of Man, by the local ethnic group. The women are also organised in dance groups; however membership of such groups is once again based on ethnic-regional criteria. Comparable economic organisations in West Africa are the Tontines, or savings clubs. These are often associations organised by female market traders. The questions we raised concerning membership in an organisation were often misunderstood to mean formal membership of established organisations operating at the settlement level. Such organisations in the Ivory Coast are neither income-generating associations as in Kenya, nor are they partners for NGOs. NGOs have a very limited presence and sphere of activity in the poor areas of Abidjan.

Membership of religious organisations is similar to that of social associations and is often informal so that those questioned did report it at this point. In contrast to Brazil, Christian sects and groupings are not widely present in the Ivory Coast. The majority of the population in the Ivorian shanty towns we studied practise the Islamic faith. As a result, these groups in the Ivory Coast cannot be considered informal associations and are therefore not comparable. Therefore, we will concentrate on a more detailed explanation of the results from Kenya.

In Kenya, economic associations are the dominant form of organisation in the shanty towns; 25% of those questioned were members in such organisations. These associations are first and foremost project-orientated, e.g. self-help groups and cooperatives. We apply the term 'project-orientated self-help group' to those organisations the activities of which are centred around a common income-generating project. Cooperatives are groupings between persons in the informal sector who are self-employed and have founded common arrangements (usually a social fund, into which contributions are paid to cover loss of income due to illness, or the cost of necessary technical devices which surpass the investment potential of the individual). In Kenya, the level of organisation in women's groups in the shanty towns studied can be compared to national statistics. According to these figures, both locally and nationally, approximately one fifth of all women are organised in self-help groups. Many women's self-help groups also take on ethnic-cultural functions, such as public dances. Our interviews show that these are mostly ethnically homogenous and therefore strengthen ethnic-cultural ties. We could observe that this also may increase inter-ethnic conflicts.

Apart from economic associations, only unions (which are formally independent, but in reality are close to the governing party) and religious groupings have membership numbers worth mentioning. In Kenyan shanty towns, parties and political organisations have no in-dependent divisions. One exception during the period of research were the local groups of the opposition party FORD-Kenya in Kisumu. Their activity was, however, mostly terminated after the elections. The local associations and youth groups of the governing party, KANU, are in fact an extension of the state administration and its power monopoly, not a division of the party aimed at organising and representing local interests. By contrast, the PDCI local youth groups in the Ivory Coast represent a regular section of the party and do not act in this way. The urban poor in the Ivory Coast only seldom organise themselves in political parties because their interests are hardly represented in party competition, which is concentrated primarily on national political ques-tions. Although they represent an important voting potential for the opposition party, there are no regular meetings which could enable the urban poor to unite and represent their interests at a local level.

Parliamentary representatives usually are not active in the shanty towns either, but in town councils or the national parliament. In con-trast, the urban poor in Kenya are more likely to be mobilised by the political opposition because they hope that a change of government would also bring an improvement in their personal situation. The inhabitants of the shanty towns we studied in Nairobi and Kisumu were predominantly ethnic Kikuyu and Luo. Both these ethnic groups were strongly represented in the government under President Kenyatta (until 1978) and since President Moi has taken over have been more on the sidelines. Their organisational forms remain at the level of self-help groups using clientelistic relationships. At present, political parties in Kenya fragment the population because they employ ethnic criteria as a method of mobilisation. This has a detrimental effect on the internal social cohesion in the shanty towns and prevents the inhabitants from joining common political groupings. In the Ivory Coast, the PDCI employs similar methods, e.g. encouraging resentments towards the Burkinabé. In comparison to the two South American countries, the number active in party political groupings in both African countries is very low.

Neither Kenya nor the Ivory Coast has a history of collective land occupation, nor are there advocatory organisations which represent the interests of the settlement to the outside world as in the Latin American cases. In Kenya, as the appointed officer of the state administration, the Chief channels the articulated interests of the residents and therefore represents the centre of power in the shanty town. In particular, self-help groups continually require the assistance of the Chief. He is responsible for bringing them into contact with the Social Development Officers, who are responsible for the financial support of self-help groups and also for foreign NGOs. The Chief regulates the distribution of plots and controls who is active in what trade. All groups have to be registered with the respective Ministry (Social Works, Culture), and this registration must be approved by the local Chief. Only then are they permitted to hold meetings, which must usually be announced beforehand.

Even after the transition to a pluralistic party system in 1990, the interest articulation of the urban poor in the Ivory Coast remains in the mould cast by the former one-party rule of the PDCI. This used the foundations of traditional (village) structures to bind the entire population into a social network, at the top of which stands the Chef du Quartier. Since 1980, in so far as they possess no traditional or first settler rights, the Chef du Quartier is elected by the residents. He represents the whole settlement before the town authorities and the mayor, and is also responsible for implementing the directives of the higher state authorities. At the same time, he used to be the head of the respective PDCI section. The local women's and youth organisations, which belong to the PDCI, are primarily employed to implement directives. In ethnically heterogeneous settlements, *chefs* from other ethnic-regional and national groupings sit alongside the Chef du Quartier and make up the local action committee, which was also integrated into the PDCI party structure. The ethnic-cultural groups in this way articulate their interests in the settlement's internal structures.

Urban shanty settlements in Kenya and the Ivory Coast are, therefore, under strong state control. The authorities' control over the activities in the settlements as well as the hierarchical organisation of interest representation prevent the formation of independently operating political groups. Even though the urban poor have only rudimentary access to the political process and government action within these structures, they have yet to question the basic power structure which still is widely perceived as legitimate. In contrast, in Chile and Brazil, local neighbourhood political organisations were formed in the 1960s as a reaction against the lack of formal mechanisms for interest articulation for the urban poor. Before this date, the urban poor lived in a legal vacuum. State presence in the shanty towns was limited to informal and sporadic intervention, and the favelas and poblaciones were not integrated into local governmental or interest articulation structures. In some cases, local neighbourhood organisations took over political power in the areas the state had neglected. With the help of external actors (political parties in Chile, the Catholic Church in Brazil), they filled the vacuum and became organisers of social life in their neighbourhood.[5] While the current political framework and an ethnically orientated system of values in Kenya and the Ivory Coast prevent the urban poor from forming independent political groups, the existence of numerous neighbourhood organisations in Brazil and Chile shows that, in principle, in societies where democratic rules are followed more strictly the interests of the urban poor can be organised. Their ability to assert interests in the political process in these cases is mostly dependent on the resources of a specific settlement (e.g. size and geographical position) and support from advocatory organisations.

Characteristics of the Most Important Local Groups

In the following section, the ability of South American neighbourhood organisations to influence the political process will be examined in more detail. The choice of active groups for the African cases is more difficult because there are no similar political organisations. In these cases, the urban poor articulate their interests via economic, or social and cultural groups. Therefore, we will examine those groups in the African countries which, according to our data, have the highest number of members. These are the economic associations in Kenya and local social and ethnic-cultural organisations in the Ivory Coast. As a result of the ethnic-regional representation in the local action committees, political interest representation in the shanty towns of the Ivory Coast is fragmented. In Kenya, the groups do not view themselves as organisations representing political interests, but rather as associations striving to improve the economic situation of their members via income-generating projects. These projects, which are not necessarily of a general nature, are presented to the outside authorities. The analysis of these groups aims to discover how they are integrated into the political process in their respective country and to what degree the preconditions or potential for the development and extension of group goals to general political demands exist. However, because the structure and goals of economic associations in Kenya differ from those of the social and ethnic-cultural groups in the Ivory Coast, the comparability of these groups is less than that of their counterparts in Brazil and Chile.

Latin American Urban Organisations

The term 'neighbourhood organisation' in South America encompasses a wide spectrum of organisations. They are differentiated not only by their political goals, forms of action and strategies, but also in relation to their social composition, size and programmes. In some cases they even compete against one another for the same state resources. As already mentioned above, the state authorities in the Brazilian and Chilean cities which experienced a huge influx of rural migrants (from 1940) who settled illegally on state or private land reacted neither with a stringent clearance policy, nor with a specific policy aimed at integrating the favelados and pobladores into urban society. The settlers often created a channel of communication to the state administration by the founding of independent neighbourhood organisations. Following the beginning of re-democratisation in Brazil at the end of the 1970s and in Chile at the end of the 1980s, the possibilities of forming representative neighbourhood organisations which operated according to democratic principles increased.

The establishment forms of mediation accepted by the residents as well as by the state authorities aimed to divert the increasing protest of the urban poor into institutional channels and bind them into the new democratic system. In current political practice, the neighbourhood organisations function as contact points for the public administration in the favelas and poblaciones. In this context, these groups strive to acquire state funds and aid programmes for their settlement. In their aspiration to improve the standard of living, they must find a balance between becoming a local administrative body[6] and remaining a local (independent) representative organisation. As the neighbourhood organisations are the main institution for implementing state aid programmes in the favelas and poblaciones, the legitimisation of their leaders is no longer solely dependent on election by the residents, but also on the changes achieved in the settlement, which they undertake in their function as the administrators of state-financed projects.

The great differences in organisational forms, especially in Brazil, can be explained by the specific positioning of the respective neighbourhood organisation between the extreme poles of 'the residents' organ for interest representation' on the one hand, and 'administrative institution' on the other. In north eastern Brazil, the formation of AMs remains to a high degree the result of state initiative; or they form in reaction to the existence of state aid programmes for needy areas (Cruz 1992; Fausto Neto 1993). The termination of such programmes often ended in the deactivation of the AMs. A further typical characteristic of such organisations in the north east is the use of the AM to promote certain politicians and/or parties. In such cases, AMs are formed before election campaigns as a result of personal initiative on the part of certain residents or individual politicians. According to estimates, 25% of all AMs in Aracaju (40 out of 160) were formed as a direct result of the individual activities of politicians (Souza 1995: 19). On election day, many of the organisations founded in this manner, which are not interested in improving living conditions in the favelas, but rather in securing personal benefits, end their activities until the next elections. The democratisation process in the north east thus has only resulted in a rudimentary democratisation of the favelados' representative organs so far. According to estimates, the number of independent AMs in Aracaju which are organised according to representative democratic principles is 3% (5 out of 160) (Souza 1995: 20).

In Rio de Janeiro, the revitalisation of local neighbourhood organisations at the end of the 1970s took place under different circumstances (see e.g. Assies 1993; Jacobi 1988). After 1978/79 numerous independent, democratic groups were formed in the favelas with the help of the Catholic Church and humanitarian non-governmental organisations. These succeeded in mobilising a grassroots base to improve living conditions. From 1982 onwards, noticeable changes in the attitude of the government, an increasing willingness to engage in negotiation with residents' associations and selective consideration of some of their demands in the political process affected the AMs' perception of the state and consequently their tactics. Following the withdrawal of the Catholic Church from the political arena in the middle of the 1980s, the tendency to instrumentalise neighbourhood organisations to further leadership interests reappeared. After the election of the populist Brizola as Governor of Rio de Janeiro (1982), a wide-ranging and relatively successful political coopting of the AM leadership began (Gay 1994: 31ff). In this way, many of the associations which had functioned according to democratic principles became mere organs of implementation for state policies. However, the percentage of primarily independently operating AMs remained still high. Estimates range between 10 and 15% (conversation with D. Ferreira 15.06.1999).

In comparison to Brazilian neighbourhood organisations, even before the military dictatorship, almost all the Juntas in Chile operated as democratically organised interest associations for the pobladores. During the military dictatorship, their representative function was lost because chairmen were appointed by the administration and their primary task was to control the grassroots rather than represent their interests. Following democratisation, the Juntas have been unable to regain, let alone expand, the powerful position they enjoyed before 1973. Until 1973, the various political parties encouraged self-organisation of the pobladores. In the late 1960s and early 1970s under Presidents Frei and Allende, interest mediation between the state and its citizens became monopolised by the political parties. In this phase, the ideological alignment and party political affinity of a Junta determined the chances of successful assertion of its interests. As a result, clientelistic relations between the Juntas on the one side and the political administrative system on the other were also formed in Chile. However, in contrast to Brazil, such relationships were not primarily based on a Junta chairman's or politician's calculations of personal benefit, but rather were ideologically motivated.

Following the transition to democracy at the end of the 1980s, the Aylwin government endeavoured to replace this principle of mediation with a state-regulated representative system. Informal contacts and party political affinities should no longer determine the level of funding for a neighbourhood but rather the evidence of special needs of a particular settlement (see also above). The lack of over-arching umbrella organisations reduced the Juntas' possibilities for influencing the political process. As a result, the Juntas' party affiliations lost their relevance. By introducing social emergency programmes, such as the internationally funded solidarity fund FOSIS,[7] the Aylwin government succeeded in preventing any renewed party mobilisation of the pobladores. It also successfully channelled any protest into the formal structure of relationships between the Juntas and the state bureaucracy. The Juntas thus no longer function primarily as organs of political representation for the pobladores, but rather as authorities which formulate project applications for a specific residential area. In this way, the state has succeeded in bureaucratising the pobladores' demands. Furthermore, competition for project funds prevents their political cooperation. The Juntas in Chile thus have developed from 'party orientated umbrella organisations to state regulated authorities' (Bultman 1995: 23).

The Juntas themselves remain organised according to representative democratic principles and in this way provide a forum for the pobladores to engage in political grassroots action in their own neighbourhood. The willingness of the pobladores to become active in the Juntas is to a large extent dependent on the Juntas' ability to solve local problems effectively. As a result of their diminishing influence on the political process, the Juntas in Santiago in particular suffer from a poor image amongst their own grassroots members. Rather than informal contacts and political influence, technical knowledge is now required to solve problems. In Temuco, however, the old system has not been as radically destroyed as in Santiago. Good contacts with those who make the decisions (e.g. unions, NGOs) increase the Juntas' chances of success in the local political arena.

Whereas in Chile now previously existing clientelistic party relationships have been almost completely replaced, the majority of political representatives in Brazil were not interested in the termination, but rather the integration of the AMs into the traditional clientelistic patterns. After democratisation, some AMs succeeded in creating new democratic structures for a dialogue with the public authorities. Although these were not in a position to completely replace the traditional, clientelistic interest representation structures, they were at least able to 'renew some of them, although they remain influenced and restricted by them' (Cardoso 1995: 197). The existence of particular clientelistic practices thus continues to hinder the consolidation of democratic interest representation in Brazil.

Those AMs and Juntas which are organised according to democratic principles see themselves increasingly reduced to the role of a local administrative authority. Despite their limited negotiating powers in the political process, they continue to enjoy widespread support amongst the local population, especially in Chile. The data we collected

Table 5.3 Status of voluntary organisations, Latin America (%)

The three most important groups in the quarter are ...	Brazil	Chile
political (state-oriented) groups (AMs, Juntas)	23	44
religious groups	46	7
local social and ethnic groups	11	40
no important groups	13	9
other groups	71	–

Source: Project Political Participation

in South America present a heterogeneous picture. In the Chilean poblaciones, political and social groups are not only supported by their own members, but also enjoy a good reputation amongst the other residents of the neighbourhood. Without doubt, since the withdrawal of political parties from the shanty towns, they represent the most important group there.

In contrast to Brazil, religious groups in Chile do not compete with political groups for leadership positions within a settlement, since only the latter have the competence to solve local problems. In response to the question as to the most important groups in the settlement, the number of those who named religious groupings in Brazil was almost twice as high as those who cited neighbourhood organisations. The AMs' loss of reputation in Rio de Janeiro is so dramatic that they no longer feel it necessary to register members. Those questioned in Rio de Janeiro deny the existence of any influential groups in their neighbourhood more often than those in other areas. This behaviour can be partly explained by specific factors present in the respective shanty towns which work to restrict the AMs' position in the political process (e.g. a geographically isolated area or a low number of residents mean that even during election campaigns, such settlements do not present interesting canvassing objects for ambitious politicians).

One of the reasons for the comparatively low level of relevance favelados in Rio de Janeiro assign to the AMs is connected to the increasingly violent atmosphere in the shanty towns. There, fights between rival drug gangs and between gangs and the police have become part of everyday life. They paralyse the activities of the AMs and/or considerably limit their possibilities of gaining influence in their respective neighbourhoods. Even though the Juntas in Chile are perceived as more effective working groups and have a relatively large membership, this does not mean that the 'communal spirit' is especially strong. There,

Table 5.4 Social unity, Latin America (%)

What are your feelings about the unity in the neighbourhood?	Brazil	Chile
Strong unity	7	6
Moderate unity	42	23
Moderate disunity	41	36
Strong disunity	11	35

Source: Project Political Participation

only 30% of those questioned believe solidarity between settlement residents to be strong. In Brazil the values are higher, although in comparison with earlier studies the tendency is in decline, which points to an increasing isolation and alienation within the favelas.[8] In the Perlman Study (1968/9) 52% of the 700 favelados questioned from Rio de Janeiro claimed there was a high level of solidarity in their settlement. In our study, only 7% felt this was true. Furthermore, at 32% distrust of fellow human beings, including family members, was much higher than in the Perlman Study (12%) (ibid.: 133). The AMs' activities increasingly fail to give residents a 'feeling of unity' (Zaluar 1985: 188). Since the disappearance of the common enemy – the military dictatorship – isolationist and individualistic tendencies have increased.

One way of strengthening influence in the political process is the aggregation of neighbourhood groups and their interests at the city level. In both Chile and Brazil such overarching organisations exist, in Chile at the city level, and in Brazil also at the national level. These umbrella organisations use party affiliations to increase their influence in the political process. However, at the same time, this limits their chances of persuading many grassroots organisations to join them. Such grassroots organisations are primarily interested in concrete improvements of their living standards, not in (party) political debate. AMs and Juntas only rarely view the possibility of 'horizontal' networks with other neighbourhood organisations as an opportunity to increase their own power. A further option to enhance the representation of their interests in the political process are vertical networks with other different organisations. Actors in South America who have offered themselves as potential coalition partners over the last decade include Church or non-governmental organisations, the main activities of which are oriented towards the urban poor. According to a study in 1990, 85% of the 780 neighbourhood organisations questioned had received support from humanitarian or Church organisations or individual priests (IBASE 1990: 10). Such people and organisations usually have better contacts and exude more confidence in front of the state authorities. They also have better legal and technical know-how. Settlement organisations can increase their own power resources in the political process by entering such cooperative arrangements. Furthermore, the presence of such external actors and the educational and political work they carry out during the foundation phase of organisations increase enormously their chances of survival.

An appraisal of the political negotiating power and cooperation of non-governmental organisations in re-democratised Chile remains more negative. The pobladores' higher educational level and greater experience with forms of self-help limits their need for external assistance. In addition, with the transition to democracy, (inter)national sources of finance for this (relatively) prosperous country almost dried up. As a result, many NGOs have been forced to stop their work in the poblaciones. In an attempt to maintain their organisation, many NGOs have reorientated their main areas of activity. Today, they longer carry out their own projects, but function primarily to implement state projects in the shanty towns or work as research institutes and/or private consulting companies. Over the past years, they have distanced themselves from the function they had during the military dictatorship as 'advocates for the poor', and the urban poor no longer perceive them as mediators of their interests. Since democratisation, for the first time in Brazil, and once more in Chile, residents' and neighbourhood associations offer the favelados and pobladores official participation channels which enable them to articulate their demands directly to state organs. In both countries, however, the phase of high levels of mobilisation is over and has given way to a more pragmatic and results-orientated understanding of organisation. The chances settlement organisations have to make themselves heard to state institutions and achieve a real improvement of living conditions using these channels vary according to their resources and are dependent on the negotiating situation and political framework.

Local Organisations in Africa

In the case of the Ivory Coast and Kenya, urban shanty towns have been integrated into the administrative structure since colonial times (see Illy/Oberndörfer 1981). The Chief or the Chef du Quartier is the state's representative in the settlement. The colonial governments required the cooperation of African leaders to ensure administrative control. Wherever possible, they built on existing African social structures, which in west Africa led to confirmation of the 'traditional' Chiefs. However, the integration of the Chiefs into the centralised colonial administration meant that their leadership style and tasks were adjusted to the requirements of the colonial power system. In this way, varied traditional social structures were transformed into a hierarchy dominated by the local Chief, who himself was completely dependent on the colonial government. The latter retained the power to remove local Chiefs.

Such structures, which were originally devised for the integration of rural areas, have also been useful in urban shanty towns. The end of colonial rule often simply entailed the handing over of state power to local elites, who were themselves less than eager to institute changes in the power structure. As a result, these institutions were accepted into the independent state's structures. In the Ivory Coast, ethnic Chiefs were integrated into the grassroots committees of the Party and in this manner into the Party itself. In Kenya, the Chiefs occupy the lowest level in the hierarchy of province and district administration. They are subordinate to the Office of the President which, as a superministry, unites all important administrative activities. Democratisation has done little to change these administrative structures. However, there are individual cases of town councils with an opposition majority which control the Chiefs.

The ethnic-cultural organisations in the Ivory Coast fulfil a myriad of functions. Most importantly, they provide social networks in the urban environment. In this way, new arrivals can always count on support from such organisations. Secondly, they function as organs for interest representation for their respective ethnic-cultural groups in the local committees. For example, migrant workers from Burkina Faso have very well-organised ethnic-cultural groups. The third important function is the maintenance of contacts to the rural home areas. Thus, it is not uncommon for urban ethnic groups to give financial support to projects (e.g. construction of a school) in their native region. More specific social groups, which are responsible for medical provision for example, are formed when a well-known or important person in the settlement decides to do so, either as a result of their own motivation or in conjunction with projects from the World Bank or NGOs. However, such groups have mostly been unable to establish themselves in the long term because, due to their founding history, they were not accepted by the settlement's residents or their funds were embezzled or stolen. In the case of youth groups, which until democratisation were part of the PDCI structures in the shanty towns, there have been some changes, for example in the settlement Washington in Abidjan. They unite all youth; however, for common activities, rather different political and social associations have been created. In parallel, the official youth organisations act in election campaigns for the PDCI. Other youth associations operate as ethnic organisations with contacts to other ethnic groups, especially when funds are available. Non-political organisations often only have a short lifespan. They fail due to ethnic divisions, the financial situation, youth unemployment or the departure, or death, of their founding members.

In Kenya, the number of project-orientated self-help groups is much higher than that of cooperatives. However, it is difficult to differentiate between these organisations. We also place the numerous women's groups in this category. A self-help group or cooperative usually fulfils various functions too. Its main task often consists of forming a credit cooperative amongst members. The focal point of activities is usually a commercial project, which provides members with a small income. The self-perception and goals of a self-help group are similar to those of a cooperative. The income-generating project usually takes the form of common production of some sort of article or offering a service. Women's self-help groups usually sell hand-made products, such as woven baskets or textiles, quite often at markets frequented by tourists. One of the successful male self-help groups we studied was a car cleaning cooperative in Nairobi. This group had diversified its service activities and also offered a house cleaning and painting service. Often self-help groups also build houses or huts in their neighbourhood and draw rent from these.

Acquiring a plot which can be used as a production facility for articles or for rented accommodation is often an important medium-term goal. If title deeds can be obtained, a mortgage can be raised on such property. In this way a group can gain a bank loan and engage in investment. In addition, the plot can also be offered as insurance for loans given to members for their private economic projects. Members of self-help groups in Kenya perceive the level of solidarity in a settlement as being higher than do those who are not organised. They belong to the established social networks in a shanty town. In contrast, some shanty town residents in Kenya are excluded from these networks and have no access to organised groups. Where this is the case, a certain level of individualisation can be observed amongst newcomers. Those with family members in a settlement or a contact person from their home region have access to the networks.

We asked residents which three groups were the most important for their neighbourhood. In Kenya, as expected, 50% of those questioned

Table 5.5 Social unity, Africa (%)

What are your feelings about the unity in the neighbourhood?	Ivory Coast	Kenya
Strong unity	20	20
Moderate unity	47	47
Moderate disunity	22	22
Strong disunity	12	12

Source: Project Political Participation

named economic organisations. In the Ivory Coast, ethnic-cultural and local social organisations dominated and were named by 58%. However, local political organisations were also often cited (32%). These are either the grassroots organisations of the PDCI or women's and youth associations with connections to this party.

Self-help groups in Kenya often seek cooperation with the state administration responsible for the shanty town, the Chief, or with the group of leaders (Elders, Village Chairmen), who preside over the settlement with the Chief. This is sensible, because the Chief has the power to forbid a group to operate. Furthermore, all sources of external support are channelled through the Chief. The self-help groups in Kenya employ harambees (donation campaigns) as a means to collect money for their projects. Due to their contacts with donors as well as relations to politicians who can give larger sums for the harambee, those self-help groups who foster good contacts with politicians from the governing KANU party and who support KANU are most successful. Opposition politicians in urban electoral districts often fail – in contrast to their rural party fellows – to offer similar gifts. They lack the resources which government politicians often acquire through nepotistic channels from the state budget. In addition, many women's self-help groups are also cultural groups which practise and perform traditional dances. They appear at KANU election events, liven up the atmosphere at a arazas' (residents' meeting) organised by high-level politicians, dance on national holidays and appear at the numerous ceremonies to welcome or bid farewell to the President at the airport.

The ethnic-cultural organisations in the Ivory Coast fulfil a similar function. Informal horizontal networks between settlement residents or their representatives and those employed in the town administration

Table 5.6 Status of voluntary organisations, Africa (%)

The three most important groups in the quarter are …	Ivory Coast	Kenya
political (state oriented) groups	32	3
religious groups	2	26
ethnic groups	33	6
economic groups	–	50
local social groups	25	9
other groups	7	7

Source: Project Political Participation

or politicians affect the possibilities of political influence and play an important role during conflicts. Thus, in the case of the clearance of Washington, various groups and people from the settlement tried to speak to officials on a personal level. Such contacts even extended to the wife of the President of the country. The Burkinabé association contacted their ambassador to put the settlement's case before the President. Thus, official representations as well as personal contacts and clientelistic relationships are employed for a cause. Self-help groups in Kenya are also integrated into clientelistic relationships. Their chairmen are often a part of the clientele network in a neighbourhood. If a self-help group does not possess such contacts to those in power, it is not likely to be successful; not least because lack of support from those in power signals to settlement residents that such a group is badly organised and does not work effectively. Self-help groups are rooted in a history of cooperation in pre-colonial societies as well as colonial social policies. Their current income-generating projects are a reaction to the development policy of 'help for self-help'. The main goal of their projects is to obtain funds. It is in their interest to gain access to external funding and to achieve this they often use clientelistic relations to the Chief and contacts with politicians.

In the Ivory Coast, integration of the shanty town's interest representation structures into the hierarchical party organisation of the PDCI does not mean, however, that the urban poor have special access to influence the political process. In the case of a conflict – as observed during the now-completed clearance of Washington – contacts to politicians, which often run parallel to official structures, can lead to at least partial success, as the delay in clearance demonstrated. More interesting are the perspectives for influencing the political process which arise from the multi-party system and other democratic innovations. It is possible to observe the first steps in this direction which could lead to a more lasting democratisation of civil society. Thus, in Washington the leading position of the Chef was challenged and his right to articulate the interests of the settlement was revoked. As a consequence, he was bypassed by certain groups and individuals during their campaign to prevent the clearance. Furthermore, they used the press, which, since the introduction of a multi-party system, knows how to operate in the political arena. The new framework in the Ivory Coast has led to first signs that the urban poor have widened their repertoire of strategies and interest representation.

The possibilities of political influence which self-help groups in Kenya enjoy lie first and foremost at the settlement level. The Chief works together with the Elders in the performance of his administrative tasks. To increase efficiency, he often calls upon people who enjoy respect amongst the residents, specifically the leaders of active and successful self-help groups. It depends on the character of each individual Chief how far he coordinates activities with them. Not all settlements have a weekly baraza. Where this is the case, residents are often present in limited numbers and preparation for the meeting is shared between the Chief and self-help groups. However, this co-operation with self-help groups and their leaders is not equivalent to legal rights. The Chief is not obliged to contact them. Often self-help groups are selectively integrated while others are excluded. The wide-ranging power the Chief exercises over the shanty town thus remains basically untouched. Women's self-help groups have a formal channel for political influence through their umbrella organisation Maendeleo ya Wanawake. The majority of its leadership positions are occupied by KANU women (often politicians' wives) and there is no independent organisation of interests. The leaders of Maendeleo ya Wanawake work without any input from the grassroots. Women from shanty towns, therefore, have no real chances of influencing the political process through this organisation.

Membership Profile of the Most Important Organisations

In this section the active membership of the organisations named above will be discussed in more detail. In particular, the socio-economic profile of the active members will be presented. The question of whether more critical attitudes towards political authorities and the democratic system are present in such associations will also be dealt with in chapters 6 and 7.

Brazil and Chile

As outlined in chapter 4 above, the favelados and pobladores are not homogenous groups. There are considerable differences with respect to criteria such as type of work, family income and education, not only between favelas and poblaciones, but also within individual settlements. In Chile, the indicators for those active in the juntas do not differ from the general sample. They have neither a higher level of education, nor do they have more secure employment. They do not earn more and are not older or younger than the average. In the settlements women are just as active in associations as men. As a result of the new principle of project applications, the political arena of the Juntas has been limited. Therefore, junta membership no longer promises individual advantage.

As a result, so-called 'cuenta-propristas' increasingly participate in the juntas. In this way, they hope to gain access to state funds for their (extremely) small enterprises. However, because the majority of public social measures in the poblaciones are primarily aimed at fighting extreme poverty, junta membership is no longer a priority for economically more prosperous pobladores. Motives for membership are more often connected to social and ideological values, which are expressed in above-average trust in this form of collective interest representation. In certain areas, our results are different for Brazil, however. There, neighbourhood organisations also reflect the respective settlement profile in respect to criteria of sex, age and education. However, when one looks at the employment structure of the politically active favelados, the percentage of those employed in the formal sector is disproportionately high and stands at 50%, clearly above the average of 39%.[9] During our expert interviews, another fact was revealed: the number of AM directors employed in the public sector was disproportionately high. In contrast, the self-employed had a lower level of representation.[10] Such an increased level of dependence on state institutions means that the participatory behaviour of AM and junta members may be more system stabilising and lead them to judge the political system and incumbents in a more favourable light than others questioned.

Ivory Coast and Kenya

The populations of African shanty towns are also very heterogeneous. Here, we discuss which categories of people are especially represented in the economic associations in Kenya and in social and ethnic-cultural groups in the Ivory Coast. In the Ivory Coast, persons from urban areas who have been forced to move into shanty towns from public housing are overrepresented in the membership of social and ethnic-cultural groups. There are only slight differences in the organisational level of men and women in both countries. In Kenya, men are overrepresented in unions and social organisations. Women are overrepresented in religious groups and to a certain extent in economic associations. In the Ivory Coast, men are overrepresented in the unions and slightly overrepresented in ethnic-cultural organisations. In the Ivory Coast, the percentage of those under 30 who are active in social and ethnic-cultural groups is 45% and lies above the level of the general sample, 37%. At the same time, those aged between 30 and 50 are underrepresented (44% against 52%). However, membership of those aged over 50 in ethnic-cultural and social groups is proportional to their number in the whole sample. With 38% membership against

30% for the whole sample, those aged between 30 and 50 are clearly overrepresented in the membership of self-help groups and cooperatives in Kenya. We considered the limited representation of younger members (51% members against 58% for the whole sample) as problematic. This group in particular suffers from high unemployment – 34% are neither formally nor informally integrated into economic life. In conjunction with limited integration into self-help groups or cooperatives, this group totally lacks economic security and future perspectives. A more than proportional number of members of self-help groups and cooperatives in Kenya also claimed to be active in the informal sector. This is due to the fact that many members secure their income via group projects which exist in the informal sector. In the Ivory Coast, there are no significant deviations.

To analyse the social structure of members of self-help groups and cooperatives, we divided their total expenses, which we obtained by adding together declared household expenses, into quartiles. We chose expenses because details concerning income were only available for a small section of those in employment – in the Ivory Coast for approximately half of those questioned, and in Kenya for about a quarter of the total. In the Ivory Coast, 34% of members of social and ethnic-cultural groups had monthly expenses which lay in the second-highest quartile. The remaining 64% were distributed evenly over the other quartiles. Therefore, members only had a limited income advantage. In Kenya, 35% of self-help group and cooperative members had monthly expenses in the highest quartile of over Kshs 10,000. Only 17% were represented in the lowest quartile of under Kshs 2,000. This confirms the assumption that in Kenya mostly the local elite, rather than the poorest in the settlement, are organised in self-help groups and cooperatives.

Table 5.7 Organisation and employment in Kenya (%)

Employment in Kenya	Members of economic organizations	Total
Formal sector	27	27
Informal sector	65	47
Unemployed	4	14
Not applicable	4	12

Source: Project Political Participation

Concluding Remarks

This review of the interest organisations of the urban poor must suffice to demonstrate the discrepancy between their need of organisation on the one hand, and their organisational ability on the other. Due to their dependence on political and administrative decisions (e.g. legalisation of land ownership or provision of basic infrastructure in a settlement), the urban poor are in great need of organisation. However, their cooperation in political organisations is hindered by serious impediments. In Kenya and the Ivory Coast, the current political framework makes it difficult for independent forms of collective interest organisation to develop at the settlement level. Self-help groups require approval from the state authorities, who in turn exercise tight control over such groups and, depending on their aims, suppress associations based on grassroots initiatives. The authoritarian and clientelistic system of interest mediation between the state and the urban poor in these countries has only been partly modified as a result of democratisation. At best, a pattern of 'competitive clientelism' can be observed in the new multi-party system. This leaves little room for the urban poor to form independent social and/or political groups. The normal forms of association are economic and/or ethnic-cultural groupings which function neither as collectors of the discontented of, nor as a nursery for the formation of democratic consciousness.

The central precondition for collective interest organisation in democratically organised societies is the perception of needs. However, mere recognition of the needs does not automatically lead to actions aimed at satisfying them. They must also be accepted as legitimate. For example, the often still-existing rurally orientated value system of many residents in African shanty towns works to stabilise the existing system of authoritarian and clientelistic power structures. This is because those concerned do not (yet) consider themselves members of a democratic society with civil rights; rather they view themselves as 'subjects' in a hierarchically organised state. The urban poor have not developed an interest in ending this situation of inequality because there exists a functioning system of clientelistic interest representation which offers them the opportunity to formulate their 'requests' within the existing power structure, even if they are only rarely successful.

Thus, it is not the existence of inequality as such that is the sole precondition for the formulation and organisation of interests, but rather the questioning of the basic system of social relations. The necessary efforts to increase such an awareness were made in Chile and Brazil by the Church, humanitarian NGOs and/or political parties. This was done in the hope that democratisation would extend opportunities for participation to previously excluded groups of the population and enable the urban poor to organise themselves and gain a voice in the political arena. In contrast to the African cases, the conditions in the South American countries were more conducive to the formation of independent self-help organisations because of the existence of democratically organised external actors and because of the lower level of (repressive) state control in the shanty towns. Legal insecurity and the lack of possibilities to articulate their demands in a political or legal manner led the urban poor in Brazil and Chile to strive for independent interest representation and for integration into the political system.

The existence of numerous neighbourhood organisations in the shanty towns of South America confirms that the interests of the urban poor can, in principle, be effectively organized. Their potential for organisation and conflict[11] is largely dependent on their compatibility with other interests articulated in the political arena. Thus, advocatorial interest formulation and electoral considerations can increase the potential resources of the urban poor. In addition, more grassroots participation can be enhanced, e.g. by the creation of special advisory committees at the local level, and thus have a positive effect on the urban poor's chances of asserting their interests.

Notes

1. 'The capability to organise interests is dependent on (...), whether there are certain defined groups of people who, as a result of their special social position, are interested in the political representation of specific needs' (Offe 1972: 145).

2. The local terminology will be used for these associations. Portuguese: 'associacao de moradores' (AM), and Spanish 'junta de vecinos' (junta).

3. Chile has a better network of public schools and health care services than Brazil.

4. 'Pelego' applies to the sheepskin that is placed on a horse's saddle to make a journey 'softer'. This term has been used since the 1930s to describe union functionaries who did not further the interests of their clientele, but rather those of the state by ensuring class conflict was kept 'soft' (Füchtner 1972: 108). Until the end of the 1970s, only 'pelego' unions, those linked to the political process by corporatist means, were active in Brazil. With democratisation, a new, a pluralistically organised union movement has been formed parallel to the old structures.

5. Neglect of the shanty towns by state institutions can be just as damaging as authoritarian control. For example: in Rio de Janeiro drug gangs used the lack of police presence during the uprising in 1995 to usurp this area (Fatheuer

1994: 30). For the residents this has meant the militarisation of everyday life (coopting of the AMs by drug gangs as a result of lack of state protection) (Souza 1993: 340).

6. The junta and AM members are not paid for their work. Therefore, in contrast to the Kenyan Chief, their voluntary function gives them more room to manoeuvre and they do not limit themselves to the function of a local administrative organ. In addition, the favelados and pobladores can vote the organisation leaders out of office if they do not feel adequately represented.

7. FOSIS (Fondo de Solidaridad e Inversión Social) is a public emergency programme which aims to combat extreme poverty. Programmes supported by this fund include measures to improve the infrastructure in the poblaciones.

8. In the Perlman Study different favelas, although with similar criteria, were chosen. This limits direct comparison. The data from the Perlman Study, however, offer rough indications of the attitudes of the urban poor in the 1960s in Rio de Janeiro.

9. At the same time, the category, 'not in employment' (this includes house-wives, pensioners, schoolchildren, those unable to work) is underrepresented among AM activists.

10. Thus, AM leadership is no longer, as Machado da Silva discovered in the 1960s and Eli Diniz in the 1980s (Diniz 1981: 18), a 'petty bourgeoisie' (eco-nomically independent people), demanding liberal rights from the state, but rather a group of people who are dependent on state structures for economic survival and who therefore demand welfare activities.

11. According to Offe, who coined this term, the ability of interests to assert themselves is dependent 'on the ability of an organisation to collectively with-draw its services from its respective functioning group, that is to make a plausible threat of withdrawal' (Offe 1972: 146). Our study shows that this is not completely true.

CHAPTER 6

Political Culture

Barbara Happe and
Sylvia Schmitt

§ THE following observations focus on the analysis of the political attitudes and values of the urban poor. We employ the term 'political culture´ in the sense of Almond and Verba, the pioneers of this kind of research, as the orientation pattern of a collective towards politics in general and specific political issues (Almond/Verba 1963: 14f.). The collective, upon which we base our research, does not consist of inhabitants of a particular country, but rather of the socially and economically marginalised groups of the urban poor. Our main interest is the question of whether one can speak of a specific national or even inter-continental political culture of the urban poor.

The first studies concerning the political culture of the urban poor appeared a few decades ago and were primarily based on research in Latin America. In the face of the changed political framework in many Latin American countries as a consequence of democratisation, it seems useful to examine these results once more to determine their validity and the present state of affairs. For comparative purposes, the generalisability of these results will then be tested with regard to our African cases.

In this context, the political interest of those questioned plays an important role because it can serve as an indicator for the importance of politics in their lives. Our considerations are based on the hypothesis that individuals will only be prepared to obtain political information concerning events within and outside their own neighbourhood if they have a basic interest in politics. Accordingly, a high number of individuals who are interested and active in politics indicates that democratic and not traditional or fatalistic attitudes predominate. The political issues which follow begin with an analysis of the political values and norms. The orientation towards the type of political regime provides further insight into the legitimacy of the existing democratic order and the extent of preference for authoritarian patterns. Orientations towards the regulative and participatory aspects of politics, i.e. satisfaction with the achievements of the regime and its representatives and with one's personal possibilities of influencing the political process, complete this part. Finally, on this basis we will attempt to establish the similarities and differences of the political culture of the urban poor in the four countries. In this way, the extent to which experiences with democratic interest mediation, which in the two African countries have to date only been sporadic and short in nature, have led to the creation or consolidation of democratic attitudes will be examined.

The concept of political support developed by David Easton (1965) serves as the theoretical point of reference for our empirical analysis. Easton understands the term 'political support' as the basic attitude of citizens towards the existing political order. His considerations are based on the premise that a political system cannot remain in existence without a minimum of long-term political support. Easton identifies two different forms of system support: 'specific support' and 'diffuse support'. 'Specific support' is based on the effectiveness of the political order and therefore on the satisfaction of the population with the achievements of the regime. 'Diffuse support' describes the continuing, long-term evaluation of the regime 'in its own right' as legitimate (Easton 1975: 445). Legitimacy is thus based on the belief that the existing political order and its basic values and norms correlate to one's own personal values and are therefore accepted in principle as 'right'. Furthermore, Easton distinguishes three possible objects of political support: the political society, the political regime and the authorities. Attitudes towards the nation (e.g. national pride) and towards fellow citizens characterise the political society.[1] The regime is comprised of the basic characteristics of a political order (value and norm system, power structure). 'Authorities' refers to the evaluation of the central institutional set-up and the incumbents in office.

Political systems require a certain level of legitimacy, which can be threatened by prolonged periods of political or economic crisis. This has been shown, for example, by the rapid decline in support for democracy in Brazil during the political crisis of 1992 (Moisés 1995: 127).[2] Conversely, satisfaction with the achievements of the regime can raise the long-term level of legitimacy. The relatively young democracies in Brazil, Chile, the Ivory Coast and Kenya, therefore, are interesting objects to test such relationships and whether a stabilisation or destabilisation of these regimes is to be expected. In the past years, numerous authors (e.g. Fuchs 1989, Westle 1989) have pointed out inconsistencies in Easton's concept and difficulties in assigning empirical indicators to his analytical categories. This criticism will not be repeated here, but will be mentioned where a possible mixing of elements of specific and diffuse support may occur.

The following analysis uses survey data based on this theoretical framework. The evaluation of the political system is differentiated according to the object to which the selected item is related, and also to the two motives of support (responsiveness and effectiveness). In this way, the results gained provide concrete insights into the attitudes or the urban poor towards their respective regimes and authorities, and, in this sense, into their political culture as a whole.

In a first step, questions were selected with the help of previous empirical studies (e.g. Barnes/Kaase et al. 1979, Berg-Schlosser 1979, Perlman 1976), which are generally used to measure political interest, value structures, legitimacy and effectiveness of political systems and their incumbents. In a second step, possible relationships between the individual variables were investigated. In order to check the possibility of creating more comprehensive indices, for some aspects some separate factor analyses were carried out for each country. However, these showed that different country-specific variables were assigned to the different factors, so that overarching indices could not be established. Since the definition of political culture already refers to 'the distribution of individual orientations towards political objects' which point to various attitudes present within a political community, it does not seem justified to assume *a priori* a unified political culture of the urban poor in the four countries. In order to analyse differences towards the respective political objects and issues within a country, we checked the influence of central control variables, such as age, sex, education, religion, occupation and place of residence (metropolis vs. medium-sized town). For the African countries the variable of regional, or ethnic, affiliation was added.[3]

The presentation of the quantitative results in this chapter is always combined with a qualitative evaluation, first for the respective country, and in further steps for country and finally for inter-continental comparisons of the respective differences and similarities. More general conclusions concerning the political culture of the urban poor are discussed, as far as these were obtained, in the concluding remarks.

Finally, a few remarks concerning the presentation of the survey results are necessary. During the analysis, it became clear that the variable 'place of residence' (medium-sized town vs. metropolis) exerted an influence on many aspects of response behaviour in Brazil, the Ivory Coast and Kenya. In contrast, in Chile such differences were rarely significant. In so far as differences between the two towns of a country examined turned out to be of importance these are listed in the tables. Furthermore, in some tables, the results are presented in dichotomous form; in others it seemed more useful to list all the answer categories of the survey to emphasise the tendency in the two African countries to name extreme positions.

Political Interest and Political Knowledge

Active participation in politics requires a certain specific interest, or at least the willingness to engage in discussions about local or national problems. Without such interest, citizens do not develop any relationship to their civil and political rights and the democratic system as a whole. The relative young democracies in the countries we studied - with the exception of Chile - after decades of authoritarian regimes present citizens, who until now have only been active participants in the political arena in isolated cases, with new challenges. It was only after the start of the democratisation process that social actors demanding the political mobilisation of the impoverished population made themselves increasingly heard (e.g. inChurches, political parties, NGOs). This was the catalyst which caused citizens to begin developing ideas concerning their rights and interest in important political events. Our data provide information about the level of political interest and can, therefore, serve as an indication of the ways and means by which the urban poor are linked to politics.

In each country, the proportion of those questioned who said they were not interested in politics was over 50%. Two thirds, however, took part in discussions concerning local problems and about half of them talked about national problems. It must be noted that in all four countries, men and those with a higher level of education have a stronger interest in politics than women and those with a low educational level. But women and those with a low level of education discussed local problems as often as the others. In Chile and Brazil, the residents of Santiago and Rio de Janeiro demonstrate more interest in political events at the national level than their colleagues in the smaller towns. In contrast, in the African towns, the size of city did not have any influence on political interest. Between 13% (Brazil) and 20% (Ivory Coast) of those questioned did not take part in any form of political discussion and they emphasised their lack of interest in politics in general. From their perspective, they saw no link between daily life and 'politics'. The significant correlation between political interest and discussion of national problems shows that the urban poor associate political interest more with the national than the local level. The widespread lack of interest in politics is due not least to the fact that the urban poor have difficulty recognising the connection between their own lives and the national political decision making arena. This is because their daily life is hardly taken into consideration in political debate and practice.

This does not necessarily mean that the urban poor do not follow political news or only have scanty knowledge of important political events or holders of office. In Kenya and the Ivory Coast in particular, they are – even though in the Ivory Coast they often do not even possess a radio – informed about the most important political events at the national level. At least two thirds of those questioned know the name of the current president, of the dominant political party, and of

Table 6.1 Political interest and political information (%)

	Brazil	Chile	Ivory Coast	Kenya
Generally speaking, would you say you are very interested/somewhat interested/ not really interested in politics?				
Very interested	8	7	19	13
Somewhat interested	41	30	19	30
Not interested	51	63	62	57
Do you talk to othersabout issues that affect the community as a whole?				
Yes	60	62	54	62
Do you ever talk withother people about problems which your countryhas to face today?				
Yes	63	51	46	47
Do you regularly follow political news?				
Yes	32	57	46	31
Who keeps you informed about things happening outside this location?				
Radio	68	77	54	77
TV	77	90	43	22
Newspapers etc.	28	42	27	30
Friends/colleagues	33	3	38	20

Source: Project Political Participation

another African head of state. However, the number reading a daily newspaper is quite limited, because newspaper distribution in the smaller towns still is very restricted; radio reception often is limited to one public channel. Knowledge of state presidents and the governing party is highest in Kenya. In both African cases, this situation is due to the dominant role of the long-term reigning presidents and their (state) parties. The somewhat lower percentage for the Ivory Coast is related to the change of power after the death of the founding president in December 1993. In contrast, almost complete coverage with mass communications systems in Brazil is not enough to provide the favelados with basic information via TV and radio about national and international politics. Similarly in Chile, the widespread viewing of political news (57%) is not reflected in the knowledge of the current political leaders in the country and the world.

In all four countries, men and those with a higher level of education generally demonstrate a better level of political knowledge. The right answers to questions concerning matters outside the country, such as the name of the US president and that of another African, or Latin American head of state, were given in Brazil and Chile most often by those residing in the metropolis. The Brazilian 'nordestinos' compensate for this information deficit with a better knowledge of local affairs; those in the smaller African towns of Man and Kisumu are also more likely to know the name of their mayor than their compatriots in the metropolis. These results demonstrate that for the majority of the urban poor, especially for women and those with a low level of formal education, politics at national level resembles a power struggle between 'gladiators' (Milbrath 1977) in an arena which they do not wish to mould actively. They remain mostly 'observers', even if their applause

Table 6.2 Political knowledge (%)

	Brazil	Chile	Ivory Coast	Kenya
Name of the acting president	69	96	87	94
Name of the ruling party	18	49	75	92
Name of the mayor	62	54	66	47
Name of an African/ Latin American president	11	43	72	76
Name of the president of the USA	20	33	37	42

Source: Project Political Participation

is sought after. In part they remain at a conscious distance from politics because they do not feel politicians and political parties take their problems seriously.

Value Structures

The following analysis of value structures shows the basic foundations of political culture in the four countries. Central democratic values, such as freedom, equality and justice, form the basis for any truly democratic regime. In the past, however, often more authoritarian attitudes which were linked to the traditional rural value systems could be found. In this context, Mangin (1970) formulated the concept of the 'peasant in the city', whose structure of values is characterised by distrust of new technologies and scientific innovations, a tendency towards fatalism, strong religious beliefs and a lack of orientation towards the future. The validity of these propositions are now tested with the help of our data.

Our surveys show that the urban poor in Chile and Brazil have distanced themselves almost totally from rural value structures. Contacts to rural (native) regions are, in contrast to the African countries (especially in comparison with Kenya), much more sporadic, in so far as relatives still live in the countryside (see chap. 2). Accordingly, the favelados and pobladores are slowly forgetting the behavioural patterns which are common there (see Perlman 1976). The debate concerning the continuation of rural value systems amongst those inhabitants who have migrated to the towns in the two African countries continues. Since the 'relationship between socio-economic environment and value priorities (...) [is] not one of immediate adaptation' (Inglehart 1992: 126), personal experience with and in the rural milieu moulds the system of values of the individual in Africa more than in the two South American states, in which the urbanisation process began decades earlier. 'Substantial time delay plays a role, because a person's basic values continue to reflect the conditions which predominated during their youth' (ibid.: 126). Breaks in this traditional thought pattern can be observed amongst the younger generation and those with a higher level of education in the Ivory Coast and Kenya.

In the following section, values such as obedience to authority, a deterministic view of the world or lack of future orientation, which belong to those value structures viewed as typically rural, will be examined. In all four countries, there is a high level of acceptance of strong leadership. Thus, 86% of the Brazilian favelados prefer a strong leader to the democratic decision making process with its long debates and numerous laws. In none of the other three countries was this value as high, and in national surveys approximately 50% of Brazilians agree with similar statements.[4]

In Brazil, the parliamentary system does not represent an attractive alternative, for either the favelados or any other group in the population, to the presidential system. In a referendum concerning the system of government in 1993, 56% of the voters chose the presidential system, and only 25% voted in favour of a parliamentary system. The remaining 19% of votes were either invalid or abstentions (Thibaut 1996: 231 ff.). As will be shown later, parliamentarians have a bad image in public opinion. Strong leaders are thought to solve problems more effectively and quickly than the protracted parliamentary process.[5] In national surveys in Brazil in 1993, 50% agreed with the statement that the country would be better off if there was only one political party (Moisés 1995: 120). Thus, in the Brazilian context, the call for strong leaders is not only a reflection of obedience to authority amongst the favelados.

In Kenya, the introduction of the multi-party system did not entail increased democratic transparency and effectiveness in the political process. The violent political protests on the streets of Nairobi in 1998 clearly demonstrated again that the newly established multi-party system is neither willing nor in a position to aggregate adequately the interests of the different groups of the population. The evaluation of strong leadership personalities in the Kenyan case is heavily dependent on the ethnic affiliation of those questioned. Thus, the members of the ethnic group in Kisumu mostly belonging to an opposition party were considerably less in favour of strong leaders than in Nairobi. As long as the parliamentary alternative to an authoritarian style of leadership is widely characterised by inability and corruption, the preference for

Table 6.3 Authority (%) '*A few strong leaders can make a country better than all the laws and talk.*'

	Brazil		Chile		Ivory Coast		Kenya	
	M	T	M	T	M	T	M	T
Strongly agree	20	45	12	14	42	28	74	46
Agree somewhat	67	40	46	57	30	30	12	26
Disagree somewhat	10	9	38	25	14	19	4	6
Disagree strongly	3	6	4	4	14	22	11	22

M=Metropolis; T=Town
Source: Project Political Participation

authoritarian leaders continues to prevail. Under such conditions specific support for the new 'democratic' regime does not grow.

At the time of the survey, the Ivory Coast was still influenced by the charismatic leadership figure of the first President, F. Houphouét-Boigny, who died in December 1993. The opposition movement, which since the beginning of the 1990s had presented a credible alternative, again lost much of its support in the middle of the 1990s and with it the idea of a more democratic form of state as an alternative to continued leadership by the (former) state party. The principle of 'palabre'[6] is an explicit tool of leadership of the state president in the Ivorian context and is compatible with a strong leader as the head of state. The present president renewed this tradition with the 'Days of Dialogue', during which he listens to criticism and complaints about the country's problems. 'In tours around the country, he [the president] would meet local elites, listen to their grievances, and promise redress. The systematic recourse to clientelism was the hallmark of these ritualized face-to-face contacts between the ruler and his subjects' (Bratton/Walle 1997: 64).

It should be noted, that the high level of support for a strong leader is partly based on the long tradition of a powerful president as the head of state. Even today, representatives in the national parliaments view their function and task - as in Brazil and Kenya - less in the acceptance of government responsibility than in ensuring their own benefits. In Kenya and the Ivory Coast, responses vary between the metropolis and the medium-sized town. In Abidjan, this is a result of the high level of support for the late president and the comparatively better living conditions and opportunities in the city.

In contrast to the other three countries, Chile already had experienced a more or less functioning competition between political parties in the 20th century. This gave the enfranchised population the opportunity to influence the choice of political leadership and the policies they implemented. But despite this much longer democratic tradition, almost two thirds of the pobladores prefer a strong leader as the head of state. This also is a surprise because of the highly 'traumatic' experiences with a repressive military regime under the leadership of General Pinochet. But it can be seen as a result of the general disillusionment with politics, which has taken place since 1992, and the lack of a grassroots base of the major political parties. Since democratisation, the parties - from the pobladores' point of view - have not been effective in their role as mediator between state and society. Discontent with the ways and means democracy currently functions in Chile correlates in this case ($r=0.3$) with support for a strong leader.

To summarise: strong leadership personalities in Brazil, the Ivory Coast and Kenya continue to be respected and their rule is perceived as legitimate partly because of existing traditions. In Brazil, the high level of support is also partly due to the long tradition of populist and charismatic leaders. Opposition to authorities legitimated by tradition and charisma is growing slowly everywhere, but because of the existing weaknesses (tendencies towards corruption in Kenya and Brazil, and a stronger orientation towards consensus in the Ivory Coast), it has only brought the beginnings of change to the thoughts of the urban poor so far. In Chile, the pobladores' majority support for a strong leader is an expression of their discontent with the current party system, which will become clearer later on.

In the studies of the 1960s and 1970s, the residential areas of the urban poor were viewed as 'enclaves of rural parochialism in the city' (see Perlman 1976: 130). The main characteristics of such 'parochialism' were viewed as religious fervour and fatalistic value structures, which are often closely associated with one another. In their answer to the question whether one's own life is largely pre-determined, the respondents in our survey gave widely ranging responses. While approximately two thirds of those questioned in the Ivory Coast and Kenya believed in predetermination, the majority of the Latinos believe that they can shape their own destiny. Such value structures, which are ascribed to the rural milieu, have almost totally disappeared among the Chilean pobladores. Only 19% still believe personal destiny is predetermined. Such value patterns increase significantly in older age groups and amongst those with a low level of education in Chile and Brazil.

Fatalistic attitudes are closely associated with church affiliation. Thus, membership in the Pentecostal Church increases the rejection of such

Table 6.4 Determinism (%) '*When a person is born, the success, he/she is going to have is already decided.*'

	Brazil		Chile		Ivory Coast		Kenya	
	M	T	M	T	M	T	M	T
Strongly agree	9	23	4	4	58	59	64	49
Agree somewhat	40	21	15	15	14	8	7	15
Disagree somewhat	43	33	67	63	13	11	4	9
Disagree strongly	9	24	14	19	16	22	25	28

M= Metropolis; T=Town
Source: Project Political Participation

fatalistic attitudes in Brazil. In the almost daily meetings, pastors encourage individual activities amongst their members in order to overcome poverty. According to their belief, poverty is not God-given, but the 'work of the Devil'. In contrast, the number of those in the Catholic Church who believe in Divine Providence is considerably higher.[7] In Chile, opposite tendencies can be observed. Despite the individualistic, achievement-orientated beliefs, membership in the same evangelical groups increases the belief in predestination of life. It is noticeable that pobladores with a higher level of education, in contrast to the more educated favelados, are represented much less than average in evangelical groupings. Thus, the factor level of education in Chile – in contrast to Brazil – has more importance than the influence of religious affiliation. Spiritualism has a long tradition in Brazil. It came to the country along with African slaves, and to this day is practised also amongst those groups with higher income and status. The low values for Chile can be explained, in addition to the, on average, higher level of education, by the strong secularisation of society, in which the spiritual world plays a much more limited role.

In the Ivory Coast, the answers concerning predestination reflect the traditional value system of the lower social classes, the majority of whom migrated from a rural environment. They agreed with the statement much more strongly than their Latin American colleagues. An acceptance of one's destiny is dominant particularly amongst Muslim migrants from the north, and immigrants from Burkina Faso. In contrast to the Islamic faith, traditional African religions have a less fatalistic attitude. Thus, those questioned in Man and Kisumu are more likely to reject this concept of predestination. Age and education also influence this attitude. In both African countries, a higher level of education nurtures rejection of fatalistic attitudes, and in the Ivory Coast, it is most often the younger generation who speaks out against predestination. The modernisation of society over the last thirty years and school exchanges with France play a large role amongst the middle and younger age groups in this regard.

However, a basic attitude of fatalism does not always mean a complete acceptance of one's destiny. Rather than passively giving themselves up, the majority make plans for the future. This is exemplified, for example, by the importance placed on school education and vocational training for their children. In this respect, the plans of the urban poor in Latin America and Africa hardly differ from one another. Completion of school education or vocational training is at the top of the list of priorities parents have for their children. Gender-specific differentiation is hardly present because the same goals are given for both sons and daughters.

Between 26% and 35% of those interviewed in Brazil, the Ivory Coast and Kenya have no or only very vague plans for their children. This lack of more concrete expectations can be traced to more general pessimistic attitudes, which often result from a realistic evaluation of their own (modest) chances in life. 15% to 25% foster unrealistically high expectations and hopes for their children. Thus, for example they want their children to have careers as actors, journalists, politicians, diplomats, doctors, lawyers or soccer stars. In Kenya and Brazil, some well-known sports personalities have attained world-wide fame in spite of their simple origins, and have fed hopes of realisation of such ideas.

In Chile, parents' plans were more realistic, which can be primarily traced to the higher level of education amongst the pobladores. The percentage of illiteracy in Brazil (14%) and in the Ivory Coast (nearly 40%) in our study is considerably higher than the value for Chile (5%). That there utopian dreaming is a thing of the past is partly due to the restructuring of society, which accompanied the military dictatorship. This consisted of the organisation of relationships in all areas of society according to market principles. Those in power dreamed of creating a 'new individualistic man', who 'could maximise his benefits and move in a social sphere which is determined by the rules of the free market and competition' (Valdés 1994: 37). It is difficult to combine such an achievement-orientated society with utopian fantasies, and it is also at odds with basic fatalistic attitudes.

This presentation and analysis of the thought patterns which are ascribed to the urban poor (obedience to authority, fatalism, lack of orientation to the future) demonstrates that they do not form a homogeneous mass held hostage by a rural system of values either within a settlement, town, or country, nor indeed intercontinentally. Obedience to authority or lack of orientation to the future can only partly be

Table 6.5 Children's future (%) 'What are the plans for your children in future?''

	Brazil	Chile	Ivory Coast	Kenya
Better life	19	37	14	13
Education	41	38	35	30
Realistic plans on employment	14	15	19	11
Unrealistic plans on empoyment	15	–	16	25
Wedding and family	1	1	4	–
No plans	12	10	12	22

Source: Project Political Participation

explained by the continuing dominance of rural value structures. For the remaining part, they result from disappointing experiences with life in town and therefore do not represent a relict from bygone times in the countryside.

The acceptance of democratic norms, e.g. equality and freedom, is one of the central and crucial conditions for a democratic order. In this regard, we inquired how deeply basic democratic values are anchored in the consciousness of the urban poor and to what extent they represent a value worth fighting for. The continuing respect for traditionally legitimated authorities, which is particularly prevalent in the two African countries, indicates that unequal treatment is more widely tolerated there than in Chile or Brazil. But Table 6.6 below shows that Africans attach great importance to basic democratic rights, such as freedom of thought, and that their level of acceptance is only slightly below that of the Latinos. Thus, there is almost consensus amongst the urban poor of all four countries concerning the inviolability of these rights. In Brazil, a higher level of education and living in the metropolis have a positive influence on this attitude; in Chile it is a higher level of education and youth. The older pobladores give the political regime a similarly high level of legitimacy (see below), without supporting more strongly, however, the normative principles of democracy. The principle of freedom of thought is an exception. In particular, those who are over 50, and suffered the limiting of this basic freedom under the military regime, today give it the status of a politically untouchable element of society.

Support for basic democratic rights is relatively high throughout all

Table 6.6 Political rights (%)

	'I believe in free speech for all no matter what their views may be.'		'Everybody should have an equal chance and an equal say in political matters.'		'When the country is in great danger we may have to force some people even if it violates their rights.'	
	M	T	M	T	M	T
Brazil	93	87	91	88	41	53
Chile	95	87	–	–	23	36
Ivory Coast	86	86	64	70	44	39
Kenya	86	80	77	77	44	47

M= Metropolis; T=Town
Source: Project Political Participation

sections of the urban poor in the Ivory Coast, and is not influenced by factors such as place of residence, sex, age etc. However, in both African countries, freedom of speech is more often demanded by men than women, a fact that reflects the traditional understanding of gender roles. In addition, this basic right is more firmly anchored in the consciousness of the urban poor in Nairobi than in Kisumu. Furthermore, in Kenya, it is mainly men and those with longer school education who support the egalitarian principle in the political process.

The limitation of basic rights in emergency and crisis situations is viewed very differently by the urban poor. Only 5% of those Chileans asked thought the limitation of basic rights in emergency situations was unconditionally justified a further 25% agree with this statement. In the other three countries, almost half of those questioned agreed with limitations to basic rights in case of an emergency. In both South American countries, there is a clear divide between respondents in the metropolis and the smaller town. The experience of a repressive military regime leads Chileans and particularly residents in the big cities to react more sceptically towards limitations of basic rights. In the Ivory Coast and Kenya, support for a state of emergency (42% and 45% respectively) can be partly explained by the specifics of the political history of the African continent. The uncertain political situation in both countries, or civil war in neighbouring states, have been used by both the Kenyan and Ivorian presidents to proclaim the importance of unity and stability for their countries. In both countries, in answer to

Table 6.7 Women's rights (%)

	Brazil	Chile	Côte d'Ivoire	Kenya
'It is only natural that men should have more rights than women'	32	23	69	57
'Some people say that women should not be active in politics. Others say, they should have the same political rightsand duties as men.What do you think?'				
Same as men	88	81	67	60
Less than men	6	9	16	21
No political rights for women	7	10	18	19

Source: Project Political Participation

the question what they are particularly proud of, large groups of the population mention peace and political stability.

With respect to (political) equality of the sexes, there is a marked difference between the urban poor in Latin America and those in Africa. While the Latinos increasingly distance themselves from the traditional view of women, in Africa it is often taken for granted that men and women have different freedoms and rights. In our survey, over two thirds of the Latinos questioned acknowledge that women should have the same freedoms and rights of political participation as men.

The percentage of those who could imagine a woman as mayor of their town (90% and 91%), or as president of the country (81% and 76%) is even higher. In both countries the criteria high level of education, place of residence in the metropolis, female and young, all work in favour of stronger support for equal rights for women. In relation to rights of political participation, gender-specific differences disappear in both countries.

The question concerning less freedom for women is answered positively by a majority in Kenya, and by almost two thirds in the Ivory Coast. These answers, which reflect traditional value patterns, do not correspond, however, to the question concerning political rights of women. In Kenya, 60% of those questioned, and 67% in the Ivory Coast, voted for equal treatment of the sexes in this respect. In the Ivory Coast, 83% can imagine a woman as mayor and 62% as president of the country. In Kenya, it is noticeable that in Kisumu a more equal role for women is more easily accepted than in the capital, Nairobi. Considerably more of those interviewed (81% in Kisumu, 71% in Nairobi) can envisage a woman as mayor or even as state president (73% and 53%). A possible explanation lies in the fact that in Kisumu, citizens have already had an experience of a female mayor who is highly respected.

This analysis makes clear that some parts of the urban poor still adhere to traditional or authoritarian value systems, but also support democratic values. In the Ivory Coast and Kenya, the urban poor support democratic values in particular when these do not stand in explicit contradiction to their traditionally moulded every-day way of thinking, or when they complement traditional values. In this regard they reflect the blocked transition process of the democracies there. In contrast, the attitudes of the Chilean pobladores more often reflect the longer democratic tradition of the country. Brazil stands between these two poles. In the north east, where clientelistic structures are stronger, rural thought patterns are more prevalent. In the metropolis a change towards democratic values can be observed.

The continued existence of a regime is, however, dependent not solely on the citizens' support of its normative principles, but also on whether they view the procedural structures and the holders of office as legitimate and effective. This will be analysed in the following section.

The Legitimacy of the Political System

According to Easton, a political system is legitimate in the eyes of its citizens when it complies to their moral norms and attitudes and, therefore, seems worth supporting. Our presentation has shown that the urban poor have a relatively positive attitude towards basic democratic norms, such as equality and freedom, without – as in the two African countries – abandoning entirely more traditional values. In these cases, certain traditions may be compatible with a modern democratic understanding.

The question remains, whether the current institutional structure, the rules of the political process and the present incumbents facilitate the perception that such values are realised. In the same way as in the value structure, authoritarian and democratic elements can be found alongside one another in the institutional structure and actions of the governments, although their weighting varies according to country and continent. While in Brazil and Chile the transition to a democratic system has been accomplished, in the Ivory Coast and Kenya one can only speak of formal democratisation so far. Thus, in questions concerning the legitimacy of political systems, one must take into account that the respondents evaluate the political realities. Therefore, the political system is evaluated not automatically according to its democratic content, but in the majority of cases according to the extent it complies with their own, sometimes traditionally moulded value code.

Table 6.8 Trust in government (%) '*I usually have confidence that the government will do what is right.*'

	Brazil		Chile		Ivory Coast		Kenya	
	M	T	M	T	M	T	M	T
Strongly agree	8	4	3	8	31	22	40	26
Agree somewhat	38	17	41	47	23	19	22	25
Disagree somewhat	46	48	47	40	26	37	10	26
Disagree strongly	9	31	10	5	21	22	29	24

M=Metropolis; T=Town
Source: Project Political Participation

General trust (diffuse support) in the government is taken as an indicator for the legitimacy of the political system. The marginalisation of the urban poor in the political process does not express itself in deep distrust of the political leadership. Almost half of those questioned claim to trust their respective government in principle. Over one quarter of the Africans questioned agreed totally with this statement, in contrast to only 5–6% of the Latinos. Moderate expectations towards the political system (Ivory Coast, Kenya, Brazil), or, in contrast to previous regimes, a political leadership with integrity (Chile), can serve as possible explanations for this expression of trust.

In the Ivory Coast, trust in the correctness of government action is considerably higher in Abidjan (54%) than in Man (42%). The smaller political arena in Man allows better recognition of the merits and deficits of the municipal authority. Here it is easier to judge the achievements of the political elite and exert influence than in the city of Abidjan. Furthermore, the majority of those questioned in Man come from the region and, in contrast to the newly arrived immigrant workers in Abidjan, they find it easier to evaluate political events. In Kenya, the responses are similar to the Ivory Coast. Trust in government in the smaller town of Kisumu is considerably lower than in Nairobi. The reason for this is based more on the politically motivated discrimination against Kisumu on the part of the central government. The town is ruled by political forces in opposition to the Moi regime.

In Brazil, the 'nordestinos' are particularly distrustful of their government. Only approximately every fifth person expresses some trust, and an above-average number of those questioned chose the option 'do not agree at all'. The nordestinos are disappointed with the almost complete lack of consideration of their needs on the part of the local political elites. Their scepticism is rooted, as will be shown below, in their negative experiences with government representatives. Over the last few years, numerous corruption scandals, bad management and nepotism have caused alarm. These motives are thus similar to the ones in the African cases, but the nordestinos 'punish' deficits in government action by withholding trust more often than the Africans. In the Ivory Coast and Kenya, the urban poor still tend to view their respective presidents as an (all-powerful) god-father, who they hope will fulfil their needs, without perceiving this as one of their rights. In Brazil, the 'cariocas' of Rio de Janeiro have more sympathy for the current government than their colleagues in the north east. Although during the time of the survey, conditions in the favelas of Rio de Janeiro bordered on civil war, the higher level of trust in government points to the deeper rooting of democratic rules in the political process in the metropolis, which providesthe urban poor with better opportunities to articulate their interests.

In Chile, previously at the head of the democratic class on the South American continent, the urban poor do not generally place undivided trust in their government. The general feeling of being abandoned by the state, which has taken root since redemocratisation, is partly responsible for the pobladores' lack of trust in the political leadership. This is less pronounced in the medium-sized town of Temuco where 55% have basic trust in the government. The pobladores here have more chance of persuading (amongst other things by way of informal contacts) local politicians to take their interests into account than in Santiago. In the city of Santiago, with its five million inabitants, this access is organised in a more technocratic and anonymous manner.

In addition to the place of residence, the responses to this question were also influenced by the age of those questioned. Younger persons in Africa (under 30) most often distrusted the government the older ones (age 50 and above) placed trust in the government much more often. The more critical attitude of youth towards the state is conspicuous in both African countries. The level of education of the younger generation may play a role here, but also the economic and socio-political failure of the state during the economic crises in the 1980s. The state cannot be a guarantor of the personal future perspectives of this group, and programmes aimed at structural adjustment mean old clientele relationships are no longer universally maintainable. Those over 50 also most often place general trust in the government in Brazil and Chile. This positive relationship of the older generation, which also is apparent in other responses, is rooted in Chile in the memory of the military regime, and in Brazil and the African cases in the higher general

Table 6.9 Demands for political reform

	Brazil		Chile		Ivory Coast		Kenya	
	M	T	M	T	M	T	M	T
Strongly agree	6	3	3	5	39	34	41	27
Agree somewhat	41	23	39	33	29	23	12	21
Disagree somewhat	39	37	52	53	13	19	9	24
Disagree strongly	14	37	6	10	19	25	37	28

M=Metropolis; T=Town
Source: Project Political Participation

acceptance of existing political structures and relationships – which are viewed as 'natural'.

However, the urban poor do not only express some basic criticism of government actions; their reservations are also related to the existing political and social structures and the uneven distribution of national wealth in their countries. The statement, 'all groups can live in harmony in this country without changing the political system in any way' is met with a similar level of acceptance in the two African countries. Not only do more Africans than Latinos (51% in Kenya, 56% in the Ivory Coast) agree with this statement, they do so with much more emphasis.

In answering this question, the respondents in Africa also evaluate the co-existence of the various ethnic groups. In Kenya, as in the Ivory Coast and the immigrant communities from other African states, ethnic affiliation is unquestioned and taken for granted. After decades of ethnic proportionality under the regency of F. Houphouët-Boigny in the Ivory Coast, since the electoral campaign in the second multi-party elections, political events and increasingly social and economic daily life are being 'tribalised'. The effects of this can be seen, amongst other things, in increased police controls of the residence permits[8] of immigrant workers. Similar developments can be observed in Kenya. Ethnic criteria often decide party loyalties, and politicians present themselves in public primarily as the representative of an ethnic group. However, ethnicity in Kenya is more than a question of political consciousness. The distribution structures of regional as well as local patron-client relationships run along the lines of ethnic affiliation. National policy also always addresses the urban poor as ethnic subjects.

In Man, more residents see a need for political reform than in the metropolis. In Abidjan, the proportion of people who refuse to answer political questions is considerably higher. This is because the majority of inhabitants in the poor settlements we studied were immigrants from neighbouring African states, who require a residence permit. Their right of residence is therefore dependent on the goodwill of the state, which in turn 'increases' their willingness to only speak positively, or not at all, about the government and political situation in the country.[9] In Kenya too, responses vary according to place of residence. In the capital city, 41% see no need for action, in Kisumu this figure is only 27%.

As with regard to the previous question, this evaluation of the social status quo demonstrates that members of the younger generation in the Ivory Coast reject it more strongly and are more outspoken concerning the necessity for political change. The older generation above fifty support the existing political conditions. The negative answers reflect the experiences of the final years of the regency of F. Houphouët-Boigny, in which the country economically and politically ground to a halt. This experience of stagnation influences the evaluation of the political and social structures, which expresses itself in clearer support for political change. In Kenya, neither the age of those questioned, nor their sex or education influence the expressed opinions. Here, the major difference lies between the residents of the capital city and those of Kisumu. The inhabitants of Kisumu see more need for political change than those in Nairobi, which can be explained by their belonging to the opposition camp.

Only 36% of Brazilians and 40% of the Chileans see no need for action with respect to the co-existence of different ethnic, social, economic or political groupings. In this way, the Latinos express more open criticism of the status quo than the Africans. In Chile, the discontent of many pobladores is directed towards the situation of social inequality. In Brazil forms of racial discrimination are more prominent, although in official Brazilian statements the myth of 'racial democracy' is propagated. According to this, Brazilians are a peaceful, happy nation because of their colourful ethnic mix and therefore incapable of discrimination towards other members of society on the basis of race (see Chauí 1995: 188). In reality, forms of social and economic discrimination are part of the everyday experience for the Afro-Brazilian population - especially in the labour market. These perceptions are based on forms of social and economic – and also in Brazil partly racist – discrimination, which are mostly perceived by the Latinos as 'illegitimate'. Measures to reduce social inequality work to increase contentment with the status quo, as the comparison between the two Brazilian towns demonstrates. In contrast, discrimination based on ethnic affiliation is more often accepted in Africa. The ethnically polarised party systems in the Ivory Coast and Kenya mean that ethnic affiliation also decides voting behaviour. The distribution of material benefits according to such criteria can strengthen ethnic cleavages, if those in positions of political responsibility do not ensure a certain proportionality.

Acceptance of the current political and social situation and the structural determination of one's personal impoverished situation is also reflected in the answers to a question about equality of opportunity between rich and poor. In spite of very different socio-economic conditions and chances of social mobility, more than half of those questioned in all four countries – in Kisumu the percentage is somewhat lower at 40%, in the Brazilian towns the values are highest at 70% – do not believe that chances of success in life are equally distributed. In response to this question in Nairobi and Man, almost 50% disagree most strongly with this statement. In view of the general acceptance of unequal situations in life, this percentage is remarkable. Scepticism concerning the opportunities for one's own children to attain success in life reflects a realistic evaluation of the government's lack of endeavours in this area. For example, for many years the school system in the Ivory Coast has been inadequate. In the settlements in Abidjan, only a few parents can afford their children's school attendance (uniforms and tuition fees). In contrast, in Man, the possibilities of access to the school system for (farmers') children are more favourable. In the poor settlements in Kenya, schooling is normally continued until the end of Standard 8, but the classes are too numerous and the level of teaching is often inadequate. Increasingly, Churches or NGOs finance the schools. Afterwards, parents can hardly afford to send their children to secondary schools. This is especially true in Kisumu. Nevertheless, approximately half of those questioned in Africa believe their children have the same opportunities as those from rich families. The veiled attitude often behind such evaluations is that one's personal social situation is determined by oneself rather than structural factors. Muslim beliefs also work to influence this attitude. In both African societies, class barriers are more penetrable and have less influence on one's situation in life than in South America. The solidarity of family networks means that vertical connections are possible and chances of social improvement more realistic.

The responses of the Latinos bear witness to a realistic evaluation of their chances in life. It is noticeable that consciousness of the structural determination of their own situation is more prevalent amongst the

Table 6.10 Equal chances (%) *'I believe that my children have the same chance to succeed as children of a rich family.'*

	Brazil		Chile		Ivory Coast		Kenya	
	M	T	M	T	M	T	M	T
Strongly agree	6	10	10	12	25	35	36	32
Agree somewhat	29	16	34	29	18	13	12	29
Disagree somewhat	42	34	42	44	20	5	5	15
Disagree strongly	24	41	15	15	37	47	47	25

M=Metropolis; T=Town
Source: Project Political Participation

younger generation and those with a higher level of education. 42% of the pobladores and 30% of the favelados believe in the equality of opportunity of rich and poor families. In contrast to the Perlman study, a negative development can be observed. Three decades ago, half of the favelados questioned still believed in equal opportunity (Perlman 1976: 178). Due to the well-developed school system and the prosperous economy in Chile, the conditions for social improvement are in fact more favourable than in the crisis-stricken, infrastructurally poor Brazil. In contrast to 19% of the favelados, only 3% of the pobladores questioned saw themselves forced as a result of financial difficulties to move from middle-class to poor neighbourhoods. In Aracaju, which is still more strongly permeated by archaic social structures, ensuring equal opportunity is even lower on the list of priorities of politicians than in the metropolis. The holders of political office are more often obliged to work towards equal opportunity, which is reflected in larger investment in the provision of infrastructure in the favelas in the form of (pre-) schooling.

Thus, between 30% and 60% of those questioned place trust in their government and accept the existing social and political situation. In none of the four countries, therefore, are those in positions of political responsibility in any way threatened by criticism and distrust from the urban poor because more traditional values or moderate expectations towards the state do not create a desire for radical change. Younger people and those with a higher level of education, however, express reservations towards the current political and social structures and the political leadership in all four countries. Such negative judgements do not by themselves represent a desire for change of the present political system. In the majority of cases, criticism is directed towards specific aspects of the current political situation or its way of functioning. Expressed criticism can also be specifically directed towards incumbents themselves, e.g. if those in government were involved during the time of the survey in corruption scandals, or if they belong to the 'wrong' ethnic group, and thereby reduce the level of trust in government. Change of government, or the filling of leadership positions on a more equitable ethnic basis can in such cases have a positive influence on the legitimacy of a regime and its authorities.

Responsiveness and Effectiveness of Government

The citizens of a country view their political regime as responsive if it can successfully fulfil their desires and demands in the decision-making process and their participation within it. In contrast to the general legitimacy of the democratic system (examined here as 'diffuse support' of government), the term 'effectiveness' refers mainly to contentment with the concrete 'outputs' of the system and its authorities, and not to the general level of support for the regime as such (Easton 1975: 445). Especially in the precarious phase of a protracted period of transition, in which the previous regime did not completely collapse, contentment with the daily achievements of the regime and its authorities can in the medium and long term raise the general level of legitimacy of the new system. Statements such as, 'the people who rule the country are not interested in what people like me think', or, 'the elected representatives quickly lose contact with the voters after the election' can serve as indicators in determining the effectiveness of a system and evaluating its leadership (Barnes/Kaase 1979). In this respect, the urban poor are clearly more discontented than in the previous section. The attitudes of the urban poor towards government and parliamentarians in all four countries are characterised by clear distrust. Thus, the majority opinion is – in Abidjan the value is the lowest at 53% – that those in government are not interested in the concerns of the 'man on the street'. Abuse of power on the part of the political leadership is diagnosed by 80% (exception: Ivory Coast with only 66%). There is almost complete consensus with regard to the unreliability of parliamentarians and politicians. A maximum of 20% (Ivory Coast) say their representatives do not lose contact with the population after elections.

The results concerning the evaluation of one's personal possibilities to influence the political process are more differentiated. While in Brazil and Kenya, at least two thirds assume a lack of possibilities for exerting

Table 6.11 Legitimacy (%)

	'Public officials care about what people like me think.'		'Generally speaking, those we elect in parliament lose touch with people pretty quickly.'		'People like me have no say in whatthe government does.'		
	M	T	M	T	M	T	Total
Brazil	37	21	86	88	67	79	
Chile	5	24	95	93	–	–	
Ivory Coast	48	33	89	89	50	50	
Kenya	35	34	82	76			67

M=Metropolis; T=Town
Source: Project Political Participation

political influence, almost half of the Ivorians see certain chances for influencing the political process. These are primarily based on possible clientelistic and ethnic relations with the political leadership.

In general, the majority of the urban poor in Abidjan and Man feel neglected by the political leadership. However, because they do not view themselves as citizens with specific rights, they see no reason why their opinion should find consideration in the political process. For example, the sober opinion about the truthfulness of electoral campaign assurances, which after an election are 'not adhered to anyway', is widespread. The representatives in the national parliament hardly play any role in the neighbourhoods in Abidjan, unless they simultaneously hold the office of mayor. In Abidjan, only 35 of the 200 persons questioned could name their respective representatives (68% non-response). The importance of the national parliament has only increased since the entrance of the opposition following the first multi-party elections and the death of Houphouët-Boigny. To this day, political and administrative positions are perceived less as a responsibility for the general good, than as private access to public sinecures (Jakobeit 1993: 208). Those questioned in Abidjan and Man judge their representative according to this criterion. In Man, this led to a situation in which the representative of a region who was absent too often was not reelected as mayor. Conversely, the achievements and presence of the lady mayor and the representatives of the Abidjan settlement Vridi III were praised in the positive answers. The responses to the question about influence on government once more mix aspects of reality and the legitimatory evaluation of the political situation.

In Kenya too, the urban poor complain about the gulf between politicians and their problems. The inhabitants of Kisumu register distinct social and economic discrimination by the government. Differences can also be observed between the older, partly Islamic, marginal settlements and the newer ones. In the former, the distance to political authorities is viewed as less, because internal organisational networks make up for the lack of presence of politicians. This intricate network of mostly Islamic organisations also has contacts to opposition parties. Men also criticise more strongly than women the lack of contact to political authorities.

The comparatively critical attitudes of Latinos towards their political leadership are rooted in a different understanding of their political rights. During the military dictatorship clearly more favelados still agreed with the statement (63%, N=472), 'the government tries to understand and solve the problems of the normal citizen' (Perlman 1976: 176) than do so today. The years of transition have taught the urban poor to question more critically the actions of government. Chileans and Brazilians differ only slightly from one another in this respect. There is a tendency for the *pobladores'* judgement to be even more negative. Over the last few years, political parties in particular have had to come to terms with a nationwide loss of esteem. In 1991, 92% of Chileans felt they were well treated by their political parties, and 75% by the government. In 1994, the respective values were only 52% and 43% (Garretón et al. 1995: 31). Relatively speaking, the President still enjoys the most positive reputation. A total of 53% (1994) of all Chileans believe he represents their interests (ibid.: 35). This negative evaluation of the political leadership is due to its failure to fulfil the high expectations many Chileans had of the return to democracy. Discontent with the political leadership is somewhat lower in Temuco than in Santiago (see also Table 6.8).

In Brazil a contrasting situation can be observed. The cariocas of Rio are clearly more content with achievements of the past few years than the nordestinos. The inhabitants of Aracaju still confront more undemocratic political decision-making processes, in which they are assigned the role of passive observers and thus often remain dependent on arbitrary government decisions.

The latter is also true for the African cases, although while the urban poor in the Ivory Coast still take marginalisation for granted to a large

Table 6.12 Satisfaction with the political authorities, political expectations (%)

	Brazil	Chile	Ivory Coast	Kenya
On the whole, are you ... with the present political authorities in your country?				
Very satisfied	14	2	21	11
Satisfied	53	25	36	23
Dissatisfied	11	58	–	23
Very dissatisfied?	22	15	43	43
And what are your expectations for the future? On the whole do you expect the political situation will be				
Better	39	41	82	32
Same	26	43	9	25
Worse?	35	16	10	43

Source: Project Political Participation

degree, Kenyans are increasingly beginning to formulate demands for civil rights. Critical judgement of the present situation and realistic evaluation of corruption and abuse of power demonstrate for both countries a prospective (Ivory Coast) and existing (Kenya) potential for unrest. Thus, 34% and 54% respectively state that the president has too much power, and over two thirds attest to abuse of power by politicians.

In the evaluation of the effectiveness of government and its authorities, one must take into account that satisfaction with the government and its incumbents is often closely associated with personal gain. This is especially true when such a change of government does not seem to be positive as such in the eyes of the population, as is the case in both African states. Personal chances of gain within the existing regime therefore often decide its acceptance or rejection.

The majority of those questioned in Brazil (67%) and the Ivory Coast (57%) express satisfaction with the incumbents. In these cases, the majority support of incumbents despite simultaneous diagnosis of serious deficits such as abuse of power, social inequality or corruption, has different reasons. In Brazil, in particular in Rio de Janeiro, the living conditions in the favelas have noticeably improved following democratisation. The Damocles' sword of threatened clearance has disappeared and made way for specific infrastructural measures in the settlements. Our results indicate that experiences of crises and emergency situations have had a moderating effect on the expectations the favelados have of the political system.

However, the Brazilian settlements demonstrate a clear regional divide. Tendencies towards a greater level of satisfaction with incumbents, as well as greater confidence in their own possibilities of influence in the political arena, can be discerned amongst the cariocas of Rio de Janeiro. This is again evidence of more deeply rooted democratic attitudes, which were consolidated by the outputs of government over the past 15 years. In contrast, the nordestinos seem to remain trapped in authoritarian attitude patterns, not least because of the longer tradition and deeper rooting of clientelistic relationships. They are somewhat more dissatisfied with the outputs than the cariocas, but (as yet) do not question the pattern of relations responsible for the situation of social and political inequality in the same way. They also view the future more pessimistically. The number of those who expect the political situation in the country to worsen is almost half (47%), approximately equal to the number of cariocas who foresee positive development. Because the process of democratic legitimation implies persuasion, those in positions of political responsibility in the north east, who have mainly drawn attention to themselves by corruption and scandals, but at the same time try to maintain the clientelistic interest mediation structures, cannot further the growth of a new, more democratic consciousness. In contrast to the cariocas, most in the north east hope for concrete improvements of their living conditions 'from above', rather than fighting for them, and in their role as subjects, the majority do not make use of their rights of democratic participation (see Cruz 1992: 128ff., see chapter 7).

The explanations for the Ivory Coast are partly similar to those for the Brazilian north east. The majority support for the government confirms that, in principle, the respondents do not question the justi-fication of continuing authoritarian power relations and the policies of the former state party, PDCI. The answers of the Ivorians also partly reveal a lack of understanding of the role of the opposition. For some, politics in a pluralistic sense is equivalent to 'doing the dirty washing of the (political) family in public'. Such lack of understanding of the necessity of opposition is also demonstrated in the question concerning the evaluation of the multi-party system. 56% of the 309 Ivorians who answered the question sympathise with the former one-party system. Even if one takes into account the fact that the respondents may express support for the one-party system due to precaution or opportunism, these responses express the fear of social unrest and civil war, which can be precipitated by the loss of power of a previous one-party regime.[10] The high rate of refusals to answer these questions can also be explained by the self-perception of women. Muslim women in par-ticular did not answer such political questions.

The responses of the Chileans and Kenyans who are dissatisfied with the political leadership can be explained as follows. The pobladores and Chileans in general attach high priority to measures aimed at improving the living conditions of the population and overcoming poverty and unemployment. In this regard, they still expect more. However, those Chileans we questioned were not totally disillusioned: only 16% believe the political situation will (further) worsen in the future. Kenyans evaluate their government in a critical manner similar to that of the pobladores. Two thirds of those questioned were dissatisfied with the government in power. This also shows that they realistically perceive the low extent of substantive democratic changes so far. They also demonstrate disappointment about the conflict amongst the opposition parties and feel deceived because their expectations of a functioning multi-party system have not been fulfilled. The hesitant support for the multi-party system (42%) is partly explained by its recent introduction and by the structural weaknesses of the opposition parties. The future is also viewed pessimistically. 43% expect the political situation to be-come worse. The legitimacy of the government is therefore much lower than in Chile. In view of the continuing problematic political situation, the expressed pessimism seems justified.

The relationship between the legitimacy and the effectiveness of the political regimes is therefore differentiated in the countries we studied. The urban poor in Brazil are most content with their current government. The improvement of their standard of living following democratisation has led (especially in Rio de Janeiro) to the creation of a certain basis of legitimacy. The opposite is the case in Kenya. Here, many amongst the urban poor hoped that the transition to a multi-party system would lead to more emphasis on social justice, which in their eyes has not been the case. In their negative responses towards the government and their pessimistic view of the political future, the incumbents reap the rewards of their own ineffectiveness, and one-sided clientelistic behaviour. In Chile, the pobladores are dissatisfied with the achievements of their government in a manner similar to the Kenyans, but the political regime there is not in a legitimacy crisis. In contrast to the Kenyans, they do not tend towards a complete rejection of the present political structures. In the Ivory Coast the majority of the urban poor express satisfaction with the still largely authoritarian regime. The marginalisation of their interests in the political process is not really questioned, so a basically authoritarian political culture corresponds with a similar political structure.

Concluding Remarks: Is There a Political Culture of the Urban Poor?

A single over-arching pattern of political culture of the urban poor could not be discovered in our study. The relationships of the urban poor towards politics not only are the result of different socio-economic and democratic levels of development, but are rooted in different political traditions and are expressed in different patterns of political thought and action. Our analysis has shown that many critical attitudes towards politics predominate in the countries we studied. This points to a certain incongruence between the political culture and political structure in these countries, although this may not necessarily lead to a destabilisation of the system. In the respective states, the relationship between political culture and structure can briefly be characterised as follows:

In Chile, the country with the largest democratic tradition in the past, the pobladores identify very strongly with basic democratic values and are critical towards possible limitations of these. The majority support for a strong leader as the head of state is more an indication of the perception of the president as 'weak' in political practice and of an inadequate understanding of parliamentarian forms of government, rather than an authoritarian pattern of thought. Similarly, the prevailing political attitudes with a clear tendency towards goal-orientated, pragmatic actions are in conformity with the democratic political structure. The discrepancy between structure and culture is revealed in the critical attitudes towards the political leadership (especially towards the political parties), and towards the current functioning of democracy. It is basically related to the government's neglect of the interests of the urban poor and the limited chances they possess to influence the political process. In spite of largely favourable economic conditions, this discontent is founded in the 'new' form of democracy, which in many ways does not continue the democratic principles of the 1960s and instead of solidarity now proclaims individual achievements as its main goal. In view of the increasing individualisation and de-politicisation of the urban poor, the danger that this discontent could erupt in (system-threatening) protest action is not very great. Since the pobladores do not differ greatly in their attitudes from other social groups, society is not threatened with division into various sub-cultures, which can work to destabilise the stability of democracy.

Brazilian political and social culture(s) and structure(s) differ greatly from the Chilean ones. On the whole, there is consensus concerning a high level of acceptance of democratic values. Apart from this, there is a great divide between the Brazilian south east and the north east, in terms of both political structure and culture. In the metropolis, Rio de Janeiro, which is more thoroughly organised according to democratic rules, the urban poor are clearly more content with the political leadership and the political system. Even though the cariocas remain critical of their leaders, they place a comparatively high level of trust in them and have developed a democratic consciousness in conformity with the political system. Their high level of satisfaction with the incumbents and their optimistic view of the political future of the country point to positive chances for the consolidation of democracy in the metropolis. In the long term, however, Brazilian democracy is in need of more thorough political 'self-cleansing' and economic consolidation. Nevertheless, in light of the relatively weak identification with political parties and critical attitudes towards the outputs of government, one can speak of a certain incongruity between structure and culture.

The attitudes of the urban poor in the north eastern town of Aracaju differ greatly from those of the cariocas. They are characterised by a greater distance to the political system, the political leadership and its outputs. The weaknesses of this more 'formal' democracy, due to the continuation of authoritarian and clientelistic structures of interest mediation, are reflected in the evaluation of the regime. The relatively high level of satisfaction with the functioning of democracy and its representatives, which seems to stand in contradiction to the diagnosed political deficits, points to the continuation of authoritarian patterns of thought. Emotionally the majority is attached to the political leadership, which stands above in a hierarchical manner, without developing stronger active and participatory relationships. This would require the recognition of the connection between their own situation and the political sphere and a more critical perception of the existing structures of inequality. Therefore, in Brazil, two different sub-cultures exist side by side. The first represents the changes in consciousness towards a more democratic participatory political culture, while the second remains trapped in more clientelistic and 'subject' perceptions of politics. Other studies ascribe authoritarian attitudes to poorer and less educated groups in society in general (Moisés 1995: 210). Our results point to the fact that within the poor groups, cultural breaks have occurred, and are occurring, which are determined by the respective place of residence and region.

In the Ivory Coast, democratisation has to date remained mostly a formal process. However, the answer to the question concerning the consolidation of democratic attitudes is ambivalent. Our survey was conducted in the election year 1995, only five years after the introduction of the multi-party system. After the death of the founding president (December 1993), the interim president carried on government business as usual in the old manner. The regime used the devaluation of the CFA-Franc in January 1994 and the following economic upturn to consolidate its legitimacy. In this sense, real changes remained very limited. At the same time, the range of answers obtained reflects the current socio-political potential for change. More democratic attitudes are not very likely to be shaped by the present political structures, since these remain trapped in the clientelistic pattern of relations formed under the state party. The opposition parties do not contribute to a positive experience of democracy either, because they are divided and, in part, have accepted offers of participation in government. Tribalistic policies towards immigrants from neighbouring countries further strengthen the tendency to bow to the political authorities as before. The political culture of the urban poor in Abidjan and Man therefore continues to be moulded by traditional values and attitudes and is characterised by the largely unquestioned acceptance of a paternalistic and authoritarian style of leadership. This is reflected in the widespread acceptance of their situation and unquestioned legitimacy of the president and his regime. At the same time, some basic democratic values reflect the traditional understanding of equality and freedom of speech ('palabre'). Many remain also trapped in traditional role models with regard to the relation of the sexes. Women continue to experience the reduction of their activities to the household. This is especially true for Muslim women from immigrant families. Furthermore, it is noticeable that Ivorian citizens are more critical towards the government than immigrants. The former have certain expectations and demands of the government and often express disappointment with its outputs.

In contrast to the Ivory Coast, those questioned in Kenya demonstrate a constant criticism towards the political authorities and political structures. In the medium-sized town of Kisumu in particular, the responses expose an attitude of opposition towards the government and the president. However, the political culture of the urban poor remains integrated into the national context. At present, this means that although there is a multi-party system, this does not imply that the country has undergone substantial democratisation. The values and attitudes of the population in the precarious settlements, however, cannot be characterised as apathetic or fatalistic. A high level of political interest and information and a differentiated range of opinions concerning daily political life and the behaviour of the leadership clearly prove this. The support for more clientelistic leadership structures, which stands in a certain contrast, can be explained by the daily political life of the African countries and the lack of experience with democratic forms of state. Furthermore, those questioned in Kenya who practise the Islamic faith also tend to demonstrate a more traditional understanding of values in a personal and political sense.

Notes

1. The attitudes of the urban poor towards political society will not be examined in this chapter; see chapters 3 and 7.

2. The number of those supporting democracy in Brazil declined within a few months from 55% to 42%. The then president, Fernando Collor de Mello, was accused of corruption and finally forced to resign. A short time after his resignation, the number of those in favour of democracy had increased once more to 59% (Moisés 1995: 127).

3. For example, in Kenya the majority of those questioned in the medium-sized town of Kisumu belong to an opposition ethnic group (see chapter 2). In the Ivorian medium-sized town of Man, the majority of inhabitants in one of the settlements we studied are Ivorians, whereas in the other settlements there are large numbers of immigrants from neighbouring African states.

4. The statements used in these studies were as follows: 'The country would do a lot better if the military came back to power', and 'Democracy is dangerous because it can cause chaos.' (Moisés 1995: 120).

5. The Brazilian and Kenyan poor answer the question, what disturbs them most in their country often with, 'The deficits of the political system.' These include tendencies to corruption and the lack of credibility of politicians, as well as the lack of policies orientated towards poverty alleviation.

6. The 'palabre' in the Ivory Coast can be compared to open 'round table' discussions. Everyone has the right to speak and the 'Chef', in this case the president, listens to opinions and commentaries concerning the most varied problems, such as disputes over land ownership in a village, or complaints of a trade union, and then decides on these. Houphouët-Boigny had used this tradition to channel discontent.

7. In comparison with the Perlman study from the years 1968/9, we can observe a slight reduction in fatalistic attitudes amongst the favelados from 57% to 46% (1995). This cannot be taken as unequivocal evidence that fatalistic values have declined because this result could be attributable to the choice of different favelas.

8. Residence permits and controls were introduced in the 1990s. Previously, there was a more or less open invitation to the neighbouring African states to participate in the Ivorian 'economic wonder'.

9. The specific situation in the Ivory Coast and the increasingly problematic situation of the immigrant workers is dealt with elsewhere (Chapter 2).

10. Mostly young people and supporters of the highly regarded opposition leader were amongst the supporters of a multi-party system.

. . . .

CHAPTER 7

Political Participation

Norbert Kersting and
Jaime Sperberg

§ URBAN poverty usually entails exclusion not only from the economic sphere, but also from various social spheres in cultural and political life. The wave of democratisation which occurred in the 1980s and 1990s offered the urban poor the opportunity to take part in the political process. How have they made use of it? Does the right to vote offer them an extra resource in their survival strategy? Are improvements in their standard of living discernible? This chapter deals with these questions. A definition of the various forms of political participation will be followed by an analysis of the concrete patterns of participation in the shanty towns of Brazil, Chile, the Ivory Coast and Kenya. On this basis, certain characteristic 'types' of participation will be developed. In parallel to other forms of involvement, the opportunity to take part in national elections has gained special importance. The formal right to vote can increase the political importance of this section of the population. Therefore, the specific electoral behaviour and the party preferences of this group will also be examined.

The survival strategies of the urban poor are characterised by the principle of risk diversification. In this regard, we will analyse whether also various forms of participation and channels for interest articulation are chosen.

Patterns of Political Participation

There are various definitions of political participation. The lack of studies dealing with political participation in the Third World is partly due to the reduction of types of political activity to conventional forms. Thus, Verba/Nie et al. (1978: 46) define participation simply as legal forms of involvement which aim to influence the decisions of the political system. Barnes/Kaase (1979: 42) widen this notion and include also other possibly even illegal activities, which are described in their terminology as 'unconventional' participation. In accordance with their definition, we understand political participation as all voluntary activities by private persons which aim, either directly or indirectly, to influence political decisions on different levels of the political system (Kaase/Marsh 1979: 42). When applied to Third World countries, this initial definition still presents a number of problems with regard to active subjects being private persons, the voluntary nature of participation, and a clearly defined notion of politics.

Often certain actions may be included in this definition even though individuals feel obliged to carry out such political activities as a result of external pressure. Thus, for example, membership of a specific political party must be viewed in the light of the political, cultural and social context of each respective country. This is true, in particular, for the differences between our African and Latin American cases. However, even in the more authoritarian African states studied, there is some room for manoeuvre which allows individual self-help and electoral activities which lead to a certain 'politicisation' of basic problems.

A large number of definitions of political participation do not explicitly describe what is exactly meant by 'political'. It is often implied that an activity related to the state or different levels of the political system is enough. We prefer to employ an extended definition and also view as political those activities which try to solve social problems, independent of whether this occurs in self-help initiatives or via direct contacts with the political authorities. The societies studied demonstrate various levels of serious social inequality, which manifest themselves in uneven income distribution as well as poor provision of goods and services. In this perspective, participation is political when it aims to overcome this lack of provision via collective and public activities. Thus, even those activities which are often described as 'economic' or 'social' have a political character, but these activities are only political if they aim for publicity and generalise local problems (see Alemann 1994: 147). The definition of these activities as political is not dependent on whether strategies are orientated towards conflict or consensus. Neither is reference to the political authorities absolutely essential. What is essential is the creation of a public space, which can be limited to a particular area but has a general character that can serve as an example for other social groups which find themselves in a similar position.

A number of authors view the dimensions of political influence as a hierarchical model (see Lane 1959; Apter 1965; Steiner 1969). Treating political participation as a cumulative act, or as a hierarchical 'latent structure pattern', means that people who engage in difficult participatory acts at a time of conflict (see Verba 1973), and those activities which are 'further down' the hierarchical ladder, opt for means of participation which entail limited social or economic costs. Thus, it is assumed that active party members (high level of intensity) participate in elections (low level of intensity). As a result, various typologies of political participation can be discerned (see Deutsch 1961; Milbrath/ Goel 1965; Di Palma 1970). In contrast, Verba and Nie (1978) view participation as a multi-dimensional act and describe 'multiple paths' of extended participation. Participation research also has moved from institutional explanation, which mostly takes account of the possibilities of 'top-down' mobilisation, to social factors and individual attitudes (see Barnes/Kaase et al. 1979; Asher/Richardson 1984).

The various forms of political participation can be categorised. Such categorisation takes into account different aspects, such as the legal framework, different political levels (local–national), the level of organisation (individual–organised), or the level of directness (indirect–direct, representative–plebiscitarian). Categorisation according to the cost of participatory acts forms the foundation of hierarchical participation models (see Milbrath/Goel 1977). These relate to the costs which participation exacts in terms of time or personal energy and expenditure (see Verba 1973). In this way, typologies are developed to describe the varying intensities of participation, for example 'gladiators', 'transitionals', 'spectators', and 'apathetics' (Milbrath/Goel 1974; see also Muller 1982). Similar to a Roman circus, 'gladiators' are viewed as the main activists (e.g. as party leaders, candidates for public office) in the political process. 'Transitionals' form the reservoir of support. They comprise 'party and campaign workers', or 'protesters', who are midway towards 'complete activists'. 'Spectators' use their vote to decide about the office holders ('voting', 'patriotic support'). The 'apathetics' do not participate at all.

Furthermore, Barnes, Kaase et al. distinguish beetween conventional and unconventional forms of participation. Conventional forms of activity include voting in national and local elections, electoral campaign activities, organisation of intermediary groups, such as unions, parties, associations etc., and personal contacts to politicians. In short, they include ' … those acts of political involvement directly or indirectly related to the electoral process' (1979: 84; see also Nohlen 1990). Unconventional forms of participation, actions with controversial legality, such as demonstrations, blockades, building occupations, and petitioning, provide a further indicator of political engagement. Therefore, unconventional activity is defined as ' … behaviour that does not correspond to the norms of law and customs that regulate participation under a particular regime' (Kaase/Marsh 1979: 41; see also Gronemeyer 1984). The boundaries to violent action are sometimes blurred. This differentiation is especially problematic for inter-cultural comparison because cultural conventions and problems differ and it is difficult to identify suitable equivalents (see Asher/Richardson 1984: 13). Evaluations of participation are also subject to internal cultural social change, that is, changes in conventions. Thus, participatory forms appear and disappear from daily life (see Binder 1977; Klingemann 1985; Uehlinger 1988).

In the following analysis, the various forms of political participation will be presented in their respective political context. The framework of the national political system, the local administrative system, neighbourhood organisations, and the political culture of the sub-milieus determine the form, extent and intensity of participation in slum and squatter settlements. Certain forms of participation, such as political discussion amongst friends and at the workplace, are not dealt with here. Participation in organisations orientated more towards civil society is also excluded. The latter, as far as these exist, are examined separately (see chapter 5). In the following section, the main forms of political participation are divided into conventional, party-orientated, and unconventional participatory forms.

Conventional opportunities for participation include voting, political contacts, party membership, acceptance of political office and electoral campaigning. Following the wave of democratisation in the 1980s and early 1990s, *elections* were introduced as the central element of a representative democracy. As a result of the dominance of centralised structures, and depending on the constitution, local or district elections compared to national parliamentary or presidential elections often have low status. Participation in referenda, which are as yet seldom part of the constitution in the Third World, is included. *Political contacts* mainly comprise letters to politicians and the authorities, as well as personal contacts to politicians. Collecting signatures and petitioning, as well as letters to the media, which are also often included in this form of participation, are not included here. *Party membership* often constitutes merely a passive role in political parties. In contrast, *acceptance of political office* represents a higher level of engagement. Taking part in *election campaigns* is also a form of political participation, which for the most part only has a limited, or indirect influence on political decision making.

Even after the end of the bureaucratic, authoritarian regime in *Brazil* (for this term, see O'Donnell 1979), the federal presidential system is characterised by clientelistic structures. The party system demonstrates only a limited level of institutionalisation. It is organisationally weak and fragmented (Mainwaring 1999). In Brazil's 'catch-all parties' (Mainwaring 1991: 26), party discipline and programmes are far less important than the personalities who stand as a party's candidate for political office. In the favelas, the 'cabo eleitoral'[1] is charged with collecting votes for a candidate, and in exchange promises the favelados material improvements or distributes presents. This clientelistic pattern of relations between favelados and politicians is an important element of political culture in Brazil and remains widespread due to the personalised nature of politics. The possibility of electoral participation is determined by registration in the electoral register. This is practically compulsory because registration in the electoral register determines allocation of job opportunities in the civil service and the successful completion of all formalities with the authorities.

During the repressive, authoritarian phase of the Brazilian military regime, the Associacoes de Moradores (AM) and their umbrella organisations, which operate in the shanty towns, suffered persecution and their leaders were replaced by official appointees. Since the beginning of the 1980s, AMs have begun to form once more, although due to the simultaneous revival of party and political competition, they often are under the control of populist leaders or politicians. Autonomous AMs, which function as democratic interest representation organs for the favelados, are mostly found in the industrialised south east of Brazil. In contrast, in the north east of the country, they remain operative agents for the local administration. Thus, many favelados view their AMs as a so-called 'miniprefeitura', that is, a branch of the city government within the favela (Bento Rubiao 1993: 104). The leaders of the favelas have the task of ensuring improvements for their neighbourhood on the basis of their individual power resources (contacts with politicians, town administration etc.). Neighbourhood organisations are often coopted by certain politicians, who mobilise their members before elections as a means of ensuring votes. However, such loyal and dependent relations between favelados and politicians have become more short-lived and flexible, so that competition for votes between politicians has increased, a fact the favelados have used to their advantage. As a result of the highly personalised nature of elections and the dominance of political clientelism, elected representatives are relatively well-known and often visit the favelas.

While political parties in Brazil never enjoyed a prominent role, before 1973 in *Chile*, they were the major formative element in the political process. Despite the far-reaching social changes during the authoritarian phase from 1973 to 1989, the Chilean party system is, in contrast to the Brazilian one, highly consolidated and has a high level of institutionalisation (see Garretón 1995). In this context, Vial (1986: 107) speaks of the 'colonisation' of social groups by political parties. The programmatic Chilean political parties engage themselves in the organisations of civil society and in this way create stable party affiliations, even amongst the urban poor. These ties were, however, partly destroyed during the period of structural change in the authoritarian phase. The urban poor often also vote for certain personalities, but political clientelism does not (any longer) constitute a characteristic element of the political system. Following the return to democracy in Chile, the parties to some extent 'withdrew from society' and now operate in their 'very own' political arena. The Christian Democratic Party, the party voted for by most pobladores, is the only one which has maintained some form of party activity in the poblaciones.

The neighbourhood committees, juntas de vecinos, received formal legal recognition in 1968. Between 1974 and 1989, the military dictatorship integrated them into its hierarchical administrative structure and their leaders were appointed by the respective mayor (see chapter 5). After 1989, the Juntas were quickly re-democratised, which reaffirmed their position as mediation organs between residents, the town administration and the national government. The Juntas also built up separate sections to deal with and solve specific problems in small groups. Over the past few years, some of these committees ('comités de adelanto', or 'organizacions de passaje') have distanced themselves from the actual Junta and now try to solve their problems using direct contacts to public institutions. Some junta-type organisations which have come into being during illegal land occupations are exceptions and do not enjoy formal recognition, but they often have a participatory dynamic of their own and sometimes also effective problem-solving abilities. However, Juntas normally have ties to either the governing coalition or the opposition parties.

The *Ivory Coast* has party and state structures similar to those of former socialist countries, which had parallel state and party structures. Political behaviour is to a high degree dependent on the regulations of the system and the dominant clientelistic pattern of relations. Local hierarchies at the slum and squatter level often limit the individual scope of choice between different participatory forms. Political activity which deviates from the official channels, e.g. participation in protest demonstrations, often meets with repression from the state. Until the introduction of a multi-party system in 1990, practically the entire population was a member of the PDCI by birth. Party organisation pervaded all areas of society. Government and administration were basically identical with the party. Party organisations and the administrative apparatus were one and the same. Party membership fees were deducted directly from salaries in the formal sector. Since 1990, such contributions have to be paid individually. A silent wave of withdrawal followed the events and political changes of the years 1990 to 1992.

Ivorian citizens become eligible to vote and to take political office at the age of 21.[2] Until 1990, immigrants from neighbouring states, especially Burkina Faso, were allowed to take part in elections. In the last elections in 1995, immigrants were only permitted to take part in local elections. Turnout in the shanty towns is very high. Generally, political authorities are only present in the settlements during an election year. There are no neighbourhood organisations based on autonomous, grassroots initiatives. The *'chef'* of the settlement, who is directly elected by the residents, has a key position. However, candidates are still often chosen by the local party section, so that the process becomes merely an election by acclamation. The *chef*, who is elected every five years, appoints members to the Action Committee, which is often the local PDCI party section. The members of this committee are normally men (especially in Islamic neighbourhoods), who belong to different ethnic groups. Correct proportions are strictly observed. The *chef* and members of the Action Committee have access to the local political level, that is the mayor's office, and are normally employed by the town administration. Thus, they are directly dependent on the local authorities. The *chef*'s real legitimation, however, does not stem from the procedure of direct elections, but is usually rooted in traditional customs, age or membership of a respected family. Until 1990, the *chef* was at the same time party chairman for his section as well as contact person and messenger between the neighbourhood and the local council.

For a long time, in *Kenya*, one could speak of a 'no-party system'. Party membership consisted of little more than buying a membership card during a campaign. Apart from 'barazas', a public gathering under the open sky, and 'harambees', originally devised as self-help initiatives, but today often resembling a public donation campaign, there are no regular participatory opportunities for party members. Election campaigns are strongly influenced by local concerns and personalities, although in the countryside, personal contacts to parliamentary representatives enjoy special importance (see also Barkan 1987). In the urban shanty towns, recognition of representatives is lower, because in this context town authorities play a larger role. The central figure is the formally appointed 'chief'. This is solely a paid administrative position and is not linked to any form of traditional or electoral legitimacy. However, often contacts to the native rural regions and the representatives there are maintained. Therefore, in Kenya and the Ivory Coast there are no autonomous organisational forms which serve the interest representation of the poor at the local level. Instead, there is a strict, hierarchical order in which administrative and judicial tasks are taken over by the chief or chef.

Unconventional forms of participation are defined as taking part in demonstrations, strikes, payment boycotts and illegal land occupation. Participation in *demonstrations* includes both approved and illegal demonstrations. These can be initiated by different groups. Sometimes such demonstrations are merely functions for the governing party ('demonstrations of praise'). Occupation of offices (town administration etc.), demonstrations which include violence against objects or persons, as well as participation in riots were not explicitly asked about in our questionnaire. *Strikes* are a form of protest which, especially in Third World countries, often have a political dimension. In the local arena, *payment boycotts* (for rent, electricity, water etc.) can also be recorded. As the local town authorities are normally aimed at by such actions (similar to the boycotts in the South African anti-apartheid movement), this is viewed as political activity. *Squatting*, that is illegal land occupation, often entails occupation of municipal, that is public, land. In the case of occupation of private land, town authorities are often called upon to act as mediator or central authority to uphold property rights.

During the military dictatorship in *Brazil*, the right to demonstrate and hold strikes was partly suspended. In reaction to the economic problems at the start of the 1980s, a broad social movement formed in the shanty towns with the help of external organisations (NGOs, the Catholic Church). At first, the demonstrations aimed to improve living conditions and defend against clearance threats. Later, in the middle of the 1980s, they sometimes presented more political demands aimed at the regime. The urban poor, especially in the industrialised south east of the country, also participated in demonstrations in favour of the introduction of direct elections for the presidency ('direitas'). The right to strike, gather and hold demonstrations was guaranteed in the new constitution, which signified the formal completion of the transition process.

Despite the tight regulations into which the authoritarian regime in *Chile* had forced union activities, the copper workers' walkouts and protests in 1983 were the driving force behind the opposition movement against the regime. Shanty town residents were especially active in these protests, which reached their climax between 1983 and 1986. During this period, demonstrations against the military regime were part of the everyday life of residents in the poor areas. As soon as agreement between the opposition and the military regime concerning a transition to democracy was reached, protest demonstrations declined. One characteristic form of participation in Chile is squatting. Whereas squatter settlements in the other countries studied usually were the result of a long, slow process of infiltration, in Chile they are often organised, broad invasions ('invasiones'). Such occupations, which usually occur on national holidays because of the low police presence and which mostly involve young families, are often planned months in advance. Sympathetic student groups, lawyers and members of the press often try to prevent the later expulsion of the settlers.

In the *Ivory Coast*, the protest potential is lower, although slum residents were involved in the democratisation movement at the start of the 1990s. Protest against the regime culminated between 1990 and 1993. In these years, protest demonstrations were a regular occurrence. These mostly mobilised the urban intelligentsia and only to a limited degree the lower classes. As immigrants, the latter either refrain from participation in internal politics, or are integrated into the political system using clientelistic means. In addition, there were demonstrations which were initiated by the ruling party. Boycotting rent or electricity payments is very rare because provision of these is mostly private. The squatter settlements originally formed as a result of gradual infiltration rather than organised land occupation.

In contrast to the Ivory Coast, *Kenya* has a longer tradition of conflict, often violent, with the former colonial (Mau-Mau uprising) as well as the KANU regime. There was significant participation of slum residents in the democratisation movement at the start of the 1990s, which culminated in the large protest demonstration 'saba saba' on 7 July 1990. Following the removal in 1991 of the clause in the constitution which enshrined KANU as the only political party, opposition parties are once more permitted. Organised land occupation did not occur. Boycotts of rent or electricity payments are rare.

In the following section, these categories will be combined to form a specific model. This typology is based on the results of our study. One group thus can be discerned which does not participate using any of the forms we asked about and which we term *inactive* (Type I). Such an 'exit'-option (according to Hirschman's [1970] typology) can be based on either an apathetic or a cynical motivation. A further large group of *voters-only* could also be distinguished. Apart from voting, this group did not engage in any other form of participation (Type II). This 'loyalty/ voice' option can express itself in favour or against the current government. Therefore, this group can contain both a loyal voter base and protest voters. A factor analysis of resources in all four countries produced a further group which favoured party-orientated forms of participation (Type III). These include such activities as party membership, electoral campaigning, accepting office and contacts with politicians. Furthermore, statistical analysis revealed another 'pure' group of persons (Type IV), who only take part in *unconventional forms of participation*, i.e. demonstrations, strikes, payment boycotts and squatting, all of which occur in the local living and working sphere. In addition to these exclusive forms, a mixed *universally active* type (Type V) could be distinguished. This mixed type predominantly takes part in conventional party-orientated activities, but their various forms of participation encompass the whole spectrum.

In order to obtain a detailed analysis of these participation types, aspects of social structure as well as the respective resources, predominantly political knowledge and free time (operationalised using the relationship between free and working time) were examined. In addition, aspects of political culture which contribute to motivation, such as interest in politics, were taken into account.

Analysis by Country

The quantitative distribution of these participation types in the four countries shows considerable differences. In comparison to Africa, the inactive group in *Brazil* is small and, at 12%, is similar to that in Chile.

Table 7.1 Types of political participation

Exit	Loyalty / voice:			
Non active I	Voting only II	Conventional party-oriented III	Unconventional activists IV	Comprehensive activists V
No political participation		Party membership	Squatting	All forms of participation
		Election campaign	Boycott: (electricity, etc.)	
		Political incumbency	Strikes	
		Political contacts (mail, personal, etc.)	Demonstrations	
	Voting	Voting	Voting	Voting

The group of 'voters-only' was 38%, similar to the level in Chile, but higher than that in the settlements in the Ivory Coast and Kenya. The fact that electoral registration in Chile and Brazil is voluntary, but afterwards voting is compulsory, must be taken into consideration. Party-orientated participation in Brazil is around 13%, much higher than the Chilean case and about as high as that in the Ivory Coast, but much lower than that in Kenya. Approximately one fifth (19%) of activists in Brazil are 'unconventional'. This is lower than in Chile, but much higher than in the African cases. The universal participation type accounts for about 16%, the same level as in Chile, but below that of Kenya. Thus, apart from the large group of 'voters-only', Brazil demonstrates a relatively even distribution of all participation types.

Chile is characterised by the large group of unconventional activists (38%). Together with the voters-only (38%), they represent the most frequent participation types. In contrast, party-orientated participation (4%) is rare. Although there is generally a higher level of activists in Chile, the universal participation type (8%) only reaches the level of the Ivory Coast. Compared to the African cases, the number of those who are inactive (12%) is very low.

In the *Ivory Coast*, the group which does not take part in any form of participation is especially prevalent. Unconventional and neighbourhood-orientated activities are the least prominent (2%). 'Universal activists' form a somewhat larger group (7%). Conventional, party-

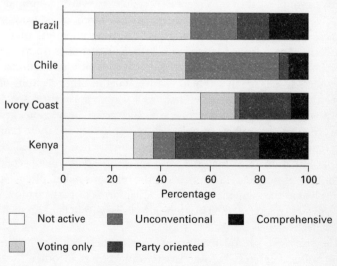

Figure 7.1 Types of participation

orientated forms of participation are relatively frequent (21%). 'Voters-only' make up the second largest group, but in comparison to the Latin American cases, this remains relatively small (14%).

In *Kenya*, those who are inactive account for more than a quarter of all those questioned (29%). The largest group of activists are party-orientated (34%). The large number of mixed types, 'universal activists', make up a relatively large group (20%). Unconventional activists are more strongly represented than in the Ivory Coast (9%), but in comparison to Latin America are still small in number. In Kenya, voters-only account for 8%.

These participatory types are influenced by different factors (age, sex, type of town, type of settlement, level of education, income, daily working hours, educational level of parents) in each of the four countries. In addition, there are significant connections to political and cultural factors (legitmation, political interest, effectiveness of the various forms of participation, evaluation of equal opportunities in society, economic and political future expectations, membership of self-help groups, willingness to engage in self-help).[3]

Brazil: Women (76%) are over-represented in the inactive group. Older women especially and those (still) not in employment belong to this type. The former are often relieved from electoral duty if they are illiterate. Younger women are often not registered because they are not available for employment and therefore experience no disadvantages from their absence from the register of job searchers. Within the inactive group, trust of strangers is very low. However, a limited level of interest in politics is at least present. The levels of education and political knowledge are also low (only 7% know the name of the US President). Apart from participation in neighbourhood groups – with the exception of some cultural groups such as samba associations – the willingness to engage in self-help is lower than in other sections of the population. Only 22% view self-help as a way to solve their problems. Those who are politically inactive are more active in religious groups. As women in this milieu often carry responsibility for their families, they tend to look for assistance to the Church when presented with a conflict situation (e.g. material worries, drug addiction of children, alcoholism of husband). Such roots in the religious milieu often express themselves in the view that unconventional forms of participation, such as payment boycotts, demonstrations, or taking part in land occupations, are ineffective.

The *voters-only* are relatively content with their living environment. Their political interest is low. Apart from voting, all other forms of participation are viewed as ineffective. Their educational level (and also that of their parents) is low. This pattern of participation is especially prevalent in Aracaju. In Aracaju, clientelistic interest representation structures dominate the political process. The almost complete absence of experience of democratic, pluralistic interest representation has prevented the emergence of more active patterns of participation. However, 14% of the members of this group are engaged in neighbourhood organisations, and the percentage of those who are willing to offer a personal contribution to solve local problems (32%) is somewhat above the average for Brazil.

Party-orientated activists often have a higher level of income and belong to those sections of the population who have a more optimistic view of the future. In this group, 69% are interested in politics. Their strong integration with the state via party activities or contacts to office holders expresses itself in a higher level of satisfaction with the political authorities. The strategy of the elites to increase the acceptance of the political system amongst the urban poor via the creation of channels of communication between the state and the favelas seems to have born fruit, at least amongst party-orientated activists. This type is strongly represented in Rio. They have strong personal initiative (45%), but participation in neighbourhood organisations is also important (20%).

Unconventional participants are characterised by their strong interest in politics (92%). Strikes, payment boycotts, squatting and demonstrations are viewed as effective. This pattern of participation is found in Rio, especially in the older settlements, because of the longer and wider horizon of experiences with such forms of action in the metropolis, and a higher level of acceptance of these by the state authorities (from the middle of the 1970s). For the same reasons, a settlement's age also acts to further the development of this participatory type. The willingness to engage in self-help is especially strong amongst the unconventionally active, and their membership of neighbourhood organisations is relatively high (20%). In contrast, daily political life in the north east is still moulded by the favelados' stronger authoritarian attitudes. These are expressed, not in legal demands, but in expectations from the state as patron.

Universal activists are more often members of the younger generation (50%) and male (63%). They are characterised by a high level of political interest (66%). They view strikes, payment boycotts and demonstrations, but also elections and party membership, as effective. They evaluate the responsiveness of those in power as higher than do the other groups. They have a high level of education and political knowledge. In addition, they are more often active in neighbourhood groups (34%) and have a high level of willingness to engage in self-help (59%). This type is somewhat more strongly represented in Aracaju. Such 'all-round activists' opt for integrative and/or expressive activities depending on the situation. The latter are chosen to give emphasis to their demands (sometimes after failed negotiations) in the political decision making process.

Chile: members of the *inactive* group are more often male (77%) and under 30 (72%) (see also Silva 2000). They see few economic prospects in the future. They view both elections and land occupation as ineffective. Their level of formal education is high, but political knowledge low (only 28% can name a Latin American statesman). They have a strong interest in self-help (88%). *Voters-only* are more often women (73%). They view payment boycotts as effective; strikes, demonstrations and squatting as ineffective. The government has a relatively high level of legitimation. Thus, they seldom register loss of contact to politicians. Despite this, equality is not perceived as existing. They demonstrate a low level of education and strong political ignorance (Latin American statesman, 4%). This type is more often found in the old slum settlements in Chile.

Party-orientated forms of participation are found amongst older sections of the population (82%) and groups who are discontented with living conditions. The members of this category are interested in politics and view their political activity as positive (political contacts, party membership, election campaign activists and acceptance of political office). They have a low level of education but a relatively high level of political knowledge (MP 64%). This type is more often found in Temuco. *Unconventional activists* are more likely to be discontented with democracy. They view strikes, demonstrations and squatting as very effective. They complain about the loss of contact with politicians. This type is often found in the Esperanza settlement in Santiago, which originated from land occupation. Unconventional activists have a relatively high level of political knowledge (Latin American statesman 56%) and their engagement in neighbourhood organisations is above average (53%). The group of people who engage in *universal participatory forms* are above average age. They have a relatively high level of interest in politics (56%). The social distance to unknown groups is quite large. They view demonstrations and squatting as effective. Their level of political knowledge is high. 60% are members of neighbourhood groups.

Ivory Coast: The *inactive* group has a high proportion of women (58%). Traditionally women play no role in political participation. In Man, a woman's world is mostly limited to the settlement, and sometimes merely to the home. Only the women of the Yacouba local ethnic group play a more active role in communal life. Members of the inactive group complain more often about the lack of equality and have a relatively low level of education. The level of satisfaction with their situation is relatively high (44%). Activism in neighbourhood organisations is relatively rare (8%) and the willingness to engage in self-help activities low (15%). *Voters-only* are characterised by a relatively high level of political lack of interest (78%). All other forms of political participation are basically viewed as ineffective (especially party membership, electoral campaigning, acceptance of political office). There is a relatively low level of willingness to engage in self-help (36%). The voters-only group encompasses a high proportion of foreigners, who otherwise possess few possibilities of active participation. The respective *'chefs'* of the groups, which are organised according to regional or ethnic criteria, represent their interests before the *chef* of the settlement and the local authorities. The wide-spread maxim 'keep quiet to avoid difficulties' leads to very limited engagement within and outside the community.

Party-orientated activists are mostly men (83%). Women participate in public life through the PDCI women's organisations. These organisations are officially open to all women, but apart from electoral campaigning, are of little importance. However, offices and functions within these organisations are only held by Ivorian women. Sometimes, such organisations are comprised solely of members of the Baoulé, the President's ethnic group. Conventionally party-orientated men often occupy functions within the party hierarchy. They are also often property owners and landlords (in Washington and Vridi) and therefore have limited interest in unconventional activity, such as payment boycotts for electricity and water. Their interest in politics is relatively high. They view participation forms such as party membership, electoral campaigning or acceptance of political office as very effective. They often have a relatively high level of education. Engagement in neighbourhood groups (42%) and personal initiative (82%) are both relatively high. *Unconventional activists* are mostly men. They have a relatively high level of education and interest in politics, but they are discontented with the government. The type engaging in universal participatory activities also demonstrates a high level of interest in politics (67%) and is characterised by a high level of discontent with those in power. This group has above-average income.

Kenya: Members of the *inactive* group are predominantely women (80%) and those with low income. The inactive group is generally satisfied with living conditions (54%). They more often view participation in elections, electoral campaigning, acceptance of political office, as well as taking part in demonstrations as ineffective. They demonstrate a low level of interest in politics (80%). Political knowledge is also limited. They are under-represented in self-help groups (16%). The type who only votes and does not engage in any other form of participation views party membership and demonstrations as especially ineffective. They also have limited political knowledge. A more than proportional number of *party-orientated activists* are men (68%). They demonstrate a high level of interest in politics, but a high level of discontent with their personal situation. They view electoral campaigning as effective. This type is often found in the old slum settlements in the medium-sized town of Kisumu (a centre of opposition). The level of political knowledge of party-orientated activists is high (MP 66%, US President 93%). They are highly involved in neighbourhood organisations (24%) and exhibit a high level of willingness to engage in self-help (50%).

The sections of the population which favour *unconventional* forms of participation are discontent with living conditions and their general situation. They see their future perspectives more negatively than other groups, but their interest in politics is higher. This type is also found more often in Kisumu. The level of political knowledge is high (MP 66%, US President 60%). The members of this category are strongly rooted in neighbourhood organisations, but demonstrate a relatively low level of personal initiative (7%) and willingness to engage in self-help. Those engaged in *universal* political activities are characterised by a high level of trust in other ethnic and social groups. They possess a high level of interest in politics and judge demonstrations as having above-average effectiveness. This type is frequently found in the old slum settlement in Kisumu. Universal activists have a high level of political knowledge (MP 87%, US President 81%). This type is rooted relatively strongly in neighbourhood groups.

Voting Behaviour

It is clear from the previous descriptions that voting is one of the urban poor's most frequent forms of political participation. Only in the Ivory Coast is the percentage of those who have taken part in elections (38%) very low. The figure is 80% for Brazil and Chile, and 69% for Kenya. In all the countries studied, competitive national elections were only reintroduced during the late 1980s or early 1990s. This was facilitated by transition to a multi-party system in the African countries, and by more meaningful democratic transitions in Latin America. The following section analyses the voting behaviour of the urban poor. Explanations will focus on political-institutional, social-structural and political-cultural factors. A key question is whether the urban poor demonstrate a voting pattern, typical for this group, which favours parties or candidates from certain political camps.

In order to explain voting behaviour and election results, the influence of the electoral and party systems in each country have to be discussed. Following this, the basic structure of motivation and attitudes which influence voting decisions will be analysed. This also includes clientelism and 'vote-buying'. First of all, the voting behaviour of the urban poor will be described. The conclusions drawn are based on statements regarding the questions, which party was chosen in the last parliamentary election and which party would be chosen in a hypothetical forthcoming election. For this reason, the analysis can only provide a limited perspective on long-term voting behaviour.

Figure 7.2 shows that, at the time of the survey in 1995, the urban poor in the Ivory Coast and Chile mostly voted for parties in the governing coalitions. In contrast, in Kenya and Brazil support for the opposition parties was strong. The high proportion of non-voters in Brazil and Chile is also conspicuous. The group of non-voters consists of those who choose to refrain from voting and those who give an invalid vote. In Brazil and Chile, where participation in elections is legally obligatory, the proportion of invalid votes is higher than the proportion of those who refuse to vote. The distinction between government and opposition voters is of limited significance in the Brazilian case. There, the parties which currently support the government were not ruling parties before the elections, and two important parties only

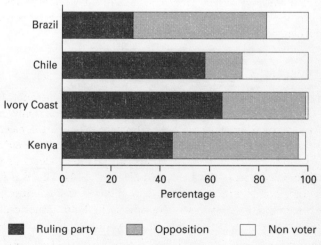

Figure 7.2 Voting behaviour, last party election

joined the governing coalition after the elections. Therefore, for this case, the parties are further placed along a left-right spectrum based on the assessment by Moises (1994). According to this scheme, left-wing parties, led by the PT (Workers Party, Partido dos Trabalhadores) and the PDT (Democratic Workers Party, Partido Democratico Trabalhista) gained 49% of the vote in the parliamentary elections in 1994. These parties do not support President Cardoso or the government he formed. The middle-ground parties, the most important mainstay of the current government, gained 34% of the vote amongst the urban poor. Parties on the right of the political spectrum only play a limited role amongst the favelados.

Apart from the Ivory Coast, the average voting turnout was 60%. In the Ivory Coast, turnout amongst the urban poor was 43%, somewhat higher than the national average (35%). Here, the presidential election was held first, then parliamentary and finally local elections. This led to a successive decline in turnout which was compounded by the relatively low level of importance the local level enjoys in comparison to the national level. In Brazil and Chile, turnout amongst the urban poor was lower than the national average, while in Kenya a somewhat higher turnout can be observed in this section of the population.

In Figure 7.4, the 'next election' question' in Chile demonstrates lasting ties to the governing coalition Concertacion, which would still gain over 50% of the votes in a future election. In the Ivory Coast, the

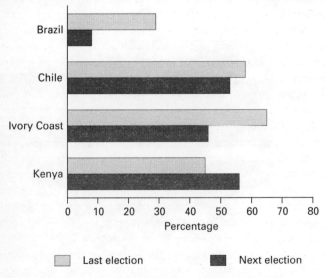

Figure 7.3 Elections–ruling parties in %

governing party, PDCI, gained a high percentage amongst the urban poor. However, this fell to under 50% in future elections. In Brazil, the governing parties only gained 34% of the vote in the last election. The low level of party ties amongst the favelados is demonstrated by the fact that only a mere 8% of those asked would give their support to these parties once more in the next election. Over half of those asked do not know who they will vote for in the next elections, an indication of the lack of a stable voter base in Brazil. This is true for the whole country and is not a phenomenon unique to the urban poor.

In Kenya, the governing KANU party gained 45% of the vote amongst the urban poor in the last elections. At the time of the survey in 1995, 56% of those asked said they would give KANU their vote in the next election. The proportion of those who are undecided is very high in Brazil, Chile and the Ivory Coast. In the case of the Ivory Coast, it should be noted that a large portion of immigrant workers had their right to vote repealed before the elections in 1995. In addition, this section of the population has a deep-seated mistrust of revealing party preferences in a survey. By observing the election results at the settlement level, certain areas could be identified as strongholds for the governing or opposition parties.

In *Brazil*, opposition parties gain the majority in all the settlements, the Favela Vidigal (the older settlement in Rio) in particular is an opposition stronghold. While ties to the governing parties are very weak, opposition parties enjoy stable support in all the settlements. In Rio de Janeiro, left-wing parties have the greatest amount of support (approx. 50%). The proportion of support for the PDT and its 'caudillo' Brizola is twice as strong as that of the PT and the workers' leader, Lula. In Aracaju, left-wing parties gain 30%, while middle-ground parties receive approx. 43% of the vote. The middle-ground parties, PSDB and PMDB, support President Cardoso and the government. In *Chile*, support for the governing coalition is only relatively low (44%) in Villa Galvarino (Santiago, old settlement). Here, the proportion of non-voters and those who are undecided whom to vote for in the next elections is especially high. Even though the proportion of votes for the government in a future election generally declines somewhat, the urban poor in Chile seem to demonstrate a lasting preference for the parties of the Concertacion. Furthermore, there are no discernible strongholds for government or opposition parties amongst the settlements studied.

In the *Ivory Coast*, Man seems to be a stronghold for the PDCI. In the first multi-party (local) elections, which were held on 1 May, 1990, the governing party gained over 70% of the vote. This popularity declines to about 50% in answer to the question concerning the next election. In Abidjan, opposition parties gain an impressive 44% support amongst the urban poor. In *Kenya*, the settlement Nyalenda (a newer settlement in Kisumu) is a bastion of the opposition because in answer to the question concerning future elections, 61% would still give their vote to the opposition party FORD-Kenya. Moreover, in Kenya, there is a high level of stability in relation to voter preferences and the opposition parties remain popular in their respective strongholds.

Who Votes for the Government and Who for the Opposition?

In Kenya and the Ivory Coast more women than men vote for the government parties, whereas gender differences in Chile and Brazil are insignificant. In Kenya, and much more so in the Ivory Coast, voters who are older than 50 tend to support the respective governing parties. In the Ivory Coast, there is a definite tendency for those under 30 to vote for the opposition. This trend can also be observed in Brazil, whereas in Chile age does not play a significant role in voter preferences. In the Ivory Coast and in Brazil, those with a higher educational level are more likely to vote for the opposition, but this trend is much stronger in Brazil. Here those amongst the urban poor with a higher level of education more often vote for left-wing parties and make up only a small proportion of non-voters. As regards employment, a higher than average percentage of those employed in the informal sector in the Ivory Coast vote for the governing party. In Brazil, workers from the formal sector are more likely to vote for left-wing opposition parties. In Kenya, and to a lesser extent in the Ivory Coast, political-cultural milieus are clearly defined according to ethnicity and religion (for this concept, see also Lepsius 1996). In Nyalenda, the majority of the Luo vote for FORD-Kenya, the party of the opposition leader Oginga Odinga, who died in 1994. The majority of the Luo are Christian. Christians, especially those of the Catholic faith, make up a large proportion of opposition voters, whereas followers of Islam mostly vote for the governing KANU party. Opposition parties can be more strongly identified with specific ethnic groups, whereas support for the governing party has a wider ethnic base, although the most important ethnic group which forms the mainstay of KANU supporters, the 'Kalenjin', were hardly present in the settlements we studied. In both the older settlements, Majengo (Nairobi) and Kaloleni (Kisumu), which have large Muslim populations, the proportion of votes for KANU was also high.

In the Ivory Coast, the political-cultural milieus are structured differently. Here, there is a clear divide between Ivorians and immigrant workers of different ethnicity from neighbouring countries. Participation amongst immigrant workers is very low, partly as a result of the loss of their right to vote. This is especially true for Ghanaians. Immigrants from Burkina Faso (Burkinabés) exhibit a somewhat higher level of voter participation, although this does not reach the level of Ivorians'. Ivorians and Burkinabés demonstrate a clear preference for the governing party, whereas other African immigrant workers split their votes almost equally between the governing and the opposition parties.

The following section first deals with structural factors which can have a decisive effect on election results. With regard to subjective and situational factors, we will then try to reveal the most important reasons for individual voting choices. However, it is clear that in the African countries a strong structural component, e.g. clientelistic relationships, serves to channel voter behaviour in a particular direction and therefore limits the scope for individual choice.

First of all, the party and electoral systems in the individual countries must be taken into account. The different organisation of electoral and party systems in the four countries influences election results in a particular manner, but has no direct influence on motivations concerning voting behaviour. Changes, or manipulation, of electoral constituencies and limitation, or extension, of voting rights can have a decisive effect on vote distribution. *Brazil's* system of proportional representation, the highly volatile party system and frequent changes of party allegiances amongst parliamentary representatives, can hardly channel election results in a particular direction. The party system is not ideologically defined and is characterised by the populist practices of individual politicians, who distribute public goods and promise services according to personal interests and tactical electoral considerations. Election results are predictable in so far as the strength of individual 'caudillos' in certain electoral constituencies is known. There is intra-party -due to open lists – as well as inter-party competition (see Mainwaring 1995: 395). Distortion of representation occurs via the preferential treatment of the least populous areas of the north and north eastern federal states because considerably fewer votes are required for a parliamentary seat in these areas.

In *Chile*, the introduction of the bi-nominal majority system (two elected representatives per constituency) by the military dictatorship has polarised the party system – the government Concertacion on the one hand, and the right-wing pro-Pinochet parties on the other. The bi-nominal electoral system favours the second-strongest party in a constituency, which in the vast majority of cases is equivalent to the right-wing pro-Pinochet opposition. In a system similar to that in Brazil, the parties present open lists in the constituencies, although right-wing parties often include 'independent' candidates in their lists. In this way, they take account of the increasing political disillusionment, and 'anti-party sentiments' in Chile. In contrast to Brazil, the personalised element is almost completely absent at the national level. This fact, combined with the isolation of the party system from influences from other social sections and professionalism in the political arena, has contributed to a broad and far-reaching distancing from parties amongst the urban poor in Chile. At the same time, an increasing techno-cratisation of politics helped defend against populist influences and achieve the goals of better governance and macro-economic stability.

The party systems in the *Ivory Coast* and *Kenya* are relatively immobile because, despite formal transition to a multi-party system, the former state parties have retained their dominant role. This is because measures to open up the political system were not based on democratic convictions but rather viewed as a means of stabilising the regime and legitimising the respective state parties. Those in power continue to influence election results via arbitrary changes in the electoral procedures. 'Gerrymander-ing', the creation of constituencies shaped according to one's needs, in these cases to favour rural over urban groups, is part of the standard repertoire of the ruling parties. In the Ivory Coast, one can observe the favouring of certain groups of immigrant workers (e.g. Burkinabés) because, despite the repeal of voting rights for foreign employees since 1994, electoral cards are still handed out to them by the political author-ities. The Burkinabés are loyal to the PDCI.

Factors of a social structural and political cultural nature can lead to long-term voter preferences (sometimes solid party ties) and maintain invariant voter decisions over a long period of time. In the four countries, variables such as socio-economic status, religion, ethnicity, regional origin, period of residence in a town, educational level, interest in politics and satisfaction with the political system or with those in power, also affect voting behaviour. However, social structural variables by themselves do not directly affect people's actions. They only affect behaviour when combined with a specific cultural and social system, in the framework of which certain behavioural patterns are deemed accept-able while others carry sanctions. Within this framework, individuals have more or less independent possibilities of action, although these are dependent on personal perceptions and individual value structures. Specific social structural factors are closely related to voting behaviour in the two African countries. There, regional origin and/or ethnicity remain decisive.

The following explanation aims to answer the question, whether a 'normal vote', which is based on a stable individual bond to a certain party over a longer period of time, can be observed amongst the urban poor. In *Brazil*, only a few long-term trends exist which explain the choice of a particular party. Left-wing voters belong to those groups in the favelas with a higher level of education. Amongst those questioned, they are less religious than average and have lived for a longer period in the town. Furthermore, they are more interested in politics and obtain political information more often from the newspapers. The longer period of residency of left-wing voters in a town points to better adaptation and integration of this group into urban living conditions. In contrast, right-wing voters are characterised by a stronger relationship to the countryside and a higher proportion of women. The level of education, interest in politics and political knowledge of this group are relatively low. In our study, most right-wing voters live in Aracaju, where 'susceptibility' to populist promises and practices is especially high. Voters for middle-ground parties express a strong interest in political news. In contrast to left-wing voters, this is not drawn from newspapers, but rather from television. Television in Brazil is an important factor which influences voting behaviour. During the election campaign in 1990, the influence of the largest television corporation in Brazil and Latin America, TV Globo, worked positively for the winning candidate, Collor.

In *Chile*, middle-ground and left-wing parties have moved closer to one another and are joined in the governing coalition, Concertacion de Partidos por la Democracia. Those who vote for the Concertacion are more content with the return of democracy in 1990 and have more trust in the government than opposition voters. Satisfaction with democracy and government policies as well as a positive evaluation of the country's political future all contribute to voting for the governing parties. We found a relatively stable majority for the Concertacion amongst the urban poor because when asked about a future election more than half would give their vote to the governing coalition. This stability is based on the general optimism which has reached even this group. The vote for the opposition, which includes both the right wing (parties which are more or less close to the former military regime), as well as the left-wing extra-parliamentary spectrum (first and foremost the Communist Party), is dependent on other factors. In this case, the evaluation of effectiveness of party membership correlates strongly with the vote for an opposition party. Opposition voters also view demonstrations as an effective means of asserting their interests. In contrast to Concertacion voters, they see no positive political developments in the future. Both the left- and right-wing oppositions are well organised and engage in selective social work in the poblaciones. Left-wing opposition voters prefer unconventional forms of participation to assert their demands, while the majority of right-wing opposition voters prefer to use party politics (via contacts to political and business figures who occupy higher positions within the hierarchy) to achieve their goals. The group of non-voters manifests a strong distrust of government and has limited political knowledge.

As previously mentioned, loyalties to ethnic groups and their political leaders are primarily responsible for the stability of voter behaviour in the African cases. Ethnicity and regional origin exert a great deal of pressure on an individual to behave according to these primordial bonds. The various other influences which occur in the urban environment are less significant. In *Kenya's* capital city, Nairobi, where the bonds to rural values and lifestyles are less apparent than in the medium-sized town of Kisumu, ethnicity and religion still mould voting behaviour. Since independence, KANU has been constantly in government. Its voters speak positively about the political regime, the political author-ities and the government. They are of the opinion that the President (Moi) does not abuse or possess too much power. In addition, they have more political contacts than opposition voters and their interest in practising self-help is low. The KANU voters' numerous personal politi-cal contacts are a further indication of the clientelistic relationship between them and the political authorities. Opposition party voters have no trust in the government, but do trust the political authorities. In this case, the latter are local authorities at the town level or individual representatives. Their interest in politics is as high as the incidence of the statement that President Moi has too much power. Both party membership and demonstrations are viewed positively. In contrast to voters for the governing party, opposition voters are more willing to engage in self-help activities. However, they only possess limited political contacts.

In the *Ivory Coast*, the higher proportion of votes for opposition parties in Abidjan can be explained by the fact that the primordial bonds of numerous ethnic and immigrant groups have been partly broken down, and that the clientelistic system does not function as effectively here as in Man. PDCI voters have a great deal of trust in the government and in the political authorities. In contrast, opposition voters have little trust in the government and express the opinion that abuse of power is rife. They are usually under 30 and view party membership as an effective means to assert their interests.

Party programmes such as those common in western Europe can only be found in a rudimentary form in some of the countries. Parties which are based on specific ideologies include the PT in Brazil and the majority of Chilean parties, apart from the pro-Pinochet party, UDI, and the populist UCCP, which was founded in 1990. However, knowledge of these programmes, let alone an identification with the major political aims of these parties, is lacking amongst the urban poor. Moreover, in Chile nowadays a wide-spread lack of political interest and a negative evaluation of parties can be found. Political parties in Africa, and partly in Brazil, have party programmes, but these do not have much meaning for a party's definition nor do they affect voting behaviour. They are 'catch-all' parties, which usually serve as political machines for individual candidates. In contrast to Chilean parties and the PT, which see themselves as class parties and try to form lasting links with certain strata of the population, the other parties represent broad social groupings, which are usually structured around a certain regional leader.

The fight for survival, which the urban poor must master each day, expresses itself mostly as an increase in pragmatism. They give their vote to those candidates who, according to their resources, promise the best results for the group or whole settlement. This output orientation is partly a consequence of poverty and partly expresses the orientation towards personalities. Right-wing and populist 'catch-all' parties benefit most often from this tendency. The relationship between orientation towards personalities and expectations of certain outputs to specific voting behaviour does not always result in a 'floating vote'. In the case of the dominant governing party in Kenya and the Ivory Coast, voters do not normally change party allegiance if they are discontented; rather they may use the possibility of intra-party competition to choose a different candidate from the same party.

The *Brazilian* case demonstrates that the pragmatic orientation and reference to personalities result in 'floating votes'. Here, short-term factors play a much more important role in determining voter behaviour than in the other countries. Voters react strongly to the offers made by different candidates through their representatives, cabos eleitorias, at the local level. Programmatic differences are of limited importance. Even in the election of a PT candidate, promised material improvements can play a decisive influence. In *Chile,* a certain output orientation, similar to that in Brazil, can also be found amongst the poorest groups. This is used first and foremost by right-wing parties, who often engage in advertising campaigns without naming the party. Although clearly defined party links with specific political cultural milieus were the norm before 1973, these largely disappeared during the military regime. The previously mentioned disillusionment with politicians and political parties can be traced to the fact that the urban poor cannot exert any influence on the decisions of the local and national government using party political channels (any more). The disappearance of the clientelistic element, which dominates in the other three countries, has led to an apolitical reaction (see Barreto 1996). Paradoxically, it is the initiators of the modernisation process, the representatives of the dictatorship who now sit in parliament, who have filled this vacuum and are trying to build personalised political relationships. The majority of the urban poor today vote for moderate left-wing and middle-ground parties, i.e. the current governing parties, because they have had direct experience of the responsiveness of the system through numerous social projects and state programmes. In this way, the Chilean state has partly filled the 'clientele vacuum' with welfare measures. However, these measures are usually awarded according to general technocratic criteria and therefore do not take into account the local organised interest groups such as the juntas de vecinos anymore. Those groups which are excluded from social policies are increasingly disillusioned with politics. Following the failure of the extreme left to mobilise the masses and topple the dictatorship, the pobladores prefer the most successful transition party, the Christian Democrats, which has provided two presidents since 1990. The Christian Democratic Party is the largest political grouping within the Concertacion and follows a moderate political course while continuing the economic policies of the 'ancien regime'.

Certain events and political topics, which gain relevance before the elections, can function as intervening variables and persuade a previously stable voter base to change voting behaviour in the short term. In the Ivory Coast, the elections in 1990 were the first multi-party elections and were dominated by opposition demands for more democracy. In Abidjan, the opposition parties (mainly the FPI) gained a high proportion of the votes amongst the urban poor, even though this group had been the main bastion of support for single-party rule before. The governing party's losses in Abidjan can be traced to the general feeling that the system was breaking up, which was common at this time. The decisive factor for this development was the decision of the FPI leader, Gbagbo, to become a candidate in the presidential election, in explicit competition to the founding state president, Houphouët-Boigny. The economic crisis also contributed to bringing many 'loyal' PDCI voters onto the side of the opposition.

In the *Kenyan* case, the parliamentary elections in 1992 were also the first multi-party elections and the country experienced a series of protests against the old regime under Moi. The urban poor were an important part of the protest movement and this was converted into a high proportion of votes for the opposition parties. In *Chile*, there were no prominent political events which had a short-term influence over voter behaviour in one way or another. This is most certainly connected to the 'quiet' and conflict-free transition. In *Brazil*, the introduction of the Real as the new currency in July 1994 and the following success in the fight against inflation affected voter behaviour. The man responsible for introducing the new currency, the former Finance Minister, Cardoso, stood as presidential candidate against the leader of the PT, Luis Inacio ('Lula') and gained a clear victory.

Concluding Remarks

The special situation of the urban poor hinders their political participation. They use their resources first and foremost in the economic and social sphere. There is relatively little time for politics within their prevailing risk-minimising strategies. In addition to the general social environment, the specific country context must be taken into account. In Kenya and the Ivory Coast, clientele-orientated forms of participation, which employ political contacts and establish intensive 'exchange' relationships, are dominant. Important goals of self-help groups can be realised in this way but this also furthers the development of relations of dependency, which do not allow the possibility of an effective control of power 'from below'. Therefore, conventional forms of participation are more prevalent in Kenya and the Ivory Coast. In Chile and in Rio de Janeiro, participatory forms which are integrated into the existing institutional structures dominate. However, in Brazil both conventional as well as unconventional channels are used, although the emphasis is on the conventional form. In Chile, political activists more often engage in unconventional forms (squatting, demonstrations).

Organised self-help activities orientated towards civil society offer an alternative field of action which, under certain conditions, can also take on a political dimension. It is conspicuous that certain sections of the population in Brazil and the Ivory Coast are neither active in self-help organisations, nor do they make use of other forms of political participation. In this group, isolated, individual self-help, that is engagement in the personal social and economic sphere, seems to dominate.

After the wave of democratisation, political inclusion of the population has remained mostly limited to voting. Election results in the respective countries are also influenced by the electoral systems and the various manipulative practices of those in power. Short-term manipulations were mainly observed in Kenya and the Ivory Coast because here social structural specifics (primordial bonds such as ethnicity) make such manipulation easier. Political legitimation and evaluation of effectiveness are to a large degree dependent on the political, institutional structure. Political inclusion of the urban poor is, therefore, differentiated. Despite the more positive development of democracy in Latin America in comparison to the African countries, even in Latin America, new opportunities for participation of the urban poor only allow limited integration into the political and economic system. Therefore, the high level of willingness to engage in self-help ascertained in Latin America must be further supplemented by effective possibilities for exerting political influence.

Notes

1. 'Cabo' means leader. 'Cabo eleitoral' is a person who gives guidance during an election and represents a particular opinion, namely that of his candidate (see Pfeiffer 1987: 106).

2. Students at institutes of higher education can sometimes gain an attestation of maturity, which allows inclusion in the electoral register even though they are below the required age.

3. In the following, only those variables which have a significant correlation to participation types will be reported.

CHAPTER 8

Multi-Level Analyses

Dirk Berg-Schlosser

§ THE previous chapters have provided a detailed analysis of the most important aspects of our study: situation in life, forms of interest organisation, central areas of political culture and concrete forms of participation, in relation to a few main influential factors. In this chapter, the most important results will be examined in the wider context of the different levels of our study, in order to define the range of the respective results and certain to discern more easily aspects which lend themselves to generalisation. In accordance with the multi-layered design of our analysis, we begin at the level of the individual settlements, then describe town-specific similarities, followed by looking at the influence of the respective age of a settlement, before finally turning to country-specific aspects. Finally, where applicable certain continental commonalities are discussed.

Our results, basically, are only valid for the specific settlements studied and cannot claim to be representative for other settlements, towns or countries. But because our original choice of cases has been made according to a 'most different systems design', this strong contrasting at least delimits the possible range of our findings at each level. In this way our multi-level analysis can provide important indications of the relative importance of each respective level as an independent factor of influence (possibilities and problems of such a 'multi-level design' are described by Przeworski/Teune, 1970, p. 47 ff.). In this sense, it represents an important and, to date in this form, unique base for complementary and continuing studies at different levels. Therefore it has a varying, but complementary value for town, country or regional experts, and respective organisations, in relation to the concrete living conditions, aspects of infrastructure, ties to local political organisations and institutions, and the democratic potential of the urban poor in these countries. In this way, both the horizontal (inter-sectoral and interdisciplinary), and vertical (according to the different levels) links of our study can be made clear.

We begin, as generally in our research, with a view 'from below', but not at the 'micro' level of those individuals questioned, but at that of the respective settlements. The settlements chosen which in nearly all cases the project leaders were able to visit and compare, demonstrate a high degree of phenotypical similarity. They are all in marginal positions either at the periphery of the respective town, or in topographically problematic zones, such as steep slopes or river banks which are threatened with flooding. Their external appearance is considerably different from the established business centres and 'better' residential areas. With the exception of the settlements which arose as a result of planned land occupation in South America, the roads or paths networks are often very irregular and confusing. Infrastructure, as far as it exists, is very rudimentary and often 'improvised' in one way or another. The differences between the Latin American and African settlements, where hardly any households have their own drinking water or access to electricity, are, however, considerable (see chapter 3).

Living Conditions and Social Relationships

The concrete living conditions in the respective settlements are determined accordingly. Those questioned generally name their individual poverty as the greatest personal problem (see chapter 4). In this respect, the initial situation is similar. When naming the greatest problem of the settlement, the picture becomes more differentiated. Even though physical infrastructure clearly takes first place everywhere, in the older settlements in the Brazilian and Chilean metropolises, and in the medium-sized Brazilian town these problems are much less acute. In contrast, problems of higher criminality, especially in the old settlement in the Chilean metropolis, are more frequent and in the Brazilian settlements are combined with a lack of social infrastructure (e.g. kindergartens, health centres etc.).

With respect to satisfaction with their general situation in life and future economic perspectives (see chapter 4), such specific settlement, or town aspects are less important. Brazil is characterised by a majority who are generally content with life, in contrast to the objectively and subjectively worse situation in Kenya and in particular in the Ivory Coast. Chile occupies midfield. Optimism for the future is especially prevalent in the Ivory Coast, followed by Chile, while in Kenya expectations are clearly lower. Brazil occupies the middle ground here.

Social trust in Brazil and Chile is generally lower. Trustworthy people

Table 8.1 Social distance (%)

	Brazil				Chile				Ivory Coast				Kenya			
	Metropolis		Town		Metropolis		Town		Metropolis		Town		Metropolis		Town	
	new	old	new	old	new	old	new	old	new	old	new	old	new	old	new	old
Family members	57	45	43	57	56	68	56	45	24	29	23	39	53	43	30	32
Friends	33	31	45	38	21	23	33	42	62	53	58	42	38	35	54	41
Neighbours	6	5	12	6	8	3	2	7	4	5	5	9	3	2	4	10
People of the same ethnic group	2	7	–	–	3	–	–	4	9	2	12	6	6	2	12	16
Other	2	12	–	–	12	5	10	1	2	11	3	3	–	–	–	2

Source: Project Political Participation

here are mostly limited to immediate family members. In the African cases, personal friendships are added to these. In the medium-sized African towns, membership of the same ethnic group also plays a greater role (see Table 8.1). Such differences are also reflected in the question concerning social solidarity. In both African cases, a much stronger feeling of community in the settlement is articulated, although this is considerably lower in the non-ethnically homogeneous settlement in the medium-sized Kenyan town than in the metropolis. In contrast, in the Ivory Coast, harmony in the medium-sized town is greater. In the old settlement in the Chilean metropolis, strong distrust predominates. The new settlement in the metropolis demonstrates greater solidarity due to the communal land occupation and continued existence of organisational structures (see next section). In the medium-sized Chilean town, social solidarity is somewhat greater, but in no way comes close to the African levels. Similarly in Brazil, the medium-sized town generally demonstrates higher levels than the metropolis, especially in the new settlement. However, it remains considerably below the African settlements.

Interest Organisation

A central element of our research concerns the forms of social and political organisation in the settlements studied, and therefore the potential for possible self-help or other activities. The concrete historical conditions and specific influential factors in the individual settlements are discussed in greater detail in Chapter 5. Here, we are once more interested in multi-level comparisons and the possible range of the discernible patterns.

The general level of organisation can be classed as relatively high, even though on average only somewhat less than half of all those questioned are active members of an organisation. But specific town and country differences come quickly to the fore with regard to the particular type of organisation (see Table 8.2). In Kenya, economically oriented forms of organisation dominate (e.g. self-help cooperatives in the informal sector), followed by religious groupings, which are very varied in this country. In the Ivory Coast, organisations based on ethnic criteria prevail, especially in the metropolis, where they partly unite groups of (foreign) immigrants. In addition, there is a relatively high level of local social and political organisation, which, especially in the medium-sized town of Man, can be traced to the dominant position of the governing party and its local dignitaries. In Chile, neighbourhood organisations, which are also active in a general political sense, clearly

Table 8.2 Membership in organisations (%)

	Brazil				Chile				Ivory Coast				Kenya			
	Metropolis		Town		Metropolis		Town		Metropolis		Town		Metropolis		Town	
	new	old	new	old	new	old	new	old	new	old	new	old	new	old	new	old
Religious organisations	5	2	5	17	3	8	4	4	4	–	17	6	7	2	7	9
Ethnic organisations	–	–	–	–	–	–	–	–	39	39	28	21	–	–	1	2
Economic organisations	–	–	–	–	–	–	–	–	–	–	–	–	24	23	29	36
Local political organisations	31	22	16	2	38	7	55	43	14	10	39	32	–	–	–	–
Local social organisations	1	–	–	1	16	11	5	10	25	36	11	27	1	4	–	–
Trade unions	1	2	–	3	–	–	–	3	18	7	6	15	2	2	4	3
None	61	72	78	76	44	75	36	40	–	10	–	–	65	68	59	49

Source: Project Political Participation

dominate ('juntas de vecinos'). In this country, these look back on a long tradition, which could not be effectively broken, even by the military regime. However, the desolate situation in the old settlement in the metropolis, which is characterised by great heterogeneity and strong fluctuation, is very different from the new settlement, which owes its foundation and continued existence to these very organisations (see Sperberg 2000). Brazil also has a strong tradition of active neighbourhood organisations ('associacoes de moradores'), especially in the metropolis. However, social activities here are more limited to samba and carnival groups. In the old settlement in the medium-sized town, religious groups, some of them evangelical, are also often present (see Happe 2000).

Apart from personal organisation membership, similar patterns can also be discerned concerning the most important organisations in the settlement (see Table 8.3). In Kenya, local social and religious organisations are most important. In the Ivory Coast, local ethnic and social groupings once more dominate. In Chile, neighbourhood organisations are dominant, with the clear exception of the old settlement in Santiago, where general social activities predominate. In Brazil, the loss of influence of the neighbourhood organisations is noticeable. The increasingly strong local religious groups stand in contrast to this, more so in the medium-sized town than in the metropolis.

When we asked about possible personal initiatives to solve problems in the neighbourhood, just over half stated that they could not contribute anything (see Table 8.4). Specific town and country differences can again be observed. In the Ivory Coast and Kenya, especially in the medium-sized town of Kisumu, these values are clearly above average. In contrast, in Chile, individual possibilities of action are generally evaluated much more highly. In this regard, the newly founded settlement in Santiago, which is based on successful communal land occupation, is again conspicuous. In Brazil, the difference between the (clearly more active) metropolis and the (highly passive) medium-sized town of Aracaju in the more traditional north east of the country is also remarkable.

Approximately one third of those questioned primarily view the respective political authorities as one of the major possibilities for solving local problems. This is stronger in the old settlements in Kenya and in the medium-sized towns in the Ivory Coast, Chile and Brazil. Nearly one third also make their own concrete suggestions. Here it is once again conspicuous that in Chile and Brazil possible collective action is given relatively high importance, especially in the metropolis.

Table 8.3 Most important organisation in the settlement (%)

	Brazil				Chile				Ivory Coast				Kenya			
	Metropolis		Town		Metropolis		Town		Metropolis		Town		Metropolis		Town	
	new	old	new	old	new	old	new	old	new	old	new	old	new	old	new	old
Religious organisations	39	33	49	63	2	9	10	17	6	–	3	1	19	19	18	39
Ethnic organisations	–	8	–	–	2	2	–	1	36	36	32	29	8	5	3	6
Economic organisations	–	–	–	–	4	–	2	1	2	–	–	–	5	8	3	13
Local political organisations	21	17	36	20	51	20	70	59	24	14	14	38	6	8	1	1
Local social organisations	4	13	6	13	34	48	11	16	31	36	11	26	48	34	73	37
Political parties	1	6	–	–	–	–	–	–	–	6	–	–	–	–	–	–

Source: Project Political Participation

Political Culture

In addition to possible self-help activities and forms of interest organisation, this study places special emphasis on the 'political culture' of the urban poor, that is the subjective attitudes and values with regard to the political system and its incumbents in each country (see chap. 6). First of all, this is a question of general political interest. This lies at roughly 40% amongst all those questioned and, even in comparison to states of the First World (see e.g. Barnes/Kaase 1979), is quite high and contradicts prevailing clichés of widespread political apathy in such settlements. This is true in a similar form for both continents, although with country-specific differences. In the Ivory Coast, political interest is generally lower, which can mostly be explained by the high proportion of immigrants from neighbouring countries, which was also reflected in our survey. At first glance, the generally low level of political interest in Chile, the country with the longest democratic traditions, is surprising. In this case, following the phase of the renewed transition to democracy, a deep disillusionment with politics and political parties and a strong tendency towards personal, predominantly economic interests and activities, can be observed in nearly all strata (see Sperberg 2000). In Brazil, the great discrepancy between the active metropolis and the passive medium-sized town is again conspicuous.

Concrete political information is differentiated accordingly. The name of the respective head of state and that of the respective mayor is known by more than half of all those questioned. The current governing party can only be named by a very small number in Brazil. This points to the relatively low importance of political parties and strong fluctuations in the party system there. Somewhat more surprising for outside observers is perhaps the result that in the African countries, despite a generally lower level of formal education and higher levels of absolute poverty, information about external political facts and events, which manifests itself in knowledge about foreign statesmen, is much higher than in the Latin American countries. Similarly surprising is the fact that nearly 60% of those questioned in Kenya, and 80% in the Ivory Coast, in both cases an even higher percentage in the medium-sized town, know the name of their parliamentary representative. Such values are much lower in Chile (24%) and Brazil (12%), especially in the respective metropolis. Such results contradict the simple expectations of 'modernisation theory' and point to the greater importance of informal communication in the African countries, such as the well-known 'radio trottoir' or the daily exchange of information in the minibusses ('matatus') in Kenya.

The political-cultural bases of democracy and the satisfaction with the new regimes show great discrepancies, despite renewed formal democratic structures in all the countries (see Table 8.4). In Kenya, satisfaction with the current 'democracy', in so far as it actually deserves this designation, is at its lowest. This is expressed in particular in the medium-sized town of Kisumu, a bastion of the opposition party FORD-Kenya. In contrast, at the time of the survey in the Ivory Coast, a general legitimacy of the regime could be observed. In Brazil, satisfaction with democracy was at its highest, but there is once more a strong contrast between the metropolis, Rio de Janeiro, and the traditional, poorer north-east of the country. In Chile, the generally very low level is again astonishing. In addition to a general disillusionment with politics, this is mainly explained by higher expectations in the face of continuing important inadequacies of the new regime, such as the military's remaining political influence.

A general support for democracy is also manifested in some important basic values. The right of freedom of speech is supported by nearly all those questioned, with slightly lower values for the African cases. Equal opportunity in politics is also generally approved of. However, in this respect, Kenya and in particular the Ivory Coast, with their more hierarchic, ethnic traditions, demonstrate considerably lower values. The limitation of basic rights as a result of possible emergency measures is viewed as justified by almost half of all those questioned. The strong rejection of this item in Chile, as the 'most burned children' in the recent past, is conspicuous.

Such basic values of democracy and satisfaction with the regime have to be distinguished from contentment with the current incumbents. Despite a number of different questions in this regard, our results come to basically the same conclusions as before. Responses were even more outspoken when we asked directly about the possible abuses of power by the respective holders of office. In all countries there was a high level of affirmation (more than 80%). Only in the Ivory Coast was

Table 8.4 Satisfaction with democracy (%)

| | Brazil | | Chile | | Ivory Coast | | Kenya | |
	M	T	M	T	M	T	M	T
Satisfied	70	46	32	30	61	51	35	25

M=Metropolis; T=Town
Source: Project Political Participation

this percentage somewhat lower at 60%. On the one hand, this is an expression of a certain political cynicism on the part of those questioned, on the other, given the concrete conditions in many states, also of political realism. This was aptly described by graffiti in one settlement: 'The clown has changed, the circus remains the same'.

The question whether the powers of the respective state president are too great, just right, or too few, gave a more differentiated picture. In Kenya, especially in the opposition-orientated Kisumu, this was clearly answered in the positive, which also correlates with the more general evaluation of the Moi regime as authoritarian. In contrast, in Chile, a clear majority viewed the competencies of the president as too limited. This is without doubt a reflection of the continued influence of the former holders of power, the military and its supreme commander Pinochet. In the Ivory Coast and Brazil, evaluations are more or less evenly distributed, although in Rio de Janeiro, the competencies of President Cardoso, e.g. towards influential large estate owners in the north east and also towards the military, are more often viewed as too limited.

In answer to the open question concerning concrete points of criticism about the conditions in the country, deficits in politics clearly occupied first place in Kenya and Brazil. In Chile it was poverty and general social inequality. This was also strongly criticised in Brazil. The values for the Ivory Coast are once more generally somewhat lower. Here, economic aspects are more strongly criticised. Criminality was given special importance in the Brazilian metropolis.

The question whether certain influential groups exert too much influence on government was answered in the affirmative by more than two thirds in Kenya and the Ivory Coast, and by 60% in Brazil. Only in Chile did a clear majority deny this. This points to the different, but still strongly clientelistic structures in the first three countries. This is also reflected in the question whether one would look for political help from friends or influential people. In both Kenya and the Ivory Coast, one third viewed this as very sensible. In contrast, the great majority in Chile did not view this as very promising. In Brazil, the values were somewhere in between.

Strong criticism of the economic system was present in all cases. The vast majority of those questioned were of the opinion that enterprises make too much profit and wages are unjust. The spectrum ranged from over 80% in Kenya, and up to 99% (!) in Chile. In the respective metropolis, the values were somewhat higher than in the medium-sized towns. Responses concerning the general equality of opportunity in the social sphere and chances of improvement for their children were differentiated (see Table 8.5). In Kenya, the majority (55%) was of the opinion that such chances of improvement did indeed exist, in contrast to 45% in the Ivory Coast, 42% in Chile, and only 30% in Brazil. The values were generally somewhat higher in the metropolis than in the medium-sized towns.

The question about equal opportunity also had gender-specific aspects. An attempt was made to discern these using four questions with different levels of concretisation. In answer to the question, whether women naturally have fewer rights than men, a clear majority in the Ivory Coast (69%) and Kenya (57%) answered affirmatively. In Brazil, the percentage was still 33%, in Chile only 23%. Agreement in the African metropolis was even higher than in the medium-sized towns. In Latin America this was the other way round. A more differentiated question about political rights for women, however, produced a clear majority for political equality. The range of variation lay between 60% in Kenya and 80% in the Latin American states. Finally, in answer to the question whether they could imagine a woman as mayor of their town, 75% in Kenya, 83% in the Ivory Coast, and 90% in Chile and Brazil respectively answered positively. However, only 62% in Kenya and the Ivory Coast, 76% in Chile, and 80% in Brazil could imagine a woman as president of the country.

When we asked whether there was social harmony in the country, the highest rate of agreement was in the metropolis in the Ivory Coast (more than two thirds). In Kenya, more than half also agreed, although this was somewhat lower in the medium-sized town. In both countries, this question basically relates to ethnic co-existence, which includes immigrants in the Ivory Coast. In Brazil and Chile on the other hand, there was clear rejection (more than 60%). This is related to the much-berated socio-economic inequalities in both countries, and the strong political polarisation with respect to attitudes towards the former military regime in Chile.

In contrast, the question concerning national pride was most clearly answered in Chile, an indication of a generally strong sense of national identity. There, nearly 60% mentioned the country, compatriots or national symbols as objects of pride, followed by 42% in Brazil. In Kenya and the Ivory Coast, the (relative) political stability (each approximately one third), and economic development (12%) occupied first place.

Finally, the political future is viewed with clear optimism in the Ivory Coast (approx. 80%), while the number of sceptics in Kenya (43%) is by far the highest. In Chile, the vast majority assumes the situation will remain the same (43%), or improve (40%). In Brazil, optimism

Table 8.5 Equal chance (%)

	Brazil				Chile				Ivory Coast				Kenya			
	Metropolis		Town		Metropolis		Town		Metropolis		Town		Metropolis		Town	
	new	old	new	old	new	old	new	old	new	old	new	old	new	old	new	old
Equal chance existing, agree	32	37	26	25	30	56	42	39	44	41	62	33	56	40	65	56

Source: Project Political Participation

Table 8.6 Which party did you vote for at the last election? (%)

	Brazil				Chile				Ivory Coast				Kenya			
	Metropolis		Town		Metropolis		Town		Metropolis		Town		Metropolis		Town	
	new	old	new	old	new	old	new	old	new	old	new	old	new	old	new	old
Ruling party	33	20	45	41	65	44	63	60	57	55	76	70	42	61	21	59
Other party	50	63	44	36	12	18	10	19	43	45	24	26	56	30	76	41
Not voted	17	17	11	23	23	38	27	22	–	–	–	4	2	9	3	–

Source: Project Political Participation

(39%) and scepticism (35%) are basically balanced, although the latter is stronger in the medium-sized town (47%).

Political Participation

Against this general political-cultural background we looked at the concrete forms of political participation and party preferences (see chapter 7). These also demonstrate certain 'level'-specific differences. Electoral participation was generally judged as effective (more than 75% of all those questioned). Country-specific differences were relatively few in this respect. In the Kenyan and Ivorian metropolis, this value was somewhat lower than in the medium-sized towns, which confirms stronger integration into national politics of the non-metropolitan and rural regions. In Chile, there are hardly any differences in this respect, while in Brazil this relationship is converse. The relative 'lagging behind', and social and political distance of the north-east in comparison with the metropolis is once more obvious. As expected, the evaluation of other 'conventional' forms of participation is also somewhat lower. Direct contact to politicians and participation in electoral campaigning, which is often associated with small 'gifts', is viewed by the majority in Kenya and the Ivory Coast as very effective. This is also true for party membership, which in these countries is in reality only formal.

As regards participation by more 'unconventional' forms, a considerable minority views demonstrations (43%) as effective, followed by strikes (36%). Payment boycotts are viewed more often as ineffective (12%). Land occupation is viewed as an effective means of interest assertion by almost two thirds in Chile, and almost 50% in Brazil. In contrast, only 22% in Kenya, and 14% in the Ivory Coast share this view. This once more emphasises the effectiveness of such activity in the past in the Latin American cases. The question whether, if necessary, violent action for interest articulation may be justified is answered affirmatively by 43% in Kenya and 45% in Brazil. In comparison, only 20% in the Ivory Coast and 12% in Chile agree with this. This points to a certain tradition of urban unrest in the former countries and at least to the latent potential for conflict and violence amongst the 'urban crowds'.

However, concrete behaviour, which was assessed separately, diverges from these general evaluations. On average, three quarters of those questioned take part in elections; with values around 80% in Chile and Brazil and 70% in Kenya, but only 39% in the Ivory Coast. In the last case, the high proportion of immigrants and the stricter conditions for citizen and electoral registration must once more be taken into account.

In the medium-sized African towns, the stated electoral participation is higher than in the metropolis, which reflects the realities of the last elections. In Latin America, such differences are insignificant. Participation in electoral campaigning was strongest in Brazil (24%) and Kenya (20%), against 6% in Chile and the Ivory Coast. Party membership, which in Kenya can be obtained by the single payment of a minimal contribution, is highest in Kenya with 25%, in contrast to 6% to 7% respectively in the other cases, although this value is considerably higher in the Brazilian metropolis than in the medium-sized town.

The unconventional activities which were reported mostly concerned demonstrations (around 18% in all countries) and strikes (average 11%, but only 4% in the Ivory Coast). Payment boycotts are relatively seldom (a total of 5%, with somewhat higher values for Brazil and Kenya). The different pattern of participation in demonstrations and land occupation in specific settlements is conspicuous. In the medium-sized Kenyan town and in the older settlements in the Ivory Coast, demonstrations were very common (almost one quarter of those questioned had taken part in one). In Chile it was the new settlement in the metropolis which drew attention in this respect (38%). In Brazil, participation in the metropolis (approx. 24%) was clearly higher than in the medium-sized town (12%). Organised land occupation is mostly unknown in the African countries, although individual squatting sometimes took place in the medium-sized Kenyan town (12%). In this respect, the new settlement in Santiago (more than 70% of those questioned had participated), but also in Temuco, with an average 30%, stand out. In Brazil, this was limited mainly to the new settlement in the metropolis (34%).

Categorisation according to participation type produced a similar picture. The 'inactives' were clearly most prevalent in the Ivory Coast, although this depended on the high proportion of immigrants, and was stronger in the metropolis than the medium-sized town. In Kenya, the discrepancy between the metropolis (more than 50% inactive) and the medium-sized town is also conspicuous. In contrast, the values in Chile and Brazil are clearly lower. This emphasises once more the greater importance of non-metropolitan and rural regions for politics in the African cases. 'Voters-only' in Chile are especially frequent, although the new settlement in Santiago clearly diverges from this. Here, with a value of 65%, 'unconventional' activities related to the residential area are clearly in the fore. Such activities are also particularly frequent in the Brazilian metropolis, with 30% in contrast to around 12% in the medium-sized town. Conventional and party-related activities show a more even pattern of distribution. 'Universal' activists are more often found in the old settlement in Kisumu (39%), with more opposition activities, and in the Brazilian metropolis (23%), due to the previously mentioned reasons.

Party political preferences are the final aspect in this regard. These also reflect contentment with the changes that have occurred and the elected representatives, or, conversely, protest and opposition currents. In both African cases, the results concerning presidential and party elections were nearly identical, although this is hardly surprising given the dominance of the president and the respective governing parties in these countries (see Table 8.6). In Kenya, the reigning president Moi and his governing party, KANU, are clearly dominant in the two older settlements, a fact that speaks for the efficiency of the party and above all of the administrative apparatus (which is basically identical with the government). This is also true for Kisumu, which otherwise belongs more to the opposition camp, but the older settlement there is more ethnically heterogeneous than the town as a whole. In the Ivory Coast, the reigning president and his party are generally dominant, in particular in the medium-sized town. In both countries, this confirms the relative continuity with the previous situation, despite the introduction of a multi-party system. In Kenya, however, the situation is more tense because the opposition forces, taken together, had a majority but were unable to form a united front or agree on a common presidential candidate.

In contrast, in Chile and Brazil, the residents of the marginal settlements clearly supported the changes that have been introduced. This is especially true of the new presidents Ailwyn (75%) and Cardoso (50%). In Chile, there is general support, while in Brazil it is stronger in the metropolis. In the two countries, the party political landscape is more heterogeneous, also with regard to the respective government camps. This is reflected in differentiated party support, especially in Brazil. Here, a clear majority voted, in particular in the metropolis, for parties other than that of the president.

The preferences indicated with regard to future elections also reflect these differences. In Kenya, support for KANU, particularly in the metropolis, has once more increased, which corresponds to the result of the 1997 elections. In contrast, at the time of our survey, support for the governing party, PDCI, in the Ivory Coast was clearly already beginning to decline. In Chile, the governing parties were able to maintain their ground, while in Brazil, Cardoso's party coalition was hardly paid any attention. The number of those who were undecided, or non-voters, is particularly high in this case. This emphasises once more the strong personalisation and great fluctuation between parties in Brazilian politics.

CHAPTER 9

The Urban Poor as a Target of Development Policy

Norbert Kersting

§ SINCE the 'second development decade' (1970–1980) the poor of the marginal settlements in the Third World have increasingly become the focus of discussions concerning development policies. Urban poverty in developing countries is increasingly viewed as a phenomenon of social exclusion. Development policies are orientated toward the principle of 'full inclusion' (Luhmann 1980: 31). Certain aspects reinforce each other and cause a precarious situation (multiple vulnerability). Cultural, social and economic exclusion also has an effect on political participation. This chapter deals with the way development policy can counter such tendencies towards marginalisation. The general aims of development policy will be presented first. Then, these development strategies will be examined to see whether and how far they are orientated towards the situation, interests and political possibilities of the urban poor, which were explored in our study. The focus is on the possibilities of participation and self-help of this group.

Development Aid and its Orientation Towards Poverty

Since the 1970s, development strategies concerned with basic needs have been oriented toward the goal of reducing absolute poverty. To this end, increasing employment, more labour-intensive production, priority for rural development, import substitution and stronger internal market development, amongst others, were strived at. Fulfilment of basic needs encompasses aspects of nourishment, health, living accommodation and education. Furthermore, demands for democratisation, participation and employment security, as well as greater redistribution, were raised. Central areas of development policy were agrarian reform, based on changes in income and ownership structures, education reform, aimed at elementary education and vocational training, and financial programmes for small enterprises and small farmers, with simultaneous support of the technologies required. After the redistribution euphoria of the 1970s, a new strategy, which aimed to combine economic growth and redistribution, came into force. In addition, aspects such as equality of the sexes and, since the UN conference in Rio de Janeiro in 1992, ecological problems and concerns over sustainable development have come to the fore (see Lachmann 1994). The second phase of structural adjustment programmes includes strategies for greater accountability and decentralisation, measures against corruption but also concepts to weaken the negative side effects of structural adjustment on the urban poor. Here, the focus lies on the development of 'social capital', self-help, empowerment, and ownership (Putnam 1993, Dembélé 2000).

The main multilateral donor in the urban sector is the World Bank. In the 1970s, its focus lay on site and service schemes and on the upgrading of informal residential areas. Since the middle of the 1980s, it has increasingly carried out integrated urban development programmes, which consist of the strengthening and creation of urban institutions, administrative reform, provision of infrastructure, land reform etc. The second important development organisation, which combats urban poverty, is UNCHS-Habitat (United Nations Centre for Human Settlement). It is mainly concerned with technical cooperation. Extensive financial programmes in the urban sector are also carried out by UNDP (United Nations Development Programme). In principle, the measures of the United Nations organisations are of a demonstrative nature. They focus on strengthening organisations and institutions, that is, advising and training in the whole area of urban management, and not, as formerly, on spatial or infrastructure planning. Since 1986, the World Bank and UNDP-UNCHS support the Urban Management Programme (UMP). Some countries have joined this programme. It aims to develop regional networks for trained specialists and institutions, and began developing new instruments and solutions for urban management. The largest bilateral donor is USAID (US Agency for International Development). Financial and technical cooperation is coordinated through its Office of Housing and Urban Programmes. Until now, its emphasis has been on helping medium-sized towns and providing suitable accommodation. For the past few years it has tried to increase cooperation with non-governmental organisations (NGOs).

Bilateral development policies in the 1990s had one over-arching target of combating poverty via self-help. Here it focuses on the improvement of the economic and social situation of people in the developing countries and especially poor sections of the population. The productive and creative abilities of the poor should be given special support, to contribute to the reduction of absolute poverty and facilitate a dignified quality of life. Self-help and participation are the pillars which support developmental work. Basically, combating poverty was divided into three areas: In the political dialogue, system change should be encouraged by advising governments within the framework of structural adjustment programmes, but also by the initiation of self-help organisations. Here the support of structural reforms should improve the chances of indirect and direct strategies for combating poverty. An indirect combating of poverty can happen in some projects, where the target group is not clearly defined. Here trickle-down effects are often assumed, which take into account impoverished environments. In projects aimed directly at combating poverty, at least half of the population who benefits is poor. They are reached directly without any further steps of implementation (e.g. via credits, water provision, infrastructure, employment), or indirectly via measures aimed at infrastructure provision (teacher training, advisors, health service).

In OECD development aid in general a small percentage, around 10%; of all projects are bilateral, self-help-orientated programmes. The four main criteria for poverty orientation are as follows: Are the poor the target group? Are their living conditions improved? Are the poor involved? Is there an impoverished environment (is productive potential supported)?

Self-help-orientated projects' combating of poverty encompasses more intensive personal participation in a special form of individual responsibility and self-help organisation of the group.

Also bilateral development policies view participation as a precondition for the long-term success of projects (see OECD/DAC 1995). It emphasises the differences of the groups involved (target groups, mediators, as well as the intensity of the possibilities of participation in the project, e.g. information, consultation, and self-determination. At the final, highest level, the aspect of 'ownership', that is responsibility for the project, comes to the fore. This encompasses self-help participation in the sense of actual work. The extension of the ability to articulate interests (empowerment) is often viewed as the main factor of success and is also a goal of development policy.

Here ecological local and urban development tries to identify, test, plan and evaluate development projects, especially in the area of combating urban poverty by the provision of housing, regional planning, water provision etc. Especially since the UN Conference on Environment and Development (UNCED) in Rio de Janeiro in 1992, the Agenda 21 has put more emphasis on the urban development and environment.

Here problems of migration as well as internal growth, but also the advantages of large conglomerations are considered. The negative results of urbanisation such as the increase in urban poverty, lack of living accommodation, increased environmental damage, the growing need for urban services and infrastructure, but also increased criminality and violence and uneven spatial development are recognised. Nevertheless, the negative trends of urbanisation should not only be overcome via greater support of rural areas and medium-sized towns, because towns can also have positive effects on the whole of society. Approximately 60% of GNP and 80% of economic growth of developing countries is created in towns. Towns are important regional and extra-regional markets. Small and medium-sized towns can take on various functions of provision and development for rural areas. Urban services also facilitate the fulfilment of basic needs for the poorer sections of the population, and reproductive behaviour also changes in the towns: the birth rate drops. The main challenges and future tasks are the overcoming of urban poverty; the strengthening of local administration, i.e. greater local autonomy and decentralisation; the improvement of physical and social infrastructure; the mobilisation and participation of the population, with special consideration for the needs and problems of women; and the improvement of the macro-economic and political framework for urban development. Finally, limitation and repair of the environmental damage caused by urban development is emphasised. In order to achieve this catalogue of goals, bilateral development policies state that the capabilities of the actors in the political arena, at the national and regional as well as the local level, must be strengthened. At town neighbourhood level, the aim is to achieve careful use of resources and improvement of living conditions of the poorer groups of the population. Close cooperation between financial cooperation and technical cooperation is striven for.

The experiences of the last development decade show that such integrated development programmes can be successful. In addition, support at different levels (national, local and neighbourhood) should come into effect without, as before, trying to deal with a wide spectrum of different problems and tasks. This often overwhelmed the project organisation. Thus, development cooperation in this area is now limited to a few strategic, project components. The former strong orientation towards quantitative aspects and the speedy provision of accommodation often meant target groups were not properly addressed. This should be better achieved by increased participation of target groups in the planning process. One important aspect is related to strengthening local authorities, in a financial as well as an organisational and structural sense. It must be seen that public administration is often characterised by clientelistic and personal interest structures. Thus, non-governmental organisations and grassroots groups should increasingly be addressed as the representatives for the poorer groups and those who suffer discrimination. Another important goal is integration of the projects into wider programmes to ensure solutions are not limited to individual towns, but can also be applied elsewhere. This requires interventions at the national, local, and neighbourhood levels. The respective institutions at the local level (mayor, local representatives), employees in the administration, non-governmental organisations, as well as representatives of private interests (e.g. residents' associations), are important targets for development cooperation.

Strengthening local self-administration also entails decentralisation at the national and regional level, which requires an increase in personnel and financial responsibility of local authorities, as well as increasing the role of municipal groups. Thus, measures aimed at improving the planning and control of spatial development are important. At the local level, these comprise improved personnel development and qualification of administrative personnel, as well as modernisation of the organisational structure. Self-help groups should also be integrated into the processes which determine local policy. A further important area is reform of local finances. Some of the competencies for raising taxes, fees and contributions, which to date have remained at the national and regional levels, should be delegated to the local authorities. This also entails a 'suitable procedure for budget and investment planning', and improved tax collection etc.

Support should be given to urban infrastructure and services, as well as the development of residential areas and renovation of informal settlements. In this respect, the definition of standards and regulations at the national level is important. Basically, this means passing responsibility to local authorities, as well as creating task groups. At the local level, self-help projects, as well as testing and supporting the private operators in the creation and maintenance of infrastructure, are increasingly gaining importance.

In the framework of bilateral cooperation, financial cooperation in the 1980s was mainly directed towards over-arching sectoral projects of urban development. The majority of projects supported physical infrastructure measures, e.g. energy and water provision, garbage collection, traffic or enterprise support. Some individual programmes aimed at the renovation of poor areas were also financed. But the effects of many of these projects were not long-lived. Therefore, for the past 20 years, the focus has turned to strengthening the capacity of the urban authorities and NGOs (capacity building). The development cooperation of non-government organisations is concentrated on certain types of project, such as suitable infrastructure projects, legal advisory programmes, self-help housing, revolving credit funds, measures for further organisation development, creation of social services, etc. The possibility of cooperation within town twinning projects and also exchange of experience between extra-regional and international local authorities, are also important aspects.

Potential and Deficits of Self-Help Organisation

Poverty-orientated self-help projects often fail because the people involved are given too little opportunity of co-determination. In particular, when projects are handed over, with regard to the long-term sustainability of such programmes it often becomes evident that the target groups were not sufficiently integrated already in the planning phase. Investments often neglect the needs of the target groups, and many projects collapse when development agencies leave. The initial structural adjustment programmes (SAP) in the late 1980s and early 1990s had hardly any poverty orientated components. Only after massive protests in many countries ('IMF riots'), were new programmes with poverty-orientated development projects initiated aimed at alleviating social costs. Structural and sectoral adjustment programmes affecting the macro level thus gained new importance for overcoming poverty and unemployment (Mitullah 2000) .

The failures of urban development programmes show that multisectoral programmes are required to reduce poverty. These programmes must be aimed at the macro, meso and microlevels. They should not be limited to one sector only, and in addition to housing problems, they must also address the health sector, income generation measures, and take into account political and socio-cultural aspects. At the macrolevel, poverty-related orientations must be integrated into the political and legal framework. The meso level encompasses institutional measures that further organisation of the poor. At the micro level, the competencies of the poor must be increased ('empowerment').

Macro Level

Encouraging self-help requires various structural conditions. The majority of states in the Third World only permit limited self-determination at the local level. Suitably decentralised structures have to be tailored to the respective cultural and political background. Development policy also increasingly takes into account the political framework at the macrolevel. The important elements of democracy, which are viewed as the upholding and furthering of human rights, legal security and participation are in the forefront. According to the level of democratisation, different catalogues of measures for political cooperation and a poverty-orientated development policy are employed. In countries where conditions are close to civil war, or where the regime is extremely repressive in character, intra-state cooperation in development policy is seldom possible or useful. Under such conditions, only forms of immediate emergency aid can be considered for the urban poor. In countries where minimum standards of legality are observed, e.g. authoritarian systems with different leanings (monarchies, personal repressive autocracies, socialist one-party systems), civil society is the main target, that is NGOs. In this case, human rights groups are mainly supported. In so-called semi-competitive regimes, in addition to other measures aimed at furthering democracy, support of local self-administration can also play an important role. Furthermore, in this case, aspects aimed at supporting participation, e.g. self-help projects, are emphasised. A wide catalogue of measures in the area of democratically orientated political education is also vitally important. Support of self-help projects also includes creating places where one can learn democracy. In more consolidated democratic states (e.g. Costa Rica, India), more qualified democratic procedures can be promoted. Strong democratic feedback and public control of politics can lead to 'better governance' (World Bank) and greater public accountability, and banish nepotism and corruption (Berg-Schlosser 1995).

At the macro level, a political culture which is orientated strongly towards the state and gives the state a central role in relation to development projects hinders the encouragement of self-help. Autonomous self-help organisation can be furthered by discouraging a paternalistic, statist political style. The four countries studied here presented different patterns in relation to the willingness to engage in self-help activities and statist orientations.

These predispositions are also related to the respective strategies of governments, which actively further participation and individual initiative or, as a result of a lack of engagement in the social sphere, call forth individual and collective self-help. In some countries, the state is the central welfare authority, which intervenes in large areas of the social sphere and leaves no room for autonomously organised self-help. In addition to national patterns, there are also considerable differences within a country, e.g. between different local authorities, but also between different settlements. Thus, in addition to specific national patterns, the various styles of politics, which are either more communitarian or statist, also have local characteristics (see van Waarden 1992). It is clear that these styles of politics influence the respective engagement in neighbourhood groups (see chapter 5).

In Brazil, there is a rather low willingness to engage in self-help, 18%, even though the associacioes de moradores (AMs) are the strongest neighbourhood groups in Rio de Janeiro and, as a result of strong state support and aid, are seen by many residents as state institutions (miniprefeituras). However, the state still allows residents enough leeway for engagement. Self-help groups have shown considerable success. In Aracaju, where AMs function not so well and have a more clientelistic relationship with the town administration, which represents a paternalistic and statist style, the willingness to engage in self-help is approx. 10% lower, and the demand for state help about 10% higher than in Rio de Janeiro.

By contrast, in Chile, the willingness to engage in self-help is very high (45%). Only in Santiago's old settlement (Galvarino) is the willingness to engage in self-help relatively low. There is a great difference in the perceived responsibility for solving problems between the 5-million-strong city of Santiago, and the 200,000-strong town of Temuco. In Temuco, approx. 40% think the town authorities should solve the problems, while in Santiago, this proportion is only 13%.

In the Ivory Coast, on average self-help has the lowest level of acceptance. Only in the older settlement in Abidjan and in the newer

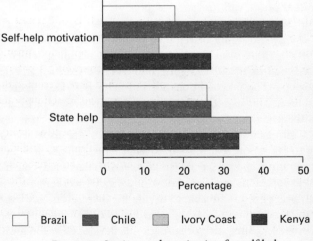

Figure 9.1 Statism and motivation for self-help

settlement in Man, is the willingness to engage in self-help somewhat greater. In relation to demands for state help, as already observed in Chile and Brazil, the proportion in the medium-sized town (Man) is higher than in Abidjan. The style of politics of the former one-party system, which attempted to dominate all social spheres, left little room for the formation of autonomous organisations and led to a strongly statist understanding of politics including the residents of marginal settlements.

In Kenya, the proportion of those willing to engage in self-help is relatively high. But, one third also think the state should solve their problems. It is conspicuous that in the old settlement in Nairobi, a very high proportion, 44%, demands state help. A single party, KANU, also dominates in Kenya; thus there is also a long tradition of expecting state help.

Support for a new understanding of statehood should be emphasised in political dialogues, and leeway for self-help groups should be guaranteed without neglecting demands. In certain cases, the normal channels, which are often based on clientelistic, paternalistic structures, should not be used, but rather autonomous advocates and organisations of civil society should be supported. Especially in the African cases, this can mean that programmes are not carried out by town and state authorities because these are too deeply involved with the former single party. Then, NGOs should take over project operation.

In addition to the basic orientation of development policy towards self-help, strong decentralisation of national policy is also important. Even though the structural adjustment programmes of the 1980s placed decentralisation of various fields of policy to the fore, the four states still demonstrate tendencies of over-centralisation. Far-reaching, detailed planning, e.g. in housing or regional policy, takes place in the central governments. This often leads to unsuitable planning which is not orientated to any particular target group and to discontent amongst the target groups. The preconditions for self-help must also be created at the local level. This basically means greater transparency of local policy. For this, the necessary instruments and capacities must be created within the town administration (capacity building). Instruments which support self-help organisation also must be strengthened. Points of contact for citizens can provide financial aid (small loans), material aid (construction materials, tools etc.), as well as know-how (social workers). It is important that target groups are able to decide for themselves to what extent they wish to make use of the different forms of self-help, participation and information. After such organisation is developed at the local level, successful pilot projects can be anchored into regional institutions, or extended to national programmes. In this way, experiences can be exchanged using municipal networks.

Meso Level

Actual power structures within society and, especially within the framework of development aid, local development agents must be taken into account during the realisation of self-help projects. These development agents are important strategic elements in the dialogue between the development planners and their clientele, who for the most part also pursue their own interests (Bierschenk/Elwert 1993). Self-help is often expressed when initiative is taken from below, that is when no initiatives come from above or external sources. The willingness to participate is most often present when individual interests are taken into account and responsibility is accepted accordingly. But self-help is therefore often an 'elite' and not a grass-roots phenomenon. It can be dominated by local, e.g. also business elites, which are more often involved (Mossmann 1994).

The cases studied show that, at the meso level, there are different preconditions for organised self-help representation. These are related to the different forms of clientelism. In the Ivory Coast and Kenya, clientelistic structures are mostly based on primordial relations, especially ethnic networks. In both countries, this becomes clear also with regard to integration in the party system. In addition to primordial relations, the single parties there also dominated the different forms of political participation as well as self-help. The creation of neighbourhood organisations and social organisations which want to operate independently of the respective party system, or wish to cross the lines of ethnic tension, is difficult. The creation of parallel organisations, which can be supported by other groups and advocates, is often hindered by the dominance of the single parties. Furthermore, in comparison to the other countries, there are fewer grass-roots Church organisations, out of which such organisations can develop. The dominance of the single parties, and the strong statism they encourage, hinders autonomous organisation as well as willingness to engage in self-help. The existing organisations in the African settlements are highly integrated into the party system. They are mostly related to cultural aspects, basic health and hygiene. The majority of members are women. The lack of existence of autonomous organisations results from the shortage of independent 'advocates'. Development projects which try to initiate self-help usually have to cooperate with the respective state or party organisations, which see themselves as advocates for the poor.

Among the Latin American cases, in Aracaju there is also a high level of clientelism and patronage ('colonelism', see Cruz 2000). The lack of interest in self-help and individually organised participation there is partly based on the low level of education, but more so on the strong statist and paternalistic orientations of the parties and the town administration. These leave little room for individual engagement, but promote single measures, such as improvement of infrastructure and housing, the planning of which has already been decided from above. The Associaoes de Moradores (AM) are also organised from above and dominated by the town administration. In contrast, in Rio de Janeiro, the town authorities have introduced measures which have led to the creation of small groups. The AMs plan and organise their neighbourhood, support further organisation and develop their own self-help projects. Even though community spirit is relatively low, there are a number of self-help activities. In contrast to Aracaju, taking the interests of the neighbourhood residents into account is not based on advocatorial or electoral tactics, but rather on a long-term development programme aimed at contributing to the improvement of the neighbourhood.

In Chile, development programmes with a more technocratic bias have a longer tradition. The projects have freed themselves from formerly existing clientelistic networks and, especially in Santiago, function as independent town development projects, which are headed by project employees who are 'autonomous' in the party political sense. In addition, the need for advocates seems to be less marked because there is a relatively high level of formal education in the poblaciones. In addition to the projects, which are directed towards fulfilment of certain techno-

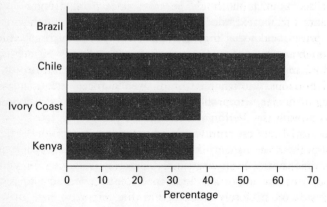

Figure 9.2 Membership in self-help organisations

cratic standards, there are also a number of welfare state measures, which contribute to the improvement of the resources of the urban poor. These are also carried out independently of party political or social, clientelistic structures. Individual welfare measures are accompanied by a marked retreat of the state from the self-help area. Thus, many new self-help projects result from this retreat and are not, as is the case with the Brazilian programmes, given support.

Participatory development programmes are often faced with the problem of a culturally based lack of possibilities of articulation and therefore lack of transparency. Thus, in many societies there is no open formulation of interests. This results in difficulties during the negotiation of compromises. There is a lack of suitable channels to articulate interests and demands and at the same time a lack of social institutions as negotiation partner. If weak interests lack the ability to articulate and organise, as well as to assert themselves *vis-à-vis* state actors, external help can become relevant. The existence of a neutral third party, which can help secure the articulation by advocacy, is important. These 'political entrepreneurs' can come from above and outside (e.g. project groups or planned neighbourhood organisations), or from below and within (traditional groups, autonomous neighbourhood movements). The presence of a critical mass within the marginal settlement with a high level of resources, special interests and motivation is crucial for formative, normative and execution phases (see Kersting 1996).

Furthering awareness of civic responsibility within the political and social elites, which can create an orientation towards general welfare and democratic empathy amongst the middle and upper classes, should also be carried out by a neutral, primarily uninterested advocate. The self-limitation of strong interests for the benefit of the inclusion of the marginalised population should be given special importance. Many organisations in the excluded sphere have contacts to church groups, parties, private and social organisations. Strong external engagement, e.g. through priests or party functionaries, creates figures of identification. More intensive organisation via regular contacts, expansion of political horizons through recognition of the social situation and a widening of demands to problems outside the residential environment occur as a result (see Perlman 1976).

Advocatorial interest representation and delegation to local leaders carry with them the danger of a take-over by an outside organisation (parties, unions etc.). Even when such 'borderliners' come from within the group and are important figures of identification, their basis of legitimacy is often closely associated with contacts to mediators in parties and authorities and is linked to corresponding strategies (see

Kersting 1999). People often use different strategies in competition for leadership positions, although those who can offer an acceptable solution to the group's demands dominate. At the local level, unconventional contacts to parties and politicians, which are based on informal clientele systems, often exist. There is more chance of asserting interests when different people or organisations compete for the support of the marginalised population within the framework of 'competitive clientelism'. This also presents parties with the opportunity to build up clientele systems and integrate autonomous neighbourhood organisations vertically into the party structure ('parallelismo'/'ventajismo'). Cooperation is often in the form of paternalistic subordination by the dominant party and integration of neighbourhood organisations into the party structure. A strategy often employed by parties is 'degraded cooptation' of marginal groups, which aims to win 'floating voters' for a short period during elections, but does not result in prolonged political inclusion.

At the local level, personal self-help in neighbourhood networks can lead to need-orientated goal achievement. In the exclusion zone of the urban poor, egalitarian social networks are found alongside clientelistic and hierarchical relations. Egalitarian reciprocal interactions most often occur in traditional neighbourhood groups. They are characterised by exchange of goods and services, ideally between equal partners. This is mostly only temporary, and usually of an informal nature, and the exchange of resources is usually very limited. It is basically neighbourhood self-help in the form of 'tit for tat'. Its general role in development policy is often limited due to lack of more significant resources (material, time and knowledge), and it is often an expression of lack of ability to engage in organised self-help.

Horizontal integration in organisations at the meso level and therefore the creation of a regional public for organisation is often blocked by the fixation of the poor on interests in their own neighbourhood. Premature horizontal integration, subordination to other institutions or cooperation with groups with similar aims, can extend goals, but also weaken the direct effect the problems have on the group. Above all, self-help projects need networks which can serve as protection (Mossmann 1994). Only such free space leads to development from below and can supplement and relieve national policy. Horizontal cooperation with other neighbourhood groups is therefore especially important, even though in the medium and long-term, there are hardly any opportunities to create a wider organisation with a membership or party structure (see Tironi 1990).

Micro Level

As the country analyses show, there is a great deal of socio-structural heterogeneity (see chapter 4) which, due to the various cross-cutting lines of cleavage, make wide-scale organisation difficult. This points to the fact that development projects in marginal settlements require intensive socio-structural analysis at the start of every project. This raises the question, whether the direction of development is orientated towards individually perceived deficits, and therefore a suitable identification with the respective project areas can be ensured, or whether development aid organisations plan projects from above which do not address the actual problems of the residents. Furthermore, the existence of different needs and heterogeneous group interests make it necessary to adapt project strategies with regard to their direction and forms of participation. In the next section, the problems in the marginal settlements will be briefly described. Are these congruent with the basic directions of development policy, e.g. support of women, ecology and environmental protection? Following this, the other important goal of participation will be discussed. Does the ability and willingness to participate exist? If development strategies do not match the interests expressed by those participating in the project, a suitable level of educational work is at least necessary for the avoidance of possible planning failures. Otherwise one must reckon with opposition, or less motivation to participate in the project, on the part of the residents.

The problems in the marginal settlements are manifold. They often influence and reinforce one another and lead to multiple vulnerability in the survival strategies of the urban poor, and a higher risk of being affected. For example, problems that occur because of a lack of health services influence the education and work spheres, and also participation in self-help projects. The problems in the marginal settlements are multi-dimensional, but they do not affect all population groups in the same way. At the same time, it must be acknowledged that not all residents follow the same goals in relation to the perception of problems and the interests in solving this state of affairs. Thus, as a result of different ownership structures, the interests of slum residents can also be very heterogeneous, which points to different interests in relation to improvements of housing and settlement infrastructure. In Chile in particular, the majority of residents own their own accommodation. In Kenya and the Ivory Coast on the other hand, only about one third own their own home in some settlements, while the majority only rent their house or flat. Tenants also need suitable housing, but they are less willing to put more of their time, money and energy into rented

accommodation. Motivation is further reduced because precarious settlements in the Latin American towns do not possess title deeds. In the
African towns, ownership relations are often unclear, but generally
solved in favour of the 'semi-legal' settlements. However, at the time of
our survey, the settlement of Washington in Abidjan was threatened
with clearance, and a short time afterwards this was carried out.

Our survey shows that the central problem areas lie in the local
sphere. Almost 90% of residents in the African marginal settlements
name physical infrastructure, mostly provision of electricity and water,
refuse collection and transport, as well as suitable accommodation, as
the main problem. In the slum settlements of the Ivory Coast, there is
a high level of discontent with provision of electricity and water. In the
Kenyan marginal settlements, two thirds of residents do not have any
kind of sanitation. In the Ivory Coast, it is approx. one quarter of
residents. However, here at least half of those questioned are content
with the level of sanitation. Only a few houses are directly connected
to the town water supply. Usually, water can be purchased in the
settlements from private providers. In both settlements in Man, it is
also possible to use a well. Provision of electricity is achieved by illegal
means in both settlements in Abidjan. In the settlement Belle-Ville there
has been general provision of electricity since 1997. In Kennedy (Man),
only one or two houses have electricity. In the settlements in Nairobi,
water can also only be purchased in canisters. The majority of households have no electricity because it is too expensive. In Mukuru Kayaba
there is no electricity at all. In comparison with the Ivory Coast, the
residents of Kenyan marginal settlements are clearly more discontent
with public transport (see chapter 3).

Interestingly, only a small proportion of African slum residents name
social infrastructure as one of the main problems. Although there are
no primary schools in the medium-sized town of Man, and the Abidjan
settlements with approx. 8,000 residents only have one school, this is
not given much attention. The same is true for Kenya, where in Mukuru
Kayaba, there is only one primary school for the approx. 30,000 residents.
Poverty, hunger, social inequality and unemployment, as well as social
relations are only identified as problem areas by a small minority in
Kenya and the Ivory Coast. However, residents identify criminality as a
problem in both countries. Nearly one third of those questioned, the
proportion is somewhat higher in the medium-sized towns, view this as
an important problem area.

Similarly, in Latin America, residents of the marginal settlements
view physical infrastructure as the main problem. This is so even though
there is almost complete provision of infrastructure in Chile. Here,

nearly every household has water and electricity, although in Esperanza (Santiago de Chile) these are the result of individual work. In Brazil, there are clear regional differences. Water and electricity are provided in both settlements in Rio de Janeiro. In contrast, in Aracaju, provision of water is deficient, especially in the new settlements, and in part only available from wells. Electricity is available for all, but is often illegally obtained. In the evaluation of sanitation, there is discontent above all in Chile. On the other hand, here there is more contentment with the neighbourhood's public transport facilities. In contrast, in Brazil, half the residents view public transport as deficient.

In Latin America, social infrastructure (schools, kindergartens, hospitals) also has a lower level of problem awareness than that of physical infrastructure. This is related to the fact that, in comparison to the African cases, provision of infrastructure is clearly better. Apart from Esperanza, the various settlements in Santiago and Temuco do not have their own primary school, but have access to the school system just outside the neighbourhood. Thus, in Chile, only a small minority views this area as a central problem. In the marginal settlements in Brazil, state as well as church primary schools are both within and very close to neighbourhoods. However, in Brazil, the expectations and hopes in relation to social infrastructure seem to be considerably higher. Nearly half of those questioned view social infrastructure as problematic.

Hunger, poverty, social inequality, as well as social relations are only named by one tenth of those questioned in Latin America. In Chile, there seems to be a special desire for justice. The problem of unemployment is only mentioned by a few. In contrast, as in the other countries, there is great fear of increasing criminality. In Chile, approx. one quarter of those questioned view this as a big problem, and this is given more importance in Santiago than in Temuco. In Brazil, fear of increasing criminality is clearly greater in Aracaju, while in Rio de Janeiro, only a quarter of those questioned defined this as a problem. This is surprising because, according to the criminal statistics for Rio de Janeiro, there are considerably higher rates of crime here than in Temuco. This indicates that in Rio de Janeiro, the population has grown accustomed to the criminal environment and arranged life accordingly, while in Aracaju, a more diffuse fear about increasing criminality dominates.

Even when the long-term problems of the marginal populations can only be solved by change in the political set-up, and therefore political apathy seems 'irrational', individual emergency situations often create political lethargy, especially amongst groups with a low level of education. An important motive which leads to participation is suitable gratification. Marginalised groups, especially the lowest strata, are extremely 'output' and 'outcome'-orientated. If suitable gratification cannot be expected, participation declines. This 'output' orientation is directed towards government action, such as legalisation of land ownership, provision of infrastructure etc. In informally organised groups without a permanent structure, the political leaders of a settlement are often the only ones to benefit from other social advantages gained from participation, such as increased social prestige, because they dominate the political participation and processes within the group. Limited 'outputs' and lack of choice within the political system force the poor to 'disengage' from the public sphere. The result is retreat into the private sphere, i.e. the recreational and social sphere. As a result of such disillusionment with politics, the population in marginal settlements is more often active in the cultural sphere, such as church groups, where the possibility of creating self-help groups exists (see also Schuurman/ Naerssen 1988).

In addition to the outputs of development projects, which must be orientated to the interests of the residents, initiatives towards participation in relation to taking part in the decision-making process and planning, and actually working in a project are of great importance. The question is, how far this is met with an corresponding willingness to participate amongst the neighbourhood residents. The various forms of participation, such as information, consultation, co-determination and self-help, are met with different levels of acceptance by the urban poor. In some development projects in marginal settlements, it is clear that even a large degree of opportunity for participation and co-determination does not lead to the expected participation. This is only due in part to the fact that urban housing policy is often subject to the control and engagement of the central government. Plans for participation, which often foresee wide-ranging cooperative self-help projects, are often carried out half-heartedly. Criticism of the concept of self-help is often based on the double burden of the lower income groups, which is an important hindrance to participation. The concept of self-help assumes freely available time and energy to work in the marginal settlements. Experience from participatory self-help projects shows that these often fail because, in addition to high financial demands, those involved also have a very limited time budget. Participation in planning and implementation often overwhelms the marginalised population, who may be 'formally' unemployed, but are actually multi-occupational. The phenomenon of widespread multi-occupation and transference of activities to non-political resources is also clearly the case in the slum and squatter settlements studied. Multi-occupation is the phenomenon in which one person has numerous jobs. These are the formal and informal activities, as well as subsistence farming, which are required to generate income. The concept also refers to the necessity of income generation by several family members within one household. This has serious implications for participation in self-help projects. As a result of multiple activities and in Africa also due to the 'maintenance of contacts' with the countryside, residents of marginal settlements have a very limited amount of time available. The assumption that slum residents have plenty of time to engage in self-help activities thus is not true for many residents.

In the settlements in the countries studied, over 80% of the residents had permanent employment. In Kenya, this was only approx. one third of residents. Individual daily working hours are especially high in Chile. Here, more than 80% work more than 8 hours a day. In Brazil, the group working less than 8 hours a day dominates. This is a result of the fact that secondary employment (only 8% of those questioned) is rarer. In contrast, in the Ivory Coast, large numbers of people have numerous places of work, both in the formal and informal spheres. The low number of second jobs in Brazil is compensated by the fact that the proportion of households where other family members also earn income is highest: 70% of households have second earners. In the other countries, this value is also over 50%. The possibilities of gaining further income or greater independence from monetary income via subsistence farming are also limited. Only one seventh possess their own garden and the same proportion have domestic animals. A great number in the Ivory Coast (38%) and Kenya (21%) require support from friends. In Brazil and Chile the number is only approx. 8%. Support by relatives is even more common. Approximately two thirds of residents in the marginal settlements in Kenya and 58% of slum residents in the Ivory Coast receive help from their extended families. In Latin America, there exist some contacts to family members in the countryside, but, apart from those of the Mapuche in Temuco, these are hardly used.

Self-help projects with preconceived time frames are often inflexible towards the working rhythm of the residents. Thus, the time factor is one the main problems in the ability to partake in self-help. It is not only true of marginal settlements in the Third World, that need and poverty weaken rather than strengthen the ability to engage in self-help (see Finkeldey 1992). Family and leisure time compete with employment, which due to long working hours, often long distances to the place of work and other secondary employment, takes up a great proportion of the day (see Olson 1968). Further participation is therefore only possible if special attractions serve to increase motivation, such as high gratification.

Participation in development projects is generally linked to the search for efficient resources using various avenues. Thus, project participation is only a form of activities above and beyond economic and social engagement, and is dependent to a great degree on the expected outputs. In the political sphere, marginalised groups seldom have the opportunity to solve short-term problems. The limited time budget hardly leaves any room for time-intensive engagement in political activities which do not directly contribute to solving a problem. Usually only in the case of an immediate threat is organised political protest initiated (see Cornelius 1978; Schmidt-Relenberg 1980).

Thus, the minimisation of risks plays a part even in participation in development projects. Without any promising alternatives or expected outputs, engagement is only possible as long as the activities are not very time-consuming. Participation is integrated into the survival strategy. Demands for participation must take into account the limited time budget and risk diversification strategy, as well as the immediate contribution to solving acute problems. The urban 'poor' are consumed by the demands of the daily fight for survival. The pressure of acute need forces under-privileged groups to look for short-term solutions to their problems. Long-term strategic interests, which could include the re-organisation of work in society, are suppressed by these immediate interests. Participation must be efficient and effective. Acute problems must be solved with only limited commitment. Thus, little time remains for symbolic forms of participation, often offered by the political side, which do not lead to problem solution.

Summary

The various over-arching sectoral concepts of international development policies in relation to combating poverty demonstrate, especially since the early 1990s, a strong trend towards self-help and participation. The World Bank and other donors strengthen strategies for decentralisation, capacity building and accountability. Programmes to weaken the negative side effects of structural adjustment reforms on the urban poor and to develop social capital, self-help, and ownership are implemented. Education and empowerment are seen as crucial measures defeating poverty. Participation is usually understood as taking part in the execution of projects (in the sense of 'sweat equities'). By contrast, co-determination, the participation in the decision-making process, is less emphasised.

Thus, there are various definitions of self-help and participation. Participation is partly viewed as taking part in the decision-making process (information, consultation, co-determination). Here, one can differentiate between 'large-scale' participation, e.g. in elections, or 'small-scale' participation, e.g. in the planning of development projects. However, participation is also viewed as actually working on the project. In addition to planning that is orientated towards the target group, the aspect of 'ownership', that is, greater identification of the target group with the development project, is also an important factor for success. Other initiatives for participation speak of obtaining outputs or contribution to project costs and are likely to lead one astray.

Development projects, which include participation in the planning process or self-help and actual work on the project, should build on the concrete potential of those involved. For this, a detailed analysis of the target group is required. Prejudices and myths about poverty and, often excessive, expectations of the ability or willingness of the target group to engage in self-help should be avoided. On the one hand, it is clear that inhabitants of marginal settlements are not a homogeneous group. On the other hand, the limited resources of the poor, in relation to social and cognitive competency, as well as their limited individual time budget, must be acknowledged. Due to multi-occupation, i.e. because of the various employment relations in the formal and informal sector of the head of household or of other family members, there is often not enough time to help in project planning. Even if the necessary institutions for support are present (capacity building) and the resources for participation, such as knowledge, can be mediated (empowerment), there are residents, who cannot be viewed as being disadvantaged, who simply have no interest in the various forms of participation. Other sections of the population are interested in getting involved in the planning process. Some groups do not have the time, ability or are not interested in taking part in the actual work of implementation. Others are less interested in the planning process because they prefer to use their labour and know-how. Good project planning keeps all these options open to the target groups. It is important that during the course of the project, participation remains open and transparent.

Development policy strategies are not only directed towards combating poverty and participation to attain their goals. Since the start of the 1980s, other overarching aims have been added, such as equality between men and women, and protection of the environment and natural resources. Projects orientated towards the urban poor show that special support for women is relatively easy to achieve because they are often more economically active and are the more active population group within the neighbourhood. In this case, attempts to create self-help groups and social networks often fall on fertile ground. By contrast, environmental protection is not viewed as a crucial issue in most of the slum and squatter settlements, even though the environmental pollution in them presents an obvious health hazard. However, these can suitably be taken into account within the framework of improvements to infrastructure, which the urban poor vehemently demand.

Cross-cutting tasks such as ecology and equality of the sexes represent an extension of the original aims of the fight against poverty. They can become contradictory when development projects simultaneously attempt to promote strong consideration of respective cultural traditions, while entertaining drastic support for the equality of men and women in the project planning stages and choice of project helpers. Such contradictions are not only at play within the logic of development policy, but also in other areas, especially during choice of personnel, where they can overwhelm the development capabilities of the various organisations.

Futhermore, development policies which are orientated towards political inclusion and the alleviation of poverty must take into account the restrictions on public expenditure and barriers to democratisation, such as the various limited resources of the state, its possible dominance by special interest groups as well as the dilemma of redistribution. However, this strategies on self help policies reminds on the current discussion on communitarism and third sector policies in OECD countries. Here and in the field of instruments of participation (see Souza 2000 on participatory budgeting in Brazil) also lessons can be learned from the experience of developing countries. So, in many countries, a potential for both redistribution and broad-based development exists.

CHAPTER 10

Conclusions and Perspectives

Dirk Berg-Schlosser

§ THE previous chapters have shown very different aspects of the living conditions of the inhabitants of urban marginalised settlements in Africa and Latin America, and their position in the current democratisation processes. These relate to their respective objective material circumstances and their subjective evaluation, concrete forms of interest organisation, their 'political-cultural' attitudes and values, and active forms of participation of both a 'conventional' and 'unconventional' nature. All this is embedded in the respective historical and political-institutional context at the local and national levels, the concrete housing and social policies for these population groups, and internal and external initiatives of non-governmental cooperation and support.

Above and beyond the detailed results in the individual chapters, a certain level of similarity and homogeneity, but also a considerable diversification and variation in the respective contexts can be observed. Such similarities are in the first instance related to the position and the external appearance of the settlements. In many respects they are peripheral and are often very 'precariously' constructed. They are self-built in topographically unsuitable areas and their legal status often remains a point of contention. The provision of infrastructure is minimal, at least in comparison to 'better' residential areas, and the majority of working conditions and relations are 'informal'. The initial impression visitors gain often reflects this and many turn away, especially as entering such settlements without local accompaniment can be often dangerous for outsiders.

This picture changes dramatically, however, when more intensive contacts can be made with the residents or, as the assistants in our project did, when repeated visits over months, and partly over years, are made and intensive personal contacts and mutual trust can be established. This extended in some cases to actual support in concrete emergency situations. If this can be achieved, a very varied world is open, which, in spite of all objective poverty, contains much spontaneity, creativity and warmth. In this way, despite all the cultural and social differences, friendly human relations with 'people like you and me' become possible.

The relationship between the external and internal world is reflected in the external environment and in the internal condition of the huts. Externally, the settlements are often dirty and, depending on the time of year and weather, muddy and covered in waste. At intervals there are stinking paths and sewage streams. However, internally the huts or flats are usually very clean and tidy, and have all the basics in a small space. Despite the poverty, a foreign visitor is often met with gestures of welcome and hospitality, such as a glass of tea or a fruit. In such encounters, the wide spectrum of individual and collective life situations becomes apparent.

Common clichés of the 'apathetic mass', or the 'social revolutionary potential' are quickly contradicted and give way to more differentiated observations, which could be placed on a broader basis using our systematic surveys and numerous 'qualitative' interviews. This also enables us to come to certain more general results and conclusions at different levels. 'Apathetic' people who do not take part in any manner in the social and political life of their environment account for only 10% of all those questioned. This is most often determined by individual fate, such as age, illness, disability, but also alcoholism or drug abuse. In the older marginal settlements, such as in Aracaju, but also in Santiago, such patterns are more clearly apparent. In contrast, older settlements, such as in Rio de Janeiro or Nairobi, also have stronger tendencies of internal improvement in the sense of 'upgrading', that is, turning the favelas into 'barrios' (areas of the town which are supplied with regular public infrastructure), and a greater level of social integration, which extends outside the settlement.

Most such neighbourhoods have a well-defined identity. This is an expression of both internal communal feelings and the respective perception by strangers from neighbouring areas or the local authorities. This is often expressed in very colourful or symbolic names, such as, in our cases, La Esperanza in Santiago, Washington in Abidjan, or, in contrast to its actual appearance, Belle Ville in Man.

The great majority of inhabitants are active in many ways, both in securing their daily existence, and in a social and political sense. In the Latin American cases, this partly happens on the basis of relatively efficient neighbourhood organisations ('juntas de vecinos', 'associacoes de moradores'), which can look back on a long tradition and which either maintained their independence during the military dictatorship, or have since regained it. Today, they often possess secure legal status and are important points of contact for many forms of activity in the neighbourhood. The chairmen and speakers are important opinion leaders and often possess party political or local administrative functions ('mini-prefecturas' in Rio). In this regard, the situation today is determined by political competition. This opens up fields of activity for both traditional 'left-wing' parties, such as the PC in Chile or the PT in Brazil, as well as for nationalist or populist currents, such as the Partido Nacional in Chile or the PDT in Rio.

In the African cases informal structures dominate. In the Ivory Coast, with its traditionally more hierarchical ethnic groups, the respective 'chef du quartier' combines traditional authority with actual administrative and organisational functions. He is also usually embedded in the long dominant structures of the single party, PDCI. In the settlements mostly inhabited by immigrants, it is usually informal ethnic, cultural associations and activities relating to the respective country of origin which are in the fore. Concrete party political activities are more seldom or, given the continuing dispute over citizenship and the right to vote, controversial. In Kenya, the local 'chiefs' are formally members of the lowest level of administration. They are also mostly involved in activities with the governing party, KANU, if for example public meetings ('barazas') take place, or larger self-help activities ('harambee') are initiated. They do not normally possess a 'traditional' form of authority. Apart from political and social activities, economic associations, such as women's cooperatives for certain products in the informal sector ('jua kali') or credit cooperatives, are relatively prevalent in Kenya.

Apart from these formal and informal, but publicly recognised and acceptable forms of organisation, there are also hidden or latent structures, which, due to their character, shun public attention. This is true, for example, for the relations of economic power in the settlement, when a few 'slumlords' let or sub-let very small accommodations, which can be observed in Kenya, or when the 'chef du quartier' in the Ivory Coast demands a fee, which serves his personal alimentation, for use of the only public water tap. In Latin America, as in one of our cases in Rio, 'drug barons' or other criminals and their gangs often control whole areas or carry out bloody conflicts with their rivals or the police. In the final analysis, the existence of such 'legal vacuums', which are no longer under the control of the state authorities, places the legitimacy of the state in general and that of its representatives in question.

Apart from such newer, to date, limited extremes, the 'political culture' of the respective settlement basically reflects important elements of the political culture in the respective countries, with certain local and regional variations. In Chile, the general consolidation of democracy can also be found in these settlements. With respect to party politics, however, it still reflects the strong social and political polarisation of the country, especially in relation to the 'legacy' of the military dictatorship and its constitutional remains. Despite existing economic and social problems, democratisation is generally perceived as 'a value in itself'. In answer to the question what democracy means to him, the chairman of a 'junta de vecinos' in Temuco replied, that during the military dictatorship he had been imprisoned for a long period of time and tortured, and now he could 'sleep well at night once more'. In Chile, therefore, there is a certain paradox. In contrast to the prevailing theories of democratic consolidation (see Linz/Stepan 1996), political culture at the grassroots level is more democratised than the intermediate level (with its still strong supporters of the Pinochet regime) and the central political institutions (with the considerable rights of veto of the military).

In Brazil, political culture is regionally split into a more authoritarian clientelistic area in the north east of the country, with its more traditional and still basically neo-feudalistic social structures, e.g. in Aracaju, and the much more industrialised, urbanised, and democratised south east, as in Rio. But, within the democratic structures stronger clientelistic and, in part, latent populist currents can also be observed. Today, these must cope with open party and personality competition in the sense of 'competitive clientelism'. In this way, in the long term, certain feedback and control mechanisms can at least be established. However, the party system itself is relatively fluid and the parties have, with the exception of the PT, weak internal organisations. The traditionally strong personalisation of Brazilian politics, which is also expressed in the strong position of the president, continues to prevail. At the federal level, the military and the traditionally orientated agrarian oligarchy in the north east have retained an influential position. To a certain extent, this confirms the observations by Guillermo O'Donnell (1996), with regard to limited, but apparently stable forms of democratisation ('democracia delegada') in numerous Latin American countries.

In the Ivory Coast, there is a great level of congruence between the political culture and the political structures (for this concept, see Almond/Verba 1963 or Eckstein 1966). However, this political culture is still more authoritarian and clientelistic than democratic. This is also shaped by the traditionally more hierarchical ethnic groups in the country and also, in the north, the influence of Islam. Under present conditions, clientelism mostly occurs within the dominant party, PDCI, which was basically moulded under the 'neo-patrimonial', in the

Weberian sense, long-lasting rule of president Houphouët-Boigny. As long as the ethnic balance within this 'consociational' structure (for this term see Lijphart 1977) was more or less maintained and enough resources for such distribution mechanisms were available, the regime proved very stable. In the face of relative economic prosperity and favourable external conditions, in comparison to the majority of the neighbouring states, this was the case for the first three decades after independence.

The 1990s brought with them a number of important external and internal changes, which damaged both the economic situation as well as political stability. The structural adjustment programmes administrated by the IMF, the drastic devaluation of the CFA-Franc and the decline in price of the main export product, cocoa, endangered the middle classes and elites of the clientelistic system, who until then had prospered. The political landscape also changed dramatically, mainly due to the externally initiated return to a multi-party system (after the conference of La Baule in 1990). The successor to the presidency after the death of Houphouët-Boigny in 1993, Bédié, no longer possessed the legitimating aura of the 'Father of the Nation', and demonstrated much less competence and skill in the way he managed the office. The current situation thus also tends towards a more 'competitive clientelism', in so far as adequate resources are available.[1]

The situation in Kenya demonstrates certain parallels to the Ivory Coast, but also a few important differences. Here, too, a single party, KANU, was in power for a long period of time under relatively prosperous economic conditions. But, due to the high level of nepotism and corruption, the 'neo-patrimonial' structures led to increasing inefficiency and economic decline. The opening to a multi-party system, which was forced by the 'donor countries' of the Paris Club in 1992, reduced the clientelistic base of KANU to regional ethnic strongholds, which increased bitterness among its adversaries even more. But the opposition parties as well are basically structured according to regional and ethnic criteria and were not in a position to offer a common alternative to the Moi regime (which is now consigned to minority status). Thus, the country finds itself in a phase of economic stagnation and political stalemate, which with regard to the recent constitutional debates seems to be difficult to solve. However, the political opening and greater freedom of political expression, which was positively evaluated in our survey, will prove difficult to revoke.

The (re-)democratisation processes which can be observed in the four countries thus offer very different pictures, as expressed in the 'view from below' by the urban poor. However, this perspective at the 'micro' level of political analysis in no way justifies the long-advocated theory of the incompatibility of poverty and democracy. In contrast, as our survey confirmed many times, democratisation represents an important element of hope and, amongst other things, an instrument for the long-term improvement of economic and political relations. Greater personal and political freedoms and legal protection of civil rights are acknowledged as valuable in their own right. Greater political competition and transparency can increase the efficiency of the regimes. A greater level of political stability and legitimacy also improves the national and international economic conditions. Even under circumstances characterised by strong clientelistic aspects, such as in the Ivory Coast and Kenya, and also partly in Brazil, the right to vote and elections represent important means of interest articulation and are a resource in the 'uneven exchange' with the respective parties and 'patrons', especially for the poorest groups amongst the population. In the words of Amartya Sen, the holder of the 1998 Nobel Prize for economics, 'A country does not have to be deemed fit *for* democracy, rather it has to become fit *through* democracy' (Sen 1999).

In this respect, our study has provided some important results and trends towards change, but also registered concrete initiatives of internal and external cooperation with and for the urban poor under very different conditions. In this way, it can serve as a base for further systematic, comparative studies using similar research instruments in other countries and regions.

In the future, intensive inter-cultural dialogues as they have been possible in our project and concluding symposium will further enhance both the methodological quality of such research and our mutual understanding of often very delicate problems and their subtle meanings. This, in a modest way, may contribute to the long-term fight against poverty and for the consolidation of democracy.

Note

1. The military putsch of December 1999 could neither be foreseen nor taken into account in our study. The subsequent presidential elections, which saw the FPI leader, Gbabgo, in front, were extremely lopsided and strong social and political tensions remain. At best again, a certain 'competitive clientelism' is being continued.

Bibliography

Adorno, Theodor. W. et al. (1950): *The Authoritarian Personality*. New York.

Alemann, Ulrich von (1975): *Partizipation, Demokratisierung, Mitbestimmung*. Opladen.

Almond, Gabriel/Verba, Sidney (eds) (1963): *The Civic Culture. Political Attitudes and Democracy in Five Nations*. Princeton.

Almond, Gabriel/Verba, Sidney (eds) (1980): *The Civic Culture Revisited*. Boston.

Antoine, Philippe/Dubresson, A./Manou-Savina, Annie (1987): *Abidjan 'côté cour': Pour comprendre la question de l'habitat*. Paris.

Antoine, Philippe/Kouamé, Aka (1994): 'Côte d'Ivoire' in: Tarver, Jean Pierre (ed.): *Urbanization in Africa: a Handbook*. Wesport: 141-64.

Apter, David E. (1965): *The Politics of Modernization*. Chicago.

Aquevedo Soto, Eduardo (1998): 'Neoliberalismo, mercado de trabajo y pobreza en Chile' in: *Estudios Latinoamericanos*, Year 5, No. 10, 175–94.

Aseka, E.M. (1990): 'Urbanization' in: Ochieng, William R. (ed.): *Themes in Kenyan History*. Nairobi: 44-67.

Asher, H.A./Richardson, B.M. (1984): *Political Participation*. Frankfurt.

Assies, Willem (1993): 'Urban Social Movements and Local Democracy in Brazil', in: *European Review of Latin American and Caribbean Studies* 55: 39–58.

Atal, Yogesh/Oyen, Else (eds) (1997): *Poverty and Participation in Civil Society*. Paris: Unesco.

Attahi, Koffi (1997): 'Decentralisation and participatory urban governance in francophone Africa' in: Swilling, Mark (ed.): *Governing Africa's Cities*. Witwatersrand University Press: 161-209.

Augel, Johannes (1985): 'Siedlungsstruktur, Sozialstruktur und Überlebensstrategien in brasilianischen Elendsvierteln' in: Augel, J. (ed.): *Leben in Armut*. Mettingen: 11–34.

Bader, Veit Michael (1991): *Kollektives Handeln. Protheorie sozialer Ungleichheit und kollektiven Handelns II*. Opladen.

Barkan, J. (ed.) (1984): *Politics and Public Policy in Kenya and Tanzania*. New York.

Barnes, Samuel H./Kaase, Max et al. (1979): *Political Action. Mass Participation in Five Western Democracies*. Beverly Hills, London.

Becker, Charles/Homer, Andrew (eds) (1994): *Beyond Urban Bias in Africa: urbanization in an era of structural adjustment*. London.

Bennholdt-Thomson, V. (1979): 'Marginalität in Lateinamerika' in: *Lateinamerika. Analysen und Berichte 3.* Berlin.

Bento Rubião (1993): *Favelas e as organizações comunitárias.* Petrópolis, Rio de Janeiro.

Berelson, B.R. et al. (1954): *Voting.* Chicago.

Berg-Schlosser, Dirk (1979): *The Social and Economic Bases of Politics in Kenya.* Berkeley.

Berg-Schlosser, Dirk (1985). *Leistungen und Fehlleistungen politischer Systeme in der Dritten Welt als Kriterium der Entwicklungspolitik.* Zeitschrift für Konjunkturpolitik: 79–114.

Berg-Schlosser, Dirk (1987): 'Politischer Klientelismus' in: Görlitz, Axel/Prätorius, Rainer (eds): *Handbuch Politikwissenschaft. Grundlagen – Forschungsstand – Perspektiven,* Reinbek bei Hamburg: 207–13.

Berg-Schlosser, Dirk (1990): 'Typologies of Third World Political Systems' in: Bebler, A./Seroka, J. (eds): *Contemporary Political Systems.* Boulder: 173–201.

Berg-Schlosser, Dirk (1997): 'Universalität der Menschenrechte?' in: Brocker, Manfred/ Nau, Heino (eds): *Ethnozentrismus.* Darmstad: 289–306.

Berg-Schlosser, Dirk/Kersting, Norbert (1988): 'Politische Aktionsformen und Einwirkungsmöglichkeiten urbaner marginalisierter Gruppen. Thesenpapier zum Workshop Habitat'. Marburg, unpublished manuscript.

Berg-Schlosser, Dirk/Kersting, Norbert (1996): 'Warum weltweit Demokratisierung' in: Hanisch, R. (ed.): *Demokratieexport in die Länder des Südens.* Hamburg: 93–143.

Berg-Schlosser, Dirk/Siegler, Rainer (1988): *Politische Stabilität und Entwicklung. Eine vergleichende Analyse der Bestimmungsfaktoren und Interaktionsmuster in Kenia, Tansania und Uganda.* Köln

Binder, L. (1977): 'Review Essays. Political Participation and Political Development' in: *American Journal of Sociology* 83, 3: 751–60.

BMZ (1990): *Sektorübergreifendes Konzept. Armutsbekämpfung durch Selbsthilfe. Selbsthilfebewegungen als Partner der Entwicklungszusammenarbeit.* Bonn.

BMZ (1994): *Hinweise zur Armutsbekämpfung.* Bonn.

BMZ (1995): *Sektorkonzept. Umweltgerechte Kommunal- und Stadtentwicklung.* September. Bonn.

BMZ (1999): *Sektorkonzept. Partizipative Entwicklungszusammenarbeit.* Bonn.

Borchert, Günter (1972): *Die Wirtschaftsräume der Elfenbeinküste. Hamburger Beiträge zur Afrika-Kunde.* Vol. 13. Deutsches Institut für Afrika-Forschung. Hamburg.

Boris, Dieter et al. (1971): *Chile auf dem Weg zum Sozialismus.* Köln

Boschi, Renato/Diniz, Eli/Lessa, Robert (1989): *Modernização e consolidação democrática no Brasil: dilemas da nova república.* São Paulo.

Bratton, Michael/Walle, Nicolas van de (1997): *Democratic Experiments in Africa. Regime Transitions in Comparative Perspective.*

Brennan, Ellen M. (1993): 'Urban land and housing issues facing the third world' in: Kasarda, John D. Parnell, Allan M. (eds): *Third World Cities. Problems, Policies and Prospects.* Newbury Park.

Brock, Lothar (1991): 'Die Dritte Welt im internationalem System' in *Handbuch Dritte Welt .1* Bonn, 3rd edn, Vol. 1: 446–66.

Brühl, Dieter (1992): 'Die brasilianische Verfassung von 1988 und die Munizipien' in: *Archiv für Kommunikationswissenschaften* 1: 41–53.

Bultmann, Ingo (1995): 'Die Nachbarschaftsbewegung und der Wandel politischer Systeme. Mexiko und Chile im Vergleich' in: Bultmann, Ingo/ Hellmann, Michaela/Meschkat, Klaus/Rojas, Jorge (eds): *Demokratie ohne soziale Bewegung? Gewerkschaften, Stadtteil- und Frauenbewegungen in Chile und Mexiko.* Unkel/Rhein, Bad Honnef: 143–234.

Butterworth, D./Chance, J. (1981): *Latin American Urbanization.* Cambridge.

Calcagnotto, Gilberto (1991): 'Die Parlaments- und Gouverneurswahlen in Brasilien 1990' in: *Lateinamerika. Analysen – Daten – Dokumentation* (8) 17/18: 65–81.

Calcagnotto, Gilberto (1994): 'Politische Kultur und Demokratisierung' in: Briesemeister, Dietrich et al. (eds): *Brasilien heute: Politik, Wirtschaft, Kultur.* Frankfurt/M.: 176–96.

Calcagnotto, Gilberto (1998): 'Das Parteienspektrum Brasiliens' in: *Der Überblick,* (34) 2: 11.

Camacho, D./Menjivar, R. (eds) (1989): *Los movimientos populares en America Latina.* Mexico.

Campbell, A. et al. (1960): *The American Voter.* New York

Campero, Guillermo (1987): *Entre la sobrevivencia y la acción política. Las organizaciones de pobladores en Santiago.* Santiago.

Cardoso, Ruth Corrêa Leite (1983): 'Movimentos sociais urbanos: balanço crítico' in: Sorj, Bernando/Almeida, Maria Hermínia Tavares de (eds): *Sociedade e política no Brasil pós-64.* São Paulo: 215–39.

Cardoso, Ruth Corrêa Leite (1988): 'Os movimentos populares no contexto da consolidação da democracia' in: Reis, Fábio Wanderley/O'Donnell, Guillermo (eds): *A democracia no Brasil: dilemas e perspectivas.* São Paulo: 368–82.

Cardoso, Ruth Corrêa Leite (1995): 'Mudança Sociocultural e Participação Política nos anos 80' in: Sola, Lourdes/Paulani, Leda M. (eds): *Lições da década de 80.* São Paulo: 193–200.

Castells, Manuel (1983): *The City and the Grassroots.* London.

CEPAL (1999): *Panorama social de América Latina 1998.* Santiago

Chauí, Marilena (1995): 'Politische Kultur und Kulturpolitik' in: Sevilla, Rafael/ Ribeiro, Darcy (eds): Brasilien: *Land der Zukunft?* Unkel/Rhein, Bad Honnef: 187–201.

Collier, P. (1998): *Social Capital and Poverty.* World Bank. Social Capital Working Paper No. 4. Washington.

Collier, Simon/Sater, William F. (1996): *A History of Chile, 1808–1994.*

Cornelius, Wayne A. (1973): 'Political Learning among the Migrant Poor: The Impact of Residential Context' in: *Sage Professional Papers in Comparative Politics,* 01–037. Beverly Hills.

Corten, André (1996): *Os pobres e o Espírito Santo: o pentecostalismo no Brasil.* Petrópolis, Rio de Janeiro.

Cruz, Maria Elisa da (1992): *Associações de Moradores: a política e os políticos.* Rio de Janeiro.

Cruz, Maria Elisa da (2000): 'Reflections on the Report 'Poverty and Democracy', paper presented at the symposium 'Poverty Reduction by Participation?'. Marburg, Institute of Political Science. July (mimeo).

Daffa, Paulus/Gerhard M. Wolts (eds) (1992): *Entwicklungshilfe dorthin!* Münster.

Dahl, R.A. (1971): *Polyarchy. Participation and Opposition.* New Haven.

Dahl, Robert A. (1989): *Democracy and Its Critics.* Cambridge, Mass.

Dahrendorf, Ralf (1994): *Der moderne soziale Konflikt. Essay zur Politik der Freiheit.* München.

De Soto, H. (1986): *El otro sendero.* Lima.

Dembélé, Ousmane (1995): 'Formes de traitement de l'habitat précaire dans l'organisation spatiale de la métropole d'Abidjan'. Abidjan. Unpublished manuscript.

Dembélé, Ousmane (2000): 'Organisation des groupes pauvres dans les quartiers precaires', paper presented at the symposium 'Poverty Reduction by Participation?' Marburg, Institute of Political Science. July (mimeo).

DESAL (1969): *Marginalidad en América Latina - un ensayo de diagnóstico.* Barcelona.

Deutsch, Karl W. (1961). 'Social Mobilization and Political Development' in *American Political Science Review,* 60 (3): 493–514.

Di Palma, Giuseppe (1970): *Apathy and Participation. Mass Politics in Western Societies.* London.

Diamond, Larry (1999): *Developing Democracy. Toward Consolidation.* Baltimore: Johns Hopkins University Press

Díaz, Alvaro (1993): 'Restructuring and the New Working Classes in Chile. Trends in Waged Employment, Informality and Poverty, 1973–1990'. UNRISD Discussion Paper 47, Genf.

Dietz, Henry (1975): *Becoming a Poblador: Political Adjustment to the Urban Environment in Lima,* Peru. Stanford.

Diniz, Eli (1981): 'Favelas: associativismo e participação social'. Rio de Janeiro: IUPERJ (mimeo).

Doimo, Ana Maria (1995): *A vez e a voz do popular: movimentos sociais e participação política no Brasil pós-70.* Rio de Janeiro.

Drakakis-Smith, Daniel (1981): *Urbanisation, Housing and the Development Process.* London.

Easton, David (1965): *A Systems Analysis of Political Life*. Chicago.

Easton, David (1975): 'A Reassessment of the Concept of Political Support' in: *British Journal of Political Science* 5: 435–57.

Eckstein, Susan (1989) *Power and Popular Protest: Latin American social movements*. Berkeley: University of California Press.

Eisenstadt, S. N./Lemarchand, R. (eds), (1981): *Political Clientelism, Patronage and Development*. London.

EIU Country Report (1995): *Côte d'Ivoire*. London.

Elwert, Georg/Evers, Hans-Dieter/Wilkens, Werner (1982): *Die Suche nach Sicherheit – kombinierte Produktionsformen im sogenannten 'informellen Sektor'*. Bielefeld.

Espinoza, Vicente (1993): 'Pobladores, participación social y cudadanía: entre los pasajes y las anchas alamedas' in: *Proposiciones*, No. 22: 21–53.

Espinoza, Vincente (2000): 'Comments on Living Conditions and Social Structures', paper presented at the symposium 'Poverty Reduction by Participation?' Marburg, Institute of Political Science. July (mimeo).

Evers, Hans-Dieter (1981): 'Zur Theorie der urbanen Unterentwicklung' in: *Dritte Welt* 1–2: 61–8.

Evers, Tilman (1980): 'Reproduktion der Arbeitskraft und stätische Bewegungen. Der Fall der illegalen Parzellierung in São Paulo' in: *Perepherie* 2 (1980), 28–47.

Evers, Tilman (1984): 'Identidade: a face oculta dos novos movimentos sociais' in: *Novos Estudos CEBRAP*, São Paulo, (2) 4: 11–22.

Evers, Tilman/Müller-Plantenberg, Clarissa/Spessart, Stefanie (1979): 'Stadtteilbewegung und Staat. Kämpfe im Reproduktionsbereich in Lateinamerika' in: Bennholdt-Thomson, Veronika et al. (eds): *Lateinamerika: Analysen und Berichte*. Vol. 3. Berlin: 118–70.

Fatheuer, Thomas (1993): 'Die Bruchlandung der Take-Off-Träume' in: Dirmoser, Dietmar et al. (eds): *Markt in den Köpfen. Lateinamerika – Analysen und Berichte* 17, Unkel/Rhein, Bad Honnef: 153–66.

Fatheuer, Thomas (1994): 'Jenseits des staatlichen Gewaltmonopols Drogenbanden, Todesschwadronen und Profiteure: die andere Privatisierung in Rio de Janeiro' in: Dirmoser, Dietmar et al. (eds): *Jenseits des Staates?* Hamburg: 23–38.

Fauré, Yves-A./Médard, Jean-François (eds) (1982): *Etat et bourgeoisie en Côte d'Ivoire*. Karthala. Paris.

Fausto Neto, Ana Maria Quiroga (1993): 'Revivendo mecanismos autoritários: as organizações de moradores na gestão de políticas públicas' in: Nascimento, Elimar Pinheiro do/Barreira, Irlys Alencar F. (eds): *Brasil urbano: cenários da ordem e da desordem*. Rio de Janeiro: 17–32.

Fernandes, Rubem César (1994): 'Governo das Almas: Denominações Evangélicas no Grande Rio' in: *Revista do Rio*: 9–22.

Flora, Peter (1999): *State Formation, Nation Building and Mass Participation in Europe. The theory of Stein Rokkan.* Oxford.

Friedmann, John (1989): 'The Latin American Barrio Movement as a Social Movement: Contribution to a Debate' in: *International Journal of Urban and Regional Research* 13, 3: 501–10.

Friedmann, John (1992): *Empowerment.* Cambridge (Mass.).

Friedmann, Reinhard (1990): *Chile unter Pinochet. Das autoritäre Experiment (1973–1990).* Freiburg.

Fuchs, Dieter (1987): 'Trends politischer Unterstützung in der Bundesrepublik' in: Berg-Schlosser, Dirk/Schissler, Jakob (eds): *Politische Kultur in Deutschland. PVS-Sonderheft* 18, Opladen: 357–77.

Fuchs, Dieter (1989): *Die Unterstützung des politischen Systems der Bundesrepublik Deutschland.* Opladen.

Füchtner, Hans (1972): *Die brasilianischen Arbeitergewerkschaften, ihre Organisation und ihre politische Funktion.* Frankfurt/M.

Gabriel, Oscar W. (1986): *Politische Kultur, Postmaterialismus und Materialismus in der Bundesrepublik Deutschland.* Opladen.

Gabriel, Oscar W. (1994): 'Politische Einstellungen und politische Kultur' in: Gabriel, Oscar W./Brettschneider, Frank (eds): *Die EU-Staaten im Vergleich. Strukturen, Prozesse, Politikinhalte.* Opladen: 96–136.

García, Ligia et al. (1994): 'Chile' in: Töpper, Barbara/Müller-Plantenberg, Urs (eds): *Transformation im südlichen lateinamerika.* Frankfurt: 148–203.

Garretón, Manuel Antonio (1995a): *Hacia una nueva era política. Estudio sobre las democratizaciones.* México DF. Santiago.

Garretón, Manuel Antonio (1995b): 'Redemocratization in Chile' in: *Journal of Democracy.* Vol. 6. No. 1: 146–58.

Garretón, Manuel Antonio/Lagos, Marta/Méndez, Roberto (1994): *Los Chilenos y la Democracia. La opinión pública 1991–1994. Informe 1993.* Santiago.

Garretón, Manuel Antonio/Lagos, Marta/Méndez, Roberto (1995): *Los Chilenos y la Democracia. La opinión pública 1991–1994. Informe 1994.* Santiago.

Gay, Robert (1994): *Popular Organization and Democracy in Rio de Janeiro – a Tale of Two Favelas.* Philadelphia.

Gibbal, Jean-Marie (1974): *Citadins et paysans dans la ville africaine. L'exemple d'Abidjan.* Presses Universitaires de Grenoble. François Maspero.

Gilbert, Alan (1993): *In Search of a Home. Rental and Shared Housing in Latin America.* London.

Gilbert, Alan/Gugler, Josef (1992): *Cities, Poverty and Development. Urbanization in the Third World.* Oxford.

Glembotski, (1985): 'Ausmaß und Wirkungschancen informeller Wirtschaftsaktivitäten in der metropolitanen Region Recife' in: Augel, J. (ed.) *1985: Leben in Armut.* Mettingen: 48–81

Gronemeyer, R. (1984): 'Partizipation' in: Kerber, H./Schmieder, A. (eds): *Handbuch Soziologie.* Reinbek: 428–31.

Guerra, Carlos (1994): 'Tejido social, conjuntos de acción y actitudes políticas en Santiago de Chile' in: Villasante, Tomás R. (ed.): *Las ciudades hablen.* Caracas: 201–18.

Hall, John A. (ed.) (1995): *Civil Society,* Cambridge, Polity Press.

Hanisch, Rolf (ed.) (1983): *Soziale Bewegungen in Entwicklungsländern.* Baden Baden.

Happe, Barbara (2000): *Armut und Politik. Politisches Denken und Handeln von städtischen Armen in Brasilien.* Mettingen.

Hillebrand, Ernst/Mehler, Andreas (1994): *Sozio-kulturelle Kurzanalyse: Côte d'Ivoire.* Hamburg.

Hippler, Jochen (ed.) (1995): *The Democratization of Disempowerment.* London.

Hirschman, Albert (1970): *Exit, Voice, and Loyalty: Responses to Decline in Firms, Organizations, and States.* Cambridge, Mass.

Hofmeier, Rolf/Schönborn (ed.) (1987): *Politisches Lexikon Afrika.* München.

Hopkins, Terence K./Wallerstein, Immanuel (eds) 1980: *Processes of the World System.* Beverly Hills.

Hunneus, Carlos (1981): *Der Zusammenbruch der Demokratie in Chile.* Heidelberg.

Huntington, Samuel P. (1996): *The Third Wave – Democratization in the Late Twentieth Century.* Norman.

IBASE (1990): *Rio de Janeiro: radiografia das lutas de bairro no Estado – 1988/1989. Mapeamento das organizações comunitárias filiadas à FAMERJ no Estado do Rio de Janeiro.* Rio de Janeiro.

IBGE (1991): *Censo Demográfico 1991. Indicadores sócio-demográficos – grandes regiões e unidades de federação.* Rio de Janeiro.

IBGE (1995): *Indicadores sociai: uma análise da década de 1980.* Rio de Janeiro.

Illy, Hans/Oberndörfer, Dieter (1981): *Sozio-kulturelle Faktoren und urbane Sozialstrukturhilfe. Überlegungen anhand der Programme des 'National Christian Council of Kenya' in Mathare Valley, Nairobi, Kenya.* Freiburg.

Imbusch, Peter (1995): *Unternehmer und Politik in Chile.* Frankfurt/Main.

Imbusch, Peter (1999): 'Chile: Die politische Konstituierung von Märkten und die Dynamisierung unternehmerischen Handelns als Zwangsprojekt' in: *Peripherie.* No. 73/74: 29–52.

IMF (1998): *Côte d'Ivoire: Selected Issues and Statistical Appendix.* IMF Staff Country Report No. 98/46,Washington, DC.

INE (1987): *Compendio Estadístico.* Santiago.

Inglehart, Ronald (1992): 'Vergleichende Wertewandelforschung' in: Berg-Schlosser, Dirk/Müller-Rommel, Ferdinand (eds): *Vergleichende Politikwissenschaft.* Opladen. 2nd edn: 125–49.

Institut National de la Statistique. Dimbo, Toé. Zanou, Benjamin (INS) (1994): *Aspects démographiques et socio-économiques des migrations Burkinabé vers la Côte d'Ivoire.* Abidjan.

IPLAN-Rio (1995): *Favelas cariocas – alguns dados estatísticos.* Rio de Janeiro.

Jacobi, Pedro Roberto (1988): *Movimentos reivindicatórios urbanos, estado e cultura política: reflexões em torno da ação coletiva e dos seus efeitos politico-institucionais no Brasil*. Rio de Janeiro.

Jakobeit, Cord (1983): 'Elfenbeinküste: Zitadelle der Stabilität oder Kartenhaus? Die Kopplung von Erfolgen und Grenzen des Entwicklungswegs sowie mögliche Perspektiven' in: *Afrika Spektrum*. Part 3, Year X. Hamburg: 257-65.

Jakobeit, Cord (1984): *Die sozio-ökonomische Entwicklung der Côte d'Ivoire seit der Unabhängigkeit*. Hamburg.

Jakobeit, Cord (1993): 'Elfenbeinküste' in: Nohlen, Dieter/ Nuscheler, Franz (eds): *Handbuch der Dritten Welt. Westafrika und Zentralafrika*. Vol. 4. 3. völlig neu bearbeitete Auflage. Bonn: 192-211.

Kaase, Max/Marsh, A. (1979): 'Political Action' in: Barnes, S.H./Kaase, M. et al.: *Political Action*. Beverly Hills: 27–56.

Kaiser, Wilfried (1995): 'Urbanisierung, Regionalentwicklung und Stadtentwicklungspolitik: Brasilien im räumlichen Wandel' in: Sevilla, Rafael/Ribeiro, Darcy (eds): *Brasilien: Land der Zukunft?* Unkel/Rhein, Bad Honnef: 67–89.

Kanté, Kébé (1994): *Die Problematik der politischen Macht und Herrschaft in der postkolonialen Côte d'Ivoire. Staat und Gesellschaft (1960–1992)*. Hamburg, Münster.

Karsch, Thomas (1993): *Zum Verhältnis von Armut, sozialen Konflikten und Sozialpolitik. Eine empirische Untersuchung in Favelas von Rio de Janeiro*. Frankfurt/M.

Kersting, Norbert (1994): *Armut und Demokratie in Zimbabwe. Urbaner Lebensstil und politische Partizipation*. Hamburg, Münster.

Kersting, Norbert (1996): *Urbane Armut. Überlebensstrategien in der 'Dritten Welt'*. Verlag für Entwicklungpolitik. Saarbrücken.

Kersting, Norbert (1999): 'Inklusion der urbanen Marginalen' in: Berg-Schlosser, D./Giegel, H.-J.: *Perspektiven der Demokratie*. Frankfurt: 289–317.

Klingemann, Hans-Dieter (1985): *Formen, Bestimmungsgründe und Konsequenzen politischer Beteiligung*. Berlin.

Koch, Gisela (1996): 'Einkommensverteilung und Inflation' in: Calcagnotto, Gilberto/Fritz, Barbara (eds): *Inflation und Stabilisierung in Brasilien. Probleme einer Gesellschaft im Wandel*. Frankfurt/M.: 293–315.

Kochendörfer-Lucius, Gudrun (1994): *Strukturelle Armutsbekämpfung durch Partizipation*. BMZ.

Kohlhepp, Gerd (1994): 'Raum und Bevölkerung' in: Briesenmeister, Dietrich et al. (eds): *Brasilien heute: Politik, Wirtschaft, Kultur*. Frankfurt/M.: 9–107.

König, Claus-Dieter (1998): *Politisches Handeln der städtischen Armen in Kenia*. Münster.

Kowarick, Lúcio (1984): 'Os caminhos do encontro: as lutas sociais em São Paulo na década de 70' in: *Presença* 2: 65–78.

Lachmann, Werner (1994): *Entwicklungspolitik*. München.

Lagos, Marta (1995): 'Cultura política y transición a la democracia en Chile' in:

Nohlen, Dieter (ed.) (1994): *Democracia y neocritica en America Latina*. Frankfurt: 160–91.

Lane, Robert E. (1959): *Political Life. Why People Get Involved in Politics*. Glencoe.

Lauga, Martín (1996): 'Chile: Demokratie zwischen Konsens und Konflikt' in: *Nord-Süd Aktuell*. Year 10, No. 1: 115–25.

Leeds, E. (1972): *Forms of Squattment and Political Organization. The Politics of Control in Brazil*. Austin.

Leiva, Fernando / Agacino, Rafael (1994): 'Mercado de trabajo flexible, pobreza y desintegración social en Chile 1990–1994' Santiago, unpublished paper.

Lepsius, M.R. (1966): 'Parteiensystem und Sozialstruktur' in: Abel, W. et al. (eds) 1996: *Wirtschaft, Geschichte und Wirtschaftsgeschichte*. Stuttgart: 56–80.

Lewis, Oscar (1966): 'The Culture of Poverty' in: *Scientific American* 215.

Linn, J.F. (1984): *Cities in the Developing World*. Oxford.

Linz, Juan J. / Stepan, Alfred (1996): *Problems of Democratic Transition and Consolidation: Southern Europe, South America, and Post-Communist Europe*. Baltimore.

Lipset, Seymour (1994). 'The Social Requisites of Democracy Revisited' in: *American Sociological Review*, 59 (1): 1–22.

Lopes de Souza, Marcelo (2000): 'Political Participation of the Urban Poor in Brazil' commentary presented at the symposium 'Poverty Reduction by Participation?' Marburg, Institute of Political Science. July (mimeo).

Lucchini, R. (1977): 'Aspects théoretiques de la marginalité social' in: *Schweizerische Zeitschrift für Soziologie* 3 (1977) 3.

Luhmann, Niklas (1980): *Gesellschaftstruktur und Semantik*. Bd 1. Frankfurt / M.

Mainwaring, Scott (1986): *Grassroots Popular Movements, Identity and Democratization in Brazil*. Notre Dame.

Mainwaring, Scott (1991a): 'Politicians, Parties, and Electoral Systems: Brazil in Comparative Perspective' in: *Comparative Politics* 24 (1): 21–43.

Mainwaring, Scott (1991b): 'Políticos, partidos e sistemas eleitorais. O Brasil numa perspectiva comparativa' in: *Novos Estudos CEBRAP* 29: 34–58.

Mainwaring, Scott (1999): *Rethinking Party Systems in the Third Wave of Democratization. The Case of Brazil*. Stanford, Ca.

Mainwaring, Scott / Share, Donald (1986): 'Transição pela transação: democratização no Brasili e na Espanha' in: *Dados (Revista de Ciencias Sociais)*, (29) 2: 207–36.

Mangin, William P. (ed.) 1970: *Peasants in the City*. Boston.

Martins, Luciano (1986): 'The "Liberalization" of Authoritarian Rule in Brazil' in: O'Donnell, Guillermo / Schmitter, Philippe / Whitehead, Laurence (eds): *Transition from Authoritarian Rule: Prospects for Democracy*. Baltimore, London: 72–94.

McClosky, Herbert (1958): 'Conservatism and Personality' in: *American Political Science Review* 52: 27–54.

McClosky, Herbert (1965): 'Consensus and Ideology in American Politics' in: *American Political Science Review* 58: 361–82.

McClosky, Herbert/Schaar, John H. (1965): 'Psychological Dimensions of Anomy' in: *American Sociological Review* 30:14–40.

McInnes, George (1995): *Hope and Despair in Urban Self-Help Building. The case of the Dandora Community Development Housing Project in Nairobi*. Nairobi.

Meinardus, Mark (1982): *Marginalität. Theoretische Aspekte und entwicklungspolitische Konsequenzen*. Saarbrücken.

Meller, Patricio (1990): 'Una perspectiva de largo plazo del desarrollo económico chileno 1830–1990' in: Blomström, Magnus/Meller, Patricio (eds): *Trayectorias divergentes*. Santiago

Menzel, Ulrich (1992): *Das Ende der Dritten Welt und das Scheitern der großen Theorie*. Frankfurt.

Merkel, Wolfgang (1999): *Defective Democracies*. Working Papers, Juan March Institute, No. 132. Madrid.

Mesa-Lago, Carmelo (1994): *Changing Social Security in Latin America. Toward Alleviating the Social Costs of Economic Reform*. Boulder, Co.

MIDEPLAN (1992a): *Población, educación, vivienda, salud, empleo y pobreza. CASEN 1990*. Santiago.

MIDEPLAN (1992b): *Participación de la comunidad en el desarrollo social. Logros y proyecciones*. Santiago.

MIDEPLAN (1994a): *Situación de la pobreza en Chile: 1987–1992*. Santiago.

MIDEPLAN (1994b): *Integración al desarrollo. Balance de la política social: 1990–1993*. Santiago.

MIDEPLAN (1998): *Evolución del empleo en Chile, 1990–1996*. Santiago.

MIDEPLAN (1999a): *Pobreza y distribución del ingreso en Chile 1998. Resultados de la VII Encuesta de Caracterización Socioeconómica Nacional (CASEN)*. Santiago.

MIDEPLAN (1999b): *Resultados de la VII Encuesta de Caracterización Socioeconómica Nacional (CASEN 1998). Focalización e impacto distributivo de los subsidios monetarios 1998*. No. 2. Santiago.

MIDEPLAN/División Social (1997): *Pobreza y distribución del ingreso en Chile, 1996. Resultados de la Encuesta de Caracterización Socioeconómica Nacional*. Santiago.

Milbrath, Lester W./Goel, M. L. (1965): *Political Participation. How and Why Do People Get Involved in Politics*. Chicago.

Milbrath, Lester W./Goel, L. (1977): *Political Participation. How and Why Do People Get Involved in Politics*. 2nd edn.

Miller, S.M. (1996): 'The great chain of poverty explanation' in: Oyen, Else et al. (eds) (1996): *Poverty. A global view*. Paris: Unesco: 569–86.

Ministerio del Interior, Subsecretaría de Desarrollo Regional y Administrativo (1992): *Manual de Gestión Municipal*. Santiago.

Minkner-Bünjer, Mechthild (1993): 'Armut und Verteilung: Herausforderung

Chiles zum Jahre 2000' in: *Lateinamerika. Analysen-Daten-Dokumentation* Vol. 10, No. 23: 69–94

Mitchell, J.C. (1987): *Cities, Societies and Social Perception.* Oxford.

Mitullah, Winnie V. (2000): 'A review of manuscript on poverty and democracy: self help and political participation in Third World countries', paper presented at the symposium 'Poverty Reduction by Participation?' Marburg, Institute of Political Science (mimeo).

Moisés, José Alvaro (1994): *Political legitimacy in Brazil in the 90s, a study of public satisfaction with the actual functioning of democracy.* Berlin.

Moisés, José Alvaro/Martinez-Alier, Verena (1978): 'A revolta dos suburbanos ou "Patrão, o trem atrasou"' in: Moisés, José Alvaro et al. (orgs.): *Contradições urbanas e movimentos sociais.* Rio de Janeiro.

Moisés; José Álvaro (1995): *Os brasileiros e a democracia. Bases sócio-políticas da legitimidade democrática.* São Paulo.

Molina, Sergio (1996): 'A public institutional framework for social policy' in: Pizarro, Crisostomo; Raczynski, Dagmar; Vial, Joaquin (eds): *Social and economic policies in Chile's transition to democracy.* UNICEF. Santiago: 153-78.

Moltmann, Bernhard (1989): 'Brasilien: Zwanzig Jahre Militärherrschaft – Lange Schatten eines ehrgeizigen Entwicklungsmodells' in: Steinweg, Rainer (Red): *Militärregime und Entwicklungspolitik.* Frankfurt/M.: 87–103.

Moltmann, Bernhard (1994): 'Das Militär: Neuorientierungen in Zeiten der Krise' in: Briesemeister, Dietrich et al. (eds): *Brasilien heute: Politik, Wirtschaft, Kultur.* Frankfurt/M.: 229–42.

Moulián, Tomás (1994): 'Limitaciones de la transición a la democracia en Chile' in: *Proposiciones* 25: 34–45.

Muller, Edward N. (1988): 'Democracy, Economic Development, and Income Inequality' in: *American Sociological Review* 53: 50–68.

Müller-Plantenberg, Clarita (1983): *Überlebenskampf und Selbstbestimmung.* Frankfurt/M.

Munzinger Archiv (ed.) (1994): *Internationales Handbuch – Länder aktuell. Côte d'Ivoire.* Ravensburg.

Nasimiyu, Ruth (1993): 'The History of Maendeleo ya Wanawake Movement in Kenya, 1952–1975' in: Khasiani, Shanyisa A. Njiro, Esther I. (eds): *The Women's Movement in Kenya.* Nairobi.

Nguessan Zoukou, L. (1990): *Régions et régionalisation en Côte d'Ivoire.* Paris, L' Harmattan.

Nie, Norman H./Verba, Sidney (1975): 'Political Participation' in: Greenstein, F.I./Polsby, N.W. (eds): *Handbook of Political Science*, Vol. 4, Reading/ Mass.

Nohlen, Dieter (1990): *Wahlrecht und Parteiensystem.* Opladen.

Nohlen, Dieter (1988): 'Mehr Demokratie in der Dritten Welt' in: *Aus Politik und Zeitgeschichte* Vol. 25–26:3–18

Nohlen, Dieter/Nuscheler, Franz (eds) (1992): *Handbuch der Dritten Welt.* Vol. 2: Südamerika. Bonn.

Nun, José (1969): 'Presentación' in: Revista Latinoamericana de Sociología 5, 2: 174–77.

Nzunga, Michael P.K. (2000): 'Comments on the living conditions and social structure', paper presented at the symposium 'Poverty Reduction by Participation?' Marburg, Institute of Political Science. July (mimeo).

O'Donnell, Guillermo A. (1979): Modernization and Bureaucratic Authoritarianism. Studies in South American Politics. Berkeley.

O'Donnell, Guillermo A. (1988): 'Hiatos, instituições e perspectivas democráticas' in: O'Donnell, Guillermo/Reis, Wanderley Fábio (eds): A Democracia no Brasil – dilemas e perspectivas. São Paulo: 72–90.

O'Donnell, Guillermo A. (1996): 'Illusions about consolidation' in: Journal of Democracy 7 (1996) 2: 34–51.

O'Donnell, Guillermo/Schmitter, Phillipe C./Whitehead, Lawrence (eds) (1986): Transitions from Authoritarian Rule. Baltimore.

Offe, Claus (1972): 'Politische Herrschaft und Klassenstrukturen. Zur Analyse spätkapitalistischer Gesellschaftssysteme' in: Kress, Gisela/Senghaas, Dieter (eds): Politikwissenschaft. Eine Einführung in ihre Probleme. Frankfurt/M.: 135–64.

Oliveira, Jane Souto de (ed.) (1993): O traço da desigualidade social no Brasil, Rio de Janeiro.

Oppenheim, Lois Hecht (1993): Politics in Chile. Democracy, Authoritarianism, and the Search for Development. Boulder, CO.

Oyen, Else et al. (eds) (1996): Poverty. A global view. Paris: Unesco.

Oxhorn, Philip D. (1995): Organizing Civil Society. The Popular Sectors and the Struggle for Democracy in Chile.

Paulais, Thierry (1995): Le développement urbain en Côte d'Ivoire. (1979–1990). Les projets de la Banque mondiale. Paris. Karthala.

Perlman, Janice E. (1976): The Myth of Marginality. Urban Poverty and Politics in Rio de Janeiro. Berkeley, Los Angeles, London.

Pfeiffer, Peter (1987): Urbanização sim, remoção nunca! Politische, sozio-ökonomische und urbanistische Aspekte der Favelas und ihre soziale Organisation in Rio de Janeiro: Entwicklung – Tendenzen – Perspektiven. Berlin.

Portes, Alejandro (1985): 'Latin American Class Structures: Their Composition and Change during the Last Decades' in: Latin American Research Review Vol. 20, No. 3: 7–39

Portes, Alejandro et al. (1989): The Informal Economy. Studies in Advanced and Less Developed Countries. Baltimore.

Potter, Robert/Ademola, Salau T. (1990): Cities and Development in the Third World. London.

Prange, Astrid (1998): 'Die Wirtschaft gibt die Richtung an' in: Der Überblick, (34) 2: 4–7.

Przeworski, Adam et al. (2000): Democracy and Development. Cambridge, New York, Melbourne.

Przeworski, Adam/Teune, Henry (1970). *The Logic of Comparative Social Inquiry*. New York.

Putnam, Robert D. (1993): *Making Democracy Work*. Princeton.

Quijano, Anibal (1974): 'Marginaler pol der Wirtschaft und marginalisierte arbeitskraft' in: Senghaas, D. (ed.): *Peripherer Kapitalismus*. Frankfurt: 298–341

Quijano, Aníbal (1984): 'Die Entstehung einer marginalen Welt in den latein-amerikanischen Städten' in: Müller-Plantenberg, Clarita/Rempel, Rolf (eds): *Soziale Bewegungen und räumliche Strukturen in Lateinamerika*. Kassel: 73–113.

Rabanal, César Rodríguez (1990): *Überleben im Slum – Psychosoziale Probleme peruanischer Elendsviertel*. Frankfurt/M.

Ragin, Charles C./Berg-Schlosser, Dirk/De Meur, Gisela (1996). 'Political Methodology: Qualitative Methods' in: Goodin, R. E.. Klingemann, H.-D. (eds): *A New Handbook of Political Science*. Oxford: 749–68.

Ravallion, N. (1997): 'Good and bad growth. The Human Development Report' in: *World Development* 25 5: 631–38.

Ribeiro, Luiz Cesar de Queiroz/Santos Jr., Orlando Alves dos (1996): *Associativismo e participação social: tendências da organização popular no Rio de Janeiro*. Rio de Janeiro.

Rocha, Sonia (1995): 'Governabilidade e pobreza. O desafio dos números' in: Valladares, Licia/Coelho, Magda (eds): *Governabilidade e pobreza no Brasil*. Rio de Janeiro.

Rocha, Sonia (1996): *Renda e pobreza: os impactos do Plano Real*. Rio de Janeiro.

Rodríguez, Alfredo/Icaza, Ana María (1993): 'Procesos de expulsión de habit-antes de bajos ingresos del centro de Santiago, 1981–1990' in: *Proposiciones* 22: 138–72.

Römpczyck, Elmar (1994): *Chile – Modell auf Ton*. Unkel/Rhein.

Room, Graham (ed.) (1995): *Beyond the Threshold: The Measurement and Analysis of Social Exclusion*. Bristol.

Samad, Syed Abdus (1996): 'The present situation in poverty research' in: Oyen, Else et al. (eds): *Poverty. A global view*. Paris: Unesco: 33–46.

Sangmeister, Hartmut (1990): 'Sklavenbefreiung und Rassenprobleme in Brasil-ien' in: *Zeitschrift für Lateinamerika* 38/39: 57–81.

Sangmeister, Hartmut (1992): 'Brasilien' in: Nohlen, Dieter/Nuscheler, Franz (eds): *Handbuch der Dritten Welt*. Vol. 2. Bonn. 219–76.

Sangmeister, Hartmut (1993): 'Messung der Armut in Lateinamerika. in: Latein-amerika', *Analysen-Daten-Dokumentation* 10, No. 23: 5–30.

Santos, Milton (1993): *A urbanização brasileira*. São Paulo.

Sassen, Sakia (1996): *Metropolen des Weltmarkts. Die neue Rolle der Global Cities*. Frankfurt.

Schäfer, Hans-Bernd (eds) (1994): *Armut in Entwicklungsländern*. Berlin.

Schenk, Michael (1982): *Kommunikationsstrukturen in Bürgerinitiativen. Empirische*

Untersu chungen zur interpersonalen Kommunikation und politischen Meinungs-bildung. Tübingen.

Schmidtchen, Gerhard (1983): 'Jugend und Staat' in: Matz, U./Schmidtchen, G. (1983): *Gewalt und Legitimität.* Opladen.

Schmitt, Sylvia (2001): *Städter und Bürger? Lebenswelten städtischer Armer in Zeiten politischer Umbrüche in der Côte d'Ivoire. Eine Untersuchung zu politischer Kultur und politischem Handeln.* Hamburg

Schulz, Ingo (1994): 'Öffentliche Verwaltung' in: Briesemeister, Dietrich et al. (eds): *Brasilien heute: Politik, Wirtschaft, Kultur.* Frankfurt/M.: 216–28.

Schuurman, Frans J./Naerssen, T. van (eds) (1989): *Urban Social Movements in the Third World.* London.

Scully, Timothy (1990): *Rethinking the Center. C,leavages Political Junctures and Party Evolution in Chile.* Notre Dame

Sen, Armatya (1999): 'Democracy as a Universal Value' in: *Journal of Democracy* Vol. 10, No. 3: 3–17.

Silva, Jeannette (2000): 'Attitudes and political interests of the Chileans at the end of the '90s', paper presented at the symposium 'Poverty Reduction by Participation?' Marburg, Institute of Political Science. July (mimeo).

Slater, David (ed.) (1985): *New Social Movements and the State in Latin America.* Amsterdam.

Sørensen, Georg (1993): *Demcracy and Democratization.* Boulder: Westview.

Sotelo, Ignacio (1973): *Soziologie Lateinamerikas.* Stuttgart.

Souza, Marcelo José Lopes de (1993): *Armut, sozialräumliche Segregation und sozialer Konflikt in der Metropolitanregion von Rio de Janeiro: ein Beitrag zur Analyse der 'Stadtfrage' in Brasilien.* Tübingen.

Souza, Maria Luiza de (1995): 'Movimentos sociais em Sergipe nas décadas de 60, 70 e 80' in: *Movimentos* (1) 1: 5–24.

Sperberg, F. Jaime (1997): *Urbane Landbesetzungen in Santiago de Chile und Buenos Aires. Soziale Bewegungen in Chile und Argentinien in den 80er Jahren.* Hamburg.

Sperberg F., Jaime (2000): *Von Stadtteilbewegungen zur Zivilgesellschaft.* Münster.

Spessart, Stephanie (1980): *Garant oder Gegner.* Saarbrücken.

Stahl, Karin (1994): 'Chile: Ein sozialpolitischer Modellfall?' in: *Nord-Süd Aktuell,* 2. Quartal: 299–313.

Steiner, J. (1969): *Bürger und Politik.* Meisenheim.

Stinchcombe, Arthur L. (1978): *Theoretical Methods in Social History.* New York.

Stren, Richard (1975): 'Urban policy and performance in Kenya and Tanzania' in: *Journal of Modern African Studies,* 13 (2).

Thibaut, Bernhard (1996): *Präsidentialismus und Demokratie in Lateinamerika: Argentinien, Brasilien, Chile und Uruguay im Vergleich.* Opladen.

Tironi, E. (1990): *Autoritarismo, modernizacion y marginalidad.* Santiago de Chile.

Tokman, Víctor E. (1990): 'The Informal Sector in Latin America: Fifteen Years

Later' in: Turnham, D. et al. (eds) (1990): *The Informal Sector Revisited*. Development Center Seminar (OECD). Paris: 94–110.

Touraine, Alain (1988): *La parole et le sang. Politique et societé en Amérique Latine*. Paris.

Uehlinger, Hans Martin (1988): *Politische Partizipation in der Bundesrepublik*. Opladen.

Urmeneta, Roberto et al. (1994): *Evolución de la calidad de vida de los pobladores 1991–1993*. Tercera Encuesta en poblaciones, Santiago, PET Doc. de Trabajo No. 102.

Valdés, Juan Gabriel (1994):'Die Chicago-Schule: Operation Chile' in: Dirmoser, Dietmar et al. (eds): *Markt in den Köpfen. Lateinamerika: Analysen und Berichte*. Vol. 17, Unkel/Rhein, Bad Honnef: 36–60.

Valladares, Lícia do Prado (1980): *Passase uma casa. Análise do programa de remoçào de favelas do Rio de Janeiro*. Ed Zahar (2nd edn).

Verba, Sidney et al. (1973): 'The Modes of Participation. Continuities in Research' in: *Comparative Political Studies* 6 (1973): 235–50.

Verba, Sidney/Nie, Norman et al. (1978): *Participation and Political Equality. A Seven Nation Comparison*. Cambridge.

Vial, G. (1986): 'Algunas condiciones para una democracia estable en Chile' in: Walker, Ignacio et al. (1986): *Democracia en Chile. Doce conferencias*. Santiago, Notre Dame: 93–115.

Vogel, Jerome (1991): 'Culture, politics and national identity in Côte d'Ivoire' in: *Social Research* 50 (2), summer: 439-56.

Weber Pazmino, G. (1990): *An Approach to Patron Client Relationship from an Anthropological Point of View*. XII World Congress of Sociology. Madrid

Westle, Bettina (1989): *Politische Legitimität – Theorien, Konzepte, empirische Befunde*. Baden-Baden.

Wiese, Bernd (1988): *Erfolge und Probleme eines Entwicklungslandes in den westafrikanischen Tropen*. Darmstadt.

Windhoff-Héritier, Adrienne (1993): 'Das Dilemma der Städte – Sozialpolitik in New York City' in: Häußermann, Hartmut/Siebel, Walter (eds): *Strukturen einer Metropole*. Frankfurt/M.: 239-63.

Wülker, G. (1991): 'Verstädterungsprozeß in der Dritten Welt' in: Opitz, P.J. (ed.): *Grundprobleme der Entwicklungsländer*. München: 70–92.

Zaluar, Alba (1985): *A máquina e a revolta. As organizações populares e o significado da pobreza*. São Paulo.

Ziemer, Klaus (1978): 'Elfenbeinküste' in: Sternberger, Dolf/ Vogel, Bernhard/ Nohlen, Dieter/Landfried, Klaus (eds): *Die Wahl der Parlamente. Vol. II: Afrika*. Erster Halbband. Berlin: 643-88.